ALSO BY DAMIEN LEWIS

With Halima Bashir:
Tears of the Desert: A Memoir of Survival in Darfur

With Mende Nazer:
Slave: My True Story

Homeland

An Extraordinary Story
of Hope and Survival

George Hussein Obama

with

Damien Lewis

SIMON & SCHUSTER

NEW YORK   LONDON   TORONTO   SYDNEY

Simon & Schuster
1230 Avenue of the Americas
New York, NY 10020

Copyright © 2010 by George Obama and Damien Lewis

First Simon & Schuster hardcover edition January 2010

SIMON & SCHUSTER and colophon are registered
trademarks of Simon & Schuster, Inc.

For information about special discounts for bulk purchases,
please contact Simon & Schuster Special Sales at
1-866-506-1949 or business@simonandschuster.com.

The Simon & Schuster Speakers Bureau can bring authors
to your live event. For more information or to book an event,
contact the Simon & Schuster Speakers Bureau at 1-866-248-3049
or visit our website at www.simonspeakers.com.

Designed by Nancy Singer

Manufactured in the United States of America

10   9   8   7   6   5   4   3   2   1

Library of Congress Cataloging-in-Publication Data is available.

ISBN 978-1-4391-7617-7
ISBN 978-1-4391-7620-7 (ebook)

Photo insert credits:
Insert pages 1, 2, 3, 4, and 6 courtesy of George Obama
Insert pages 5, 7, and 8 copyright © Damien Lewis

For my mother
G. O.

For Eva, again
D. L.

Believe nothing, oh monks, merely because you have been told it,
or because it is traditional, or because you yourselves have imagined it.
Do not believe what your teacher tells you merely out of respect
for the teacher.
But whatever, after due examination and analysis,
you find to be conducive
to the good, the benefit, the welfare of all beings,
that doctrine believe and cling to,
and take it as your guide.

GAUTAMA BUDDHA
(CIRCA 563–483 B.C.)

ACKNOWLEDGMENTS

A VERY SPECIAL thanks to the following, without whom this book would not have been possible. Lana Wong of the Shootback project and her husband, Robbie Bisset, for providing a guiding hand in the Kenyan ghetto. Julius Mwelu of the Mwelu Foundation and all his young and talented photographers, for camaraderie and for the promise of hope. Rajab Obama, Ludgard Musine, Clyde Kagondu, Jonathan Mweu, Tony Odiyo, John Ukiru, and all the others from Huruma who were of such help. Special thanks to my niece, Mwanaisha, with whom I share my Huruma home. Very special thanks to Annabel Merullo, Tom Williams, Jessica Cooper, Louisa Pritchard, and everyone at my UK agency, PFD, for believing in the telling of my story. Special thanks to Grainne Fox and Christy Fletcher of U.S. subagents Fletcher & Co. Very special thanks to my U.S. publisher David Rosenthal, for seeing such potential in my story from the very first. Special thanks to Ruth Fecych, Michelle Rorke, Tracey Guest, and all at my American publisher, Simon & Schuster, who helped make my book what it is. Thanks also to Billy Clarke, for the perceptive comments on early drafts. Thanks to Alan Trafford and Adrian Acres, and especially to Christine Major and to David John Lewis, for casting an appraising eye over the manuscript. Special thanks to Sean Ryan and Richard Foreman, fellow scribes, for such early enthusiasm and support, and for creative comments on the manuscript. Thanks to

Elizabeth Wright, Sarah Molloy, and Anne O'Mahoney at Concern, for painting the bigger picture of life in Kenya's slums. And finally, very special thanks to Eva, Chubba (David), Logs (Damien), and Podger (Sianna-Sarah)—my fine companions and playmates during the writing.

A percentage of the royalties from this book will go to fund the community organizations the Mwelu Foundation and Huruma Centre Youth Group, which work in the Kenyan slums.

CONTENTS

Homeland

AUTHOR'S NOTE

THIS IS A true story. It happened to me between the year of my birth and the present day. A very few of the names in this book have been changed, in order to protect those individuals. Kenya is at times a lawless and dangerous place, especially in the ghetto. When you read my story you will understand why such changes may have been necessary. Conversations are recreated both from my own recollections and from those of family and friends who were present at the events portrayed. Without doubt my memory is fallible, and any mistakes herein are entirely of my own making.

PROLOGUE

You know, they said this day would never come. They said our sights were set too high. They said this country was too divided, too disillusioned to ever come together around a common purpose. But on this January night, at this defining moment in history, you have done what the cynics said we couldn't do.

The man's voice boomed out from the tiny TV screen on the shelf above the bar in Kenya where racks of bottles and glasses sat protected behind thick metal bars. His speech was as strong and unyielding as those cold steel bars, the voice resonant, deep, and powerful, like a rich promise of hope.

In lines that stretched around schools and churches, in small towns and in big cities, you came together as Democrats, Republicans, and independents, to stand up and say that we are one nation. We are one people. And our time for change has come.

In the crowd behind the tall, copper-skinned man who was speaking, I could see a bunch of mostly white people—*mzungus* as we call them in Kenya—smiling and cheering ecstatically, and waving blue placards with the man's name on them, or red ones emblazoned with the slogan Stand for Change.

> *We are choosing hope over fear. We're choosing unity over division, and sending a powerful message that change is coming to America.*

This was the voice of a man who in the winter of 2008 had the promise of becoming the next U.S. president. But more than that, perhaps, this was the voice of a man who might truly make history by becoming the first black president of America. But to Kenyans like us, this was first and foremost the voice of a man who was Africa's lost son, for as far as we were concerned, he was half-Kenyan and hailed from one of the foremost tribes in our country—the Luo.

> *The time has come for a president who will be honest about the choices and the challenges we face, who will listen to you and learn from you, even when we disagree, who won't just tell you what you want to hear, but what you need to know.*

Unlike every other black Kenyan in that bar, I had a unique and special reason for listening to those words. For the man delivering this extraordinarily rousing speech was my half brother, a brother by blood, but one that I had barely known.

> *This was the moment when we tore down barriers that have divided us for too long. . . . This was the moment when we finally beat back the politics of fear and doubt and cynicism, the politics where we tear each other down instead of lifting this country up. This was the moment.*

From the wild cheering of the crowd, and his repeated appeals to them personally—"You said . . . You heard . . . You called . . ."—I felt as if the people of America knew this man far better than I, and felt a more personal connection to him, and yet he and I shared the same father. We had lived two separate lives, a world apart, yet in a sense we were joined forever by birth. And that was the strangest thing of all for me; that was both the closeness and the gulf between us.

Years from now, you'll look back and you'll say that this was the moment, this was the place where America remembered what it means to hope.

I glanced around the sparse bar, with its plain and yellowing walls. A bare concrete balcony looked out over the noisy, chaotic streets of the ghetto. Old men and young clustered around the chipped Formica tabletops, gazing at that screen and listening with something like rapture. Not a soul in that bar cared much for Kenyan politics, which seemed forever mired in corruption. But in this man—in their lost African son—Kenyans saw their own promise of hope and change that might somehow shine a light into the dark heart of Africa.

For many months, we've been teased, even derided for talking about hope. But we always knew that hope is not blind optimism. . . . Hope is that thing inside us that insists, despite all the evidence to the contrary, that something better awaits us if we have the courage to reach for it and to work for it and to fight for it.

Hope. He used that word a lot, did my big brother in America. Yet for so many years hope had been an alien concept to me. During my darkest, lost years the very concept of hope had been closed to me. It was only relatively recently that I had learned again what it meant to know and to feel the true spirit of hope.

Hope is what led a band of colonists to rise up against an empire. What led the greatest of generations to free a continent and heal a nation. What led young women and young men to sit at lunch counters and brave fire hoses and march through Selma and Montgomery for freedom's cause.

After living a life of relative privilege, I had crashed and burned in my teens, and I had lost all hope. I had migrated from the plush Nairobi suburbs to a life with the city's street kids, and from there I had been sucked into the wild chaos of the ghetto. I had lost myself in drink and drugs, and I had become a gun-toting gangster, caught in a life of violence and crime.

Hope—hope is what led me here today. With a father from Kenya, a mother from Kansas, and a story that could only happen in the United States of America.

At the mention of our country the crowd in the bar jumped to its feet, cheering wildly. What would the drinkers think, I wondered, were they to realize that Barack Obama's half brother sat in their very midst—George Obama, an unremarkable resident of the Huruma slum.

Hope is the bedrock of this nation. The belief that our destiny will not be written for us, but by us, by all those men and women who are not content to settle for the world as it is, who have the courage to remake the world as it should be . . .

While he was striving to become president of the United States, I was a slum-dwelling ex-prisoner and ex-gangster. And with each day that my big brother's fame and status grew, I knew deep within myself that my anonymity couldn't last. In a day, a week, a month, whatever, someone would inevitably make the connection— we shared the same father, but had different mothers—and venture into the closed and dangerous world of the slums to track me down.

We are the United States of America. And in this mo-
ment, in this election, we are ready to believe again.

Sure enough, the journalists and reporters came into my ghetto homeland in droves. Having my long-lost brother win the American presidency would prove both a blessing and a curse.

Not even he could erase the darkness and the shame in my past. Only I might do that, by helping build for the people of my slum homeland a better and a brighter future. And one step at a time I reckoned we were getting there.

CHAPTER I

The Beginning

"Sometimes, Georgie, I'm speaking but you're just not hearing me, are you?"

Whenever Grandma Dorcas teased me, which was often, she did so with a wide smile that lit up all her features. I'd gaze up into that big, open face of hers—the mouthful of crooked teeth and a patchwork of laughter lines around dancing eyes—and try to remember just what she had been telling me.

I'd insist that I had been listening. "I was hearing you, Dani, I was."

Dani is the word for "grandma" in the language of my tribe, the Luo; *kwara* that for "grandpa."

Grandma seemed to be more than happy to tell her stories over and over and over again, and so she'd often catch me daydreaming. More often than not she'd know that I was far away in my land of make-believe, but she never really seemed to mind.

My father had died when I was just a few months old, and as a result Grandma always seemed to be soft on me. She used a big stick on my cousins whenever they stepped out of line, but she never once beat me. My mother, Jael, would leave me in my grandparents' care for days on end, so there was plenty of time for Grandma's storytelling.

"You're a real dreamer, just like that grandfather you were named after." Grandma would ruffle my hair, affectionately. "You're a real dreamer, just like him."

This was a perfect excuse to tell me the story of how my *juogi*—my naming ceremony—had come to pass.

"You know how you came to have your name? I can't for the life of me remember if I told you." Grandma gave a sigh. "Well, just to be sure you know, this is how you came to be named George Hussein Onyango Obama. A few days after your birth . . ."

Grandma was perched on a low wooden stool, where she liked to sit when telling her stories. It was carved from a single section of tree trunk, the rough-hewn ax marks worn smooth by the rubbing of human skin and the passage of time. I was on the ground at her feet, nestled against her legs. The essence of Grandma was all around me—a smoky, spicy, musty scent that to me signified love and home.

I let my mind drift as her voice rumbled away in the background, lulling me like honeyed sunshine. I started to imagine myself on a fishing trip with my cousin, Omondi. Only this time, I was the mudfish catcher par excellence. For every one mudfish that Omondi caught, I'd catch half a dozen or more. Omondi couldn't believe it. Finally, in my world of make-believe at least, I'd earned a little respect from my tough rural cousin.

Grandma had told me the story of my naming so many times that I'd lost count. In the weeks after my birth my father, Barack Obama Senior, had waited until an ancestor appeared to him in a vision. It was my grandfather on my father's side, and so that was who I was named after.

There are twenty-three Luo subtribes, and my father was from the Jo-Alego—*Jo* being the Luo word for "people of." The subtribes intermarry freely, but the children always inherit the tribal identity of their father. Africa is a largely patriarchal society, Kenya included. A child's tribal and cultural heritage is seen as coming from the father's side. Traditionally, children are "owned" by the father's clan, and if there is a breakdown in a marriage, the offspring very often go with the father.

The Luo word for the naming ceremony, *juogi*, is also our word for *ju-ju*, the worship of spirits and ancestors. In the Luo traditional belief system there is a supreme creator, Nyasaye, and a powerful cult of the ancestor. Only ancestors who led good lives are supposed to appear in the *juogi* vision. Whoever appears in that vision is "reincarnated" via the naming and lives again on earth in the person who bears his name. That's why Grandma was forever telling me that I would grow up to be just like Grandpa Obama.

My grandfathers on both my mother's and father's sides bore the name Onyango, as do I. *Onyango* is a Luo word meaning "someone who is born in the early morning," and as my mother had told me, I was born just after dawn. On my father's side my grandpa's name was Hussein Onyango Obama, so I guess Grandma was right—I was named after him. My English first name probably came from my father's close childhood friend George.

But as a child I didn't know any of this for certain. My father had passed away during the first year of my life and it was my mother's extended family that made up my home and my life.

As with many African tribes, in the Luo the twin strands of traditional African belief and contemporary religion often run side by side. Grandma seemed to have no problems reconciling her Christianity with the Luo's more ancient beliefs. She was a great churchgoer. Every Sunday she'd don her finest robes and emerge from her hut wrapped from head to toe in rainbow colors. On her head she'd wear a traditional Luo cloth, twisted around and around and tied in a bright bow.

She'd set off for the village church like a ship under sail, all whites, reds, and yellows billowing before her. As soon as we children saw her coming, we'd run away as fast as we could. I wanted to be out playing in the rice paddy or fishing with my cousin Omondi, not sitting for hours in a hot and airless church with the preacher droning on. On the rare occasions when Grandma did hustle me off to Sunday service, I'd kill the time with serious daydreaming.

Grandma used to pepper her stories with references to God, the Bible, and Christian parables. She was forever drawing religious lessons from life as she observed it in the family compound. And each night before I went to sleep, she'd pray for me. I liked that; there was something comforting in her hushed words. After Grandma's prayers, I was tucked up in Grandma's bed, which I shared with my cousin Omondi, and Grandma slept on a thin mattress on the floor. I used to feel so secure snuggled up in Grandma's bed, my cousin close to me, and Grandma right next to us, in her hut in the family homestead, that I'd sleep through the balmy African night untroubled by dreams.

I never once saw Grandpa Onyango go to church. I don't think he disapproved of Grandma's pious ways, he was just too old and set in his own habits to do anything that he didn't absolutely want to do. In fact, he rarely left the family compound. Polygamy was normal in the traditional Luo society of their generation, and a Luo man was allowed up to five wives. Grandpa had three. Grandma Dorcas was the first and the oldest and, in theory at least, that made her the most important.

Grandpa was supposed to rotate among them, spending each night with a different wife. But in my earliest memories he was already too old to be doing any of that. Perhaps his wives competed for Grandpa's affections when he was younger, but I never heard them arguing or complaining much.

In order to win and keep several wives, you had to be wealthy. In Luo culture wealth equated to cows, and the more cows you had, the richer you were. Grandpa had forty cows, which by Luo standards meant that he was a rich man. His sons were married off to Luo girls, and for each of those marriages Grandpa would have paid a dowry of so many cattle. That he had managed to do so and keep his big herd meant that he had husbanded his resources well.

Surrounding the homestead were the fields where Grandpa grazed his cattle, plus his goats and sheep. He owned land in other parts of the village, and much of this was used for rice growing. The rice fields were rain-fed, as opposed to irrigated. If the main April-to-

June rains failed, the young rice plants would wither and die in the fields, and there would be no crop that year.

Grandpa was well educated for a Luo elder, for he had been to school, a colonial one run by the British. Despite his age his mind was razor sharp. He could remember the names of all his grandchildren, and there were dozens and dozens of them!

My mother's full name was Jael Atieno Onyango. *Atieno* means "born at night." Like many Luo, she was tall and willowy, with a quiet and graceful African beauty. She wore her hair in braids that fell to the small of her back. They swayed and danced when she walked. She was twenty-two years old when I was born; barely six months later my father was killed in a car crash on Kenya's chaotic roads. She was my father's fourth wife, and just months into their relationship fate had decreed that she would end up a single parent, with an infant son to rear.

My mother had given birth to me in Nairobi, where she was studying and working at the time. But my earliest memories are of her rural home, and my time spent daydreaming on Grandma Dorcas's knee. The village was situated in the Nyando region, a flat and fertile part of the country on the shores of Lake Victoria, in the Luo's traditional heartland. Just about everyone in the village was from one subtribe of the Luo, called the Jo-Kano.

At the start of the April rainy season the wind would blow in from the bush in a sudden, raging storm. The dry fronds on the palm trees clashing together sounded like an army of children fighting with wooden swords. Then you knew that rain was on the way, and you had no more than ten minutes to get under cover. As a wall of gray clouds rushed in from the far horizon, powerful gusts knocked down coconuts from the palms and dead branches off the trees. The only thing to do was to shelter in Grandma's house and wait for the storm to pass.

Huge drops of water would pummel the sandy earth, mashing it into the consistency of muddy coffee. The smell of the first rain on the hot ground was a strong, heady mixture of steamy, peppery dust and sunbaked earth. That unmistakable scent came with a rush of excitement. It signified a season of plenty—one of fattened cattle, creamy milk, juicy maize cobs, and lush rice fields. In the evening a chorus of croaking would envelop us, as the frogs in the waterlogged rice fields started calling to each other, ushering in the African night.

Mostly the storms would last for only a few hours, and then the sun would return, hot and crystal bright in the clear, rain-washed air. Rarely would it rain for days on end. If it did, the downpour would flood the far side of the road, but never our compound. Grandpa had built on a slightly raised site, and we would stay dry while the houses across the road sagged into the floodwater, their mud walls dissolving into piles of brown sludge. Those families would have to go stay with their relatives until the floodwaters were gone.

Our compound was large by Luo standards. It had to be, in order to accommodate the huge family that Grandpa had sired. Grandma alone had eight children, and I couldn't count all the grandchildren. My mother had been born and brought up in that bustling homestead, but she had been sent to Nairobi in her teens to attend secondary school. Once her studies were done, she'd found work in the city, and after that she had split her life between the rural and urban worlds.

My mother was proud of being Luo and she tried to teach me everything she could about the Luo traditions, culture, and history. But invariably it was Grandma who revealed to me the most about my roots, because her life was steeped in Luo tradition, and she had the time to really talk with me.

One day Grandma called me over to her favorite stool and began to tell me the story of the ancient times. This was a tale about how we Luo had ended up in Nyando, and from where we had come. It was a saga of brave warriors, perilous river-crossings, and heroic expeditions into the unknown, and for once Grandma had me gripped. I sat there hugging my legs, digging my toes into the hard-baked earth as I listened to Grandma's tale of mighty adventures.

"Many, many years ago there were no Luo in Kenya," Grandma began. "At that time we lived in a country far to the north, in the flat

and steamy swamplands. We built huts of grass and mud on the is-
lands. The waters were full of giant crocodiles that ate people, but still
we Luo braved those waters in our canoes. We were skillful fisher-
men, just as we are on Lake Victoria today. But this land in the north,
which today is called Sudan, was a place of fierce and warlike tribes.
There were great battles between the Luo and rival peoples over water, cattle, and land, and many died."

Grandma paused for a second. I felt her fingers playing with my
dusty, wiry hair. She plucked out a speck of dry grass that had lodged
there when I was playing.

"You're not listening to me, are you, little Georgie?" she prompted,
gently.

"I am, Dani, I am listening," I insisted. "There's lots of fighting
going on between us and the others. Go on."

"Well, some Luo chose to migrate south, to escape the fighting,"
Grandma continued, happy that for once I was paying attention. "In
doing so they had to navigate mighty rivers and lakes and cross high
mountains. But eventually they made it here to Kenya. Of course, this
land had its own people, but we Luo were clever, as well as being warriors. Some people we did fight, but with others we signed peace
deals, and with some we married into their clans. In that way our
enemies became our friends, neighbors, and our families even. And
that's the story of how we came to know this part of Kenya as our
home."

I glanced around me at the familiar contours of the homestead. I
told myself that it had been worth the long journey across Africa, and
the struggles that had accompanied it, to end up in a place such as
this. I loved it here.

Grandma's house was a square, mud-walled building, with a roof
of blue galvanized iron. During storms, the noise of the raindrops
pounding on the roof was deafening. The compound was set back
from the road that led through the village, and Grandma's was the
first house inside the gate, which signified that she was the most senior wife. To either side and set further back were the two houses for
Grandpa's second and third wives.

Each house had a kitchen to one side, which was constructed of mixed mud and cow dung. At the far end of the compound were half a dozen circular mud huts, with grass thatch roofs. These were the men's houses, for the unmarried young men and teenage boys. Once a boy reached adolescence, he wasn't allowed to stay in the main house with his mother and the girls. All in all, there must have been forty or more family members in the compound from three generations, with a hut or a house for everyone.

And then there were the animals. At the very center of the compound was a circular cows' enclosure made of branches driven into the ground to form a stout palisade with just one gate. Next to that was a smaller, rectangular enclosure for goats, with a wooden fence and grass thatch roof. And everywhere chickens were scratching in the dirt, trying to peck up any food. There were also half a dozen dogs. They spent the day sleeping, but at night they were alert and on the lookout for strangers.

The compound perimeter was marked by a thick, impenetrable fence made of thorn trees. The cattle were placed at the very heart of the compound, for they represented the wealth of the family. Grandma had told me scary stories about cattle raids. Luo from rival clans had come to our village with spears, clubs, and leather shields to steal cattle to pay the dowries for their sons' marriages or to increase their own herds.

My cousin Omondi was always going on about those raids. It was the job of the small boys to take the goats into the bush during the day to graze. The most dangerous thing that we'd encounter were the snakes, but they'd usually try to keep well out of our way. Omondi was always warning me to be on the lookout for the raiders. He carried a stout stick for whacking the goats if they strayed too far, but in Omondi's mind it was for heroically fighting off the raiders.

Omondi was a year or so younger than I, but he was a tough little country boy born and bred. I loved the rural life, but I hadn't been born and bred in the country. I was seen as having one foot in the city, and as a result Omondi was always the "leader" whenever we were out in the bush. I was older and almost a head taller than he, but he was in charge. If the raiders came, I was supposed to run with the goats to the compound while Omondi would stand and fight them.

While we small boys were out looking after the goats, it was the girls' job to gather firewood. The grown women would remain at home, tending the cooking fires. They'd balance a pot on three rounded hearthstones and feed the firewood in from the sides. They cooked in the open air until the rains forced them indoors. At those times the smoke got into everything—our clothes, our hair, and our skin. Everyone ended up with a salty, smoky, burned aroma. In a way I liked having the smell of the cooking fire upon me, for it too was an unmistakable scent of the village.

My favorite food was Grandma's fish stew. Grandma would buy tilapia, a popular fish about the size of an average trout, which were abundant in nearby Lake Victoria. She simmered tilapia in a tomato and onion sauce and served it with *ugali*, a stodgy maize flour mash a bit like mashed potato. Grandma was gentle, protective, and indulgent with me, for she knew that I was the grandson with the missing father. Whenever she could, she would prepare my favorite fish stew.

There was no electricity in the village, and nothing like a TV. In the evenings I'd sit outside the door to Grandma's house, enveloped in the warm, inky night. I'd scoop up the *ugali* in my hand, dip it into the bowl of fish stew, and throw the lot into my mouth. Delicious. All around the compound the watery yellow light of oil lanterns spilling out from hut doorways softened the darkness. Overhead, the stars would burn like ice-cold fire, so close that I felt as if I could reach up and touch them.

After everyone had eaten, we'd gather around the fire, and Grandma would try to teach us youngsters a Luo song or one of the legends of the tribe. When it was time for bed, she'd sing us a simple lullaby:

My child you need to sleep,
My child you need to sleep.
You've looked after the cows,
My child you need to sleep.

You've fetched in the firewood,
My child you need to sleep.
You've looked after the goats,
My child you need to sleep.
Your belly's full of food,
My child you need to sleep.
The fire's burning low,
My child you need to sleep . . .

Grandma's voice, and the soporific repetition of the verses, would lull me into the world of my dreams.

I loved it at the homestead, but I wasn't wholly part of life there. In the middle of the night I'd wake, needing to use the loo. There was no bathroom in the house, and I was scared of the night. I wasn't used to it like the other kids were. With only an oil lantern to guide me through the quiet and the dark, I had to try to find the outside toilet. The stars stared down from the wide-open sky, making me feel small and alone. Omondi, I knew, wouldn't be like that. He was a tough country kid. Nothing scared him.

When I wasn't herding goats I'd run around barefoot, playing and joking and laughing with the other kids. All we boys wore was a pair of raggedy shorts, and by the end of a morning's play we'd be covered in dust, with grass and leaves in our hair. There was a pond just outside the compound that was deep enough to wash in. The trouble was that there were water snakes in there, and if you weren't careful, one would go slithering over your foot.

Omondi and the other boys didn't seem to mind. They'd strip naked, dive in, and cavort around in the pool's depths, but I'd be rooted to the shallows, glancing around nervously for anything green and slithering. After we'd washed, Grandma would prepare tea and boiled rice for lunch. The tea was served with heaps of sugar and milk fresh from our cattle.

Grandma was forever pointing out to me the three cows that she said were mine. Apparently, they were the ones that my father had paid as dowry for my mother. Grandma explained that I would use them to pay for my own wife's dowry when I was old enough to choose a Luo woman to marry. Grandma had given each of my cows a name, and just as she did with all Grandpa's cattle, she knew each by sight.

One day Grandma decided it was time I learned to milk my cows. The other boys, Omondi included, knew how, and Grandma saw no reason why I shouldn't. The problem was that each cow was used to being milked by the one person who looked after it. Over time the milker built up a relationship with his cow, who wouldn't willingly give her milk to anyone else.

Grandma milked my cows and they were used to her touch, but she wasn't going to let that stop us. She picked out one, set a bowl beneath the animal's udder, and placed a little three-legged stool beside it. I sat down uneasily and glanced up at the vast flank of the cow, and it suddenly struck me what a real beast it was. Grandma took hold of one of the pink and wrinkled teats and tried to demonstrate to me the pulling-squeezing motion that made the milk flow.

"Come on, Georgie," she encouraged me. "Gentle but firm, gentle but firm, and try to get a rhythm going."

Under her familiar touch the first jets of warm milk squirted, pencil-lead thin, into the bowl. Each landed with a light, musical hiss. Soon Grandma had two teats on the go—one after the other, one after the other, jetting white into the bowl. She took her hand away from one of the teats and replaced it with my own, nervous fingers. The udder felt warm and rubbery and tight with milk.

"Hold firm, and do just as I'm doing," Grandma whispered.

She tried to guide my hand up and down, up and down, and with her hand over mine the milk continued to flow. I started to relax a little. Maybe I could do this. Maybe it wasn't as hard as I had feared.

"See, it's not so difficult, is it?" Grandma smiled as she took her hand away from mine. "She's all yours. She'll start to know your touch, so you can milk her whenever you like."

But once Grandma had removed her fingers, I just seemed to lose the sense of the thing, and my confidence ebbed away. I had tried my best to hide it, but I was afraid of cows, and I knew they could sense when someone wasn't relaxed and easy around them. I felt the milk stop flowing and my fingers seemed to turn to stone. Soon there were no more jets of white squirting into that bowl. I glanced up at Grandma, only to notice that the cow had turned her head and was glaring at me.

An instant later I was on my feet with the stool knocked flying, as I fled from the cow's flashing hooves. Enraged at my clumsy efforts, she had kicked out at me, and I escaped just before one of her sharp hooves got me.

Once she made sure that I was okay, my doting Grandma dissolved into fits of laughter. I guess it must have been pretty funny seeing me flee for my life from a normally docile cow. But that was it for me with cattle from then on. I vowed that I'd never milk such a beast for the rest of my life, and I never have.

In spite of such failures, Grandma remained determined to teach me the village ways. But I think she knew that I wasn't ever going to make the grade like my country cousin Omondi.

CHAPTER 2

The Last Son

When I was five years old, I started school at Nairobi South Primary. It was the hot, dry month of September 1987, and my first school uniform was gray flannel shorts, a white shirt, and shiny black shoes. In the colder, wetter months I'd wear a brown woolen sweater to keep out the chill, but I'd still have to wear those shorts. Long trousers were for grown-ups, and I wouldn't be allowed those until I reached high school.

My mother had rented an apartment in an area of Nairobi called South B. It was very basic by Western standards, the apartment block being a serried rank of bare concrete boxes with crumbling stairwells stained gray-green by the rains. Nairobi sits at a high altitude, and during the cold season the building was chilly and damp, especially at night. But in Kenya this was the kind of place where the reasonably well-off folks lived.

That first day of school I was eager to start. I thought my mother would stay with me, but she dropped me and left, and I spent much of the day in tears wondering why she'd abandoned me to a group of strangers. I was as tall, if not taller than the other boys, but I was one of the youngest in the class and the most immature. Yet I soon got over being upset. I had to, as a matter of survival. I knew if I turned into a blubbering wreck every school day, I wouldn't last for long.

From the very start I loved the breaks between lessons. We'd charge around the dusty playing field chasing a ball of paper bound with plastic and tied tightly with string. This was our makeshift football, for none of us could afford to buy a real one. I was pretty good at football. I wasn't very bulky, but like many Luo I was lean and fleet of foot, and I could run rings around most of the other boys. I loved nothing more than to whack that rag ball in a cloud of dust, straight into the back of the net.

I used to walk to school along with my friends from South B. It was only a ten-minute stroll and none of us felt in any danger. The area was pretty safe and we were only kids, so who would want to bother us? Each morning my mother would kiss me good-bye before setting off for the city wearing a smart skirt and blouse. She worked as a secretary in the treasury ministry in downtown Nairobi, which paid well by Kenyan standards. But it was still a struggle to cover my school fees, buy my school uniform, pay the rent on our apartment, and put food on the table.

The only way to make ends meet was to share the costs of our apartment. It was a two-bedroom affair, and one of my aunties and two of my older cousins moved in, which meant that there were five of us. In a way, living with our close relatives re-created in Nairobi the life we knew from the village.

There was one big advantage to having a crowded household: it meant that I was never alone, and rarely did I have a moment in which to contemplate the fact that I had no father. Because Barack Obama Senior had died when I was so young, having no father around was what I knew. While I was too young to be troubled by it, I'm sure my mother missed him, but she never once showed it or lamented her loss to me. She was too protective of me for that.

During my first year at school I studied English, math, geography, science, and Swahili, and I was keen to do well. We had electricity at home, and so my mother helped with my homework late into the evening. It was crucial to study hard, for we had tests each term. Any pupil who failed to get a pass mark had to repeat that term's lessons. Fail too often, and you'd end up being kept down a year.

There seemed little chance of that happening to me. In the first exams I came in among the top five of my class, and I was first in math. My math teacher told my mother that I was one of the most gifted pupils he had ever had. My mother was proud of my achievements. She told me that if I worked hard, I would do well, and I could do anything I wanted in life. All in all I was a happy-go-lucky child, if still something of a dreamer. I felt as if I had the world ahead of me, and with hard work I could achieve my dreams.

There are more than forty different tribes in Kenya, and living in Nairobi I was surrounded by kids from most of them. In the city, tribe didn't seem to matter as much as in a rural village. At school we never asked about which tribe anyone was from. Often I didn't even know. I chose my friends because I liked them and not because of their tribe.

Each of the tribes has its own language, and so the chances of my finding a fellow Luo speaker were small. The only way I could communicate with my friends was in English or Swahili, a language spoken widely across East Africa, and the first language of Kenya. But at my mother's insistence we kept speaking Luo at home, so that I wouldn't forget my native tongue.

One day shortly before my sixth birthday my mother sat me down for a little chat. Life was busy and it wasn't usual for her to seek a one-to-one with her young son, especially in private. She took my hand reassuringly with one of hers, and with the other she patted her tummy.

"George, soon Mama's going to have a baby," she told me. "Mama's pregnant, and there's a baby growing in here. Soon there's going to be the three of us: me, you, and a little brother or sister. Won't that be fun? We'll be more of a family then, won't we?"

"Yeah, I guess," I replied.

I didn't know quite what to say. I was a bit embarrassed, and I didn't understand what the word "pregnant" meant. Plus my mind was half on the games I'd been playing with my friends outside. I could hear them through the open window screaming and laughing.

"It'll be someone for me to play with, won't it, Mama?" I asked.

My mother smiled. "Sure it will. You'll have a little playmate. You won't be alone anymore."

"Well, that's good, Mama." I jumped up. "So can I go play with my friends?"

"Off you go." My mother smiled, then called after me, "But make sure you're in for six sharp—supper time!"

I rushed down the echoing concrete stairwell into the bright afternoon sunshine and sprinted over to join my friends. I didn't dwell too much on what my mother had said. It was somewhere far in the future, and for a young boy like me the future was another country. Of course, I was very close to my mother. I was an only child, and for five years it had just been she and I. But I didn't feel threatened by a baby brother or sister coming along. I just thought it would be nice to have a playmate. It might even be someone to help me do the chores.

When my mother would try to get me to clear the table or to wash the dishes or to run errands for her to the corner shops, I'd insist that I just had to be with my friends, for we were in the middle of playing a very important game. She would look at me strangely and shake her head. She'd tell me how I was "stubborn, just like your father." It didn't mean that much to me. I had never known my father, so how could I know if my stubborn streak had come from him?

I saw my friends with their fathers, and that gave me a sense of what having one around might mean. But in my childish mind I didn't understand that it took a mother and a father to make a baby. Like most kids of my age I just presumed that babies came out of thin air. I was more interested in how good a football player I was, or how I might wheedle some new toys out of my mother, than in where babies came from.

My mother had bought me some metal Tonka toys—cars and trucks and earth movers—plus I had a big teddy bear. But my best toy of all was my He-Man robot, a metal android action man. I had become the tough, indestructible robot boy from the city. I told myself that the next time I went to the village, I'd take my He-Man with me. It was sure to impress my cousin Omondi. I'd arrive from the urban jungle like an avenging cyber-warrior and become the leader of the entire village gang.

But before I had the chance to take my He-Man to the village, something unexpected happened at school—something that would come to have an overarching influence on my life. One day during break we were out chasing around our shadows and the raggedy football. It was a particularly wild and fiercely contested match, and I was determined to score a goal before the bell went for the end of break.

As we hurtled across the dusty ground, a car drew up at the school gates and three figures got out. None of us paid it much attention, especially me, for I had been passed the ball and was just about to score. As I made a break for the makeshift goal, the ball dancing at my feet, I heard someone calling out my name from the sidelines.

"Obama! Obama! Come here. You have visitors. Come and greet them."

I turned around. It was one of the teachers. Beside him stood a tall, elderly woman. I didn't exactly recognize her, but there was something vaguely familiar about her poise and bearing. Reluctantly, I kicked the ball across to James, a fellow player on my team and one of my best buddies. I left the field hot and sweaty from the match. I tried wiping my hands on my trousers before taking the one that the tall woman held out to me in greeting.

"You don't recognize me, do you, George?" she asked. "I'm your Auntie Zeituni. Your father's sister. And there's someone very special come to greet you."

Holding this lady's hand, I was led across to the school gate. A tall, dignified-looking man was standing there, with a darker-skinned woman at his side. I kept glancing back toward the football game, to see if my team had scored. I didn't want to be rude, but I didn't recognize or know any of these people. The lady gripping my hand had said that she was my father's sister, but as far as I could remember, I'd never met her.

These people were not a part of the life that my mother and I had built for ourselves in the home village or here in Nairobi. I was apprehensive and worried: *What do these strangers want with me?* I wondered.

We stopped in front of the smiling pair, and the tall lady holding my hand leaned down to me.

"This is your sister Auma," she told me, indicating the woman. "She used to play with you on her knee."

She turned toward the man. "And this is your brother, Barack Obama. He's come all the way from America to see you."

I gazed up at this tall man. The word "America" didn't mean anything to me. I didn't know where America was. But I did notice that he was light-skinned, and to me he looked more like a *mzungu,* a white person, than he did a black African. When he greeted me he spoke with an odd, foreign-sounding accent, so I could barely understand him. He wasn't from Kenya, that much was for sure.

I held out my hand to greet them, hoping that it wasn't too dusty from the match. I could feel the sweat dripping down my back, but whether it was from the exertion of the game or the strangeness of the situation I wasn't certain. I was unsure what to say, so I resolved to smile bravely and to say nothing. I just wanted it to be over, to no longer be the awkward center of attention. I wanted to rush back and rejoin my friends in the hot and dusty anonymity of the match.

My father had never been a part of my life. His side of the family didn't figure in my existence, and as a five-year-old kid I wasn't really interested in finding out about them. I couldn't help but sneak a glance behind me, to check if the boy to whom I had passed had scored. He should have. I'd left him with an open goal.

Before we could get much further than polite hellos, there was a shout from the direction of the school building. The headmistress came over and told the visitors that they had to leave. They needed my mother's permission to visit, she explained, without which they really shouldn't have come. There were a few words of objection from Auntie Zeituni, then all three of them seemed to agree that it was probably best to go.

After saying hurried good-byes, the three figures returned to their car, and I to the match. I could feel their eyes upon me as I rejoined my team on the field.

"What's the score?" I asked James.

"Nil–nil," he replied. "I passed to Frank. He didn't score."

"But I gave him an open goal!" I complained. "An open goal!"

James shrugged. "We've still got time to win, if you get those legs of yours moving. Who're the visitors?"

"Someone from America," I replied, my eye on the approaching ball.

"Where's America?" James asked.

"I don't know," I said. I threw up my hand to call for the pass. "Over here! Over here! My ball! My ball!"

As I called for the ball, the car with my other family in it pulled away from the curb and was soon lost to the busy Nairobi traffic. Years later I would meet my American brother again, but by then his life and my own had changed beyond all recognition.

That evening my mother was visibly upset. She had found out from the school principal about the surprise visit, and she wasn't particularly pleased. I was too young to want to probe her disquiet, or to ask her about who those people were or why they had come. As far as I was concerned, I had quite enough aunties and uncles and cousins and grandparents. My mother's clan seemed endless to me, and I didn't need any more family.

A few weeks later my mother came home with a little bundle in her arms. She had been absent for several days, and my auntie had been looking after me. I was used to being left in the care of my extended family, so it was no big deal. That little bundle turned out to be my baby brother. My mother had named him Marvin, after the soul singer Marvin Gaye.

I spent the evening gazing down into the scrunched-up face of my new playfellow. As I placed my outstretched finger in the palm of his tiny hand and felt him grip it, I just knew that Marvin and I were going to be the best of buddies. He looked to be a strong and happy baby, and he was the kid brother that I was going to run around with and take on adventures. I was so excited that I didn't go out to join my friends that evening.

I was too young to wonder who exactly Marvin's father might be. One moment little Marvin hadn't been around, and the next he was—like magic. I wasn't worried that I'd have to share my mother. I was more excited about having a playmate. With little Marvin around, I wasn't ever going to be alone anymore.

A few months after Marvin's birth my mother started having a new "friend" around to visit. Surprisingly, to my young mind at least, that visitor was a *mzungu*. Christian Bertrand was tall and well built, with short brown hair. His eyes were an incredible clear blue, like the sky over our home village after the first rains. No black Africans have eyes like that, and I couldn't believe that a grown-up's eyes could be anything other than warm pools of smoky chocolate like my mother's.

Christian had a kind face that was creased with laugh lines. They puckered and twitched whenever he smiled, reminding me of a chicken's feet scratching away in the earth. Even those laugh lines were strange to me, for a black person's skin doesn't tend to crease and wrinkle with age as much a white person's. But in spite of his otherness, Christian was fun to have around. He was forever ruffling my hair or picking me up and swinging me around by my arms in a wild "windmill."

Christian was the first white person with whom I had any real contact. I'd seen *mzungus* on the streets of Nairobi—usually tourists weighed down under giant backpacks, or the odd businessman sweating profusely in a smart suit—but that was about as near as I'd ever got to one. I'd never actually met a white person or spent time talking to one or sat down with one to share a meal.

I couldn't ask my mother who Christian was exactly, or why she had a white friend, for those aren't the kind of things a young Kenyan child can inquire of a parent. But from what I overheard when they were chatting, I learned that Christian and my mother had met in downtown Nairobi. Christian had come to Kenya to run an aid program, and his office was on the same block as where my mother worked.

Over time I became accustomed to Christian's visits, and having him around began to feel something like normal. This was fortunate, for it meant that it wasn't quite such a shock when my mother told me that Christian had found a new place for us all to live. We were going to move in with him, as one big happy family.

Christian had rented a house in a Nairobi suburb called Umoja—the Swahili word for "unity." Umoja was a fine district, the kind of place to which the affluent Kenyan middle class aspired. It was a step up for us, that much was certain. Luckily, it was still within commuting distance of my school, which meant that I wouldn't be losing all my friends in one go. All in all, moving to Umoja didn't seem such a bad idea to me.

The day of the move my biggest concern was for my metal Tonka toys, and for my He-Man robot. I refused to let the movers pack them into one of their wooden crates. I kept the hard, angular edges of those toys pressed into my lap during the drive across Nairobi, and I had my two favorite Tonka toys clutched in my hands.

Like most young boys, I was in love with speed. I loved being driven anywhere fast, or running fast in an effort to beat my friends. I used to tell myself stories about how I'd be a racing car driver when I grew up, and all the while I'd zoom my toy racing cars backward and forward through the air. That's how I passed my time on the drive to Umoja and the white-painted bungalow that was to be our new home.

At first I was too shy and embarrassed to step foot inside, but Christian enticed me in with words of welcome. The front door opened onto a hallway, which in turn led into a lounge-dining area. It had a big TV pushed against one wall, plus comfy sofas arranged around a coffee table. On the far side was a wooden dining table and chairs, set against a serving hatch that opened into the kitchen.

The best thing about that kitchen was the fridge. I stood there wide-eyed as Christian swung open the door and the white light of its insides beamed down on me. It was crammed full of all sorts of goodies, but what really drew my eye was the row of chilled sodas racked up in the door. Coca-Cola, Fanta Orange, Sprite—with a fridge like this Marvin and I had ended up somewhere close to paradise. I couldn't wait to tell my country cousin Omondi just what we had at our new house in the city, for there was nothing he could do to compete with this.

But the very best thing about the Umoja house was that Marvin and I had our own bedroom. There was a bed for me set against one wall, and opposite that a cot for little Marvin, who wasn't yet one year old. Our room was adjacent to the main bedroom, one that I soon realized my mother would be sharing with Christian.

It felt odd to me that my mother had a white man for a partner. I still found it strange seeing her with this *mzungu*. And sometimes I wondered what we were doing moving in with a guy who wasn't from our tribe, our country, or our race even. At first I couldn't understand why she wanted to be with someone who wasn't a Kenyan or a Luo. But if Christian was willing to share his Umoja home with us, surely he had to be a good guy for my mother to want to be with, I reasoned.

CHAPTER 3

Our Father

The Umoja neighborhood consisted of rows of identical white bungalows, all arranged in a neat grid, with land set aside as open areas in which the local kids could play. Our house had its own garden, which was enclosed by a wall topped off with broken glass to deter intruders. In one corner was a vegetable patch, and opposite that was a play area where Christian had put some swings and slides. But what really drew my eye were the vehicles parked just off the road.

"Those, little Georgie, they are our cars," Christian announced, pointing out the gleaming machines to one side of the gate. "Which one is it you would you like to sit in?"

Christian spoke English with a trace of a French accent, but I didn't have any problems understanding him. Even so, I was at a loss for words.

"Uh . . . I'd . . . All of them. Can I sit in all of them, please?"

Christian laughed. "*Bien sur!* But of course. Come, let me show you."

Christian mixed his English with occasional words that I didn't understand. It turned out they were in his native language, called "French." Like many kids in Nairobi I had presumed that all *mzungus* were British, the white people who had colonized our country and whom we learned about in school. But Christian explained that he was from a place called "France," where everyone spoke French.

Well, if all the people in France drove cars like Christian's gleaming vehicles, then it had to be the best country in the world, I reasoned.

"And so, we start with the Range Rover?" Christian prompted. "Okay?"

I glanced up at him and nodded, shyly: *Yes, do show me your big, he-man zooming jeep.*

Christian was dressed like a real *mzungu* in shorts that showed off a pair of tanned and hairy legs. No African man would be seen dead in short trousers, for they'd be a laughingstock. Shorts were for boys, and once you became a man, you graduated to long trousers. But for some reason we made exceptions for the white men in our country, who seemed to have no problem with dressing like schoolboys!

Christian opened the door of the jeep and lifted me up so I could sit in the front. It smelled of rich, sun-warmed leather, not like the *matatu* minibus taxis that I took around Nairobi, which reeked of hot, sweaty plastic and engine oil. The last in the row of three vehicles was a Volkswagen camper van, but sandwiched between the VW camper and the Range Rover was the most amazing machine that I had ever seen.

Christian's Peugeot 505 looked like something out of the Paris-Dakar rally. It sat high off the ground on jacked-up suspension, its front grille and headlamps forming a scowling face over massive, mud-eater knobbly tires. Projecting out front was a huge bull bar, which gave the vehicle an even tougher and more fearsome expression. Mounted on that bull bar was a big red winch—the tongue in the monster's mouth—which would be used for hauling the vehicle out of swamps or soft riverbeds. And down each side of the metallic gray vehicle were smart decals, reading DANGEL 4 x 4, whatever that might mean.

Wow! The more I looked at it, the more I couldn't believe that my mother's partner owned such a beast of a thing. It was the coolest vehicle in the whole of Nairobi. I couldn't wait to get into it and have Christian drive me somewhere. It just had to be superfast, and what could possibly stop it? If I could get him to drive me out to the home village in such a monster vehicle, Cousin Omondi would have to admit defeat.

Christian patted the bodywork lovingly. "I can see you like it, *n'est-ce pas?*"

"It's fine," I told him, glancing at the Peugeot admiringly. "It's really amazing."

"You know something, Georgie, I had it shipped all the way from France. That is where they make them like this. We could go anywhere in it—all across Africa even!"

I glanced at him in wonder. I didn't know if Christian was being serious or not. Would he really take me "all across Africa" in such an amazing beast of a thing? For now I'd be happy just to sit in it. I was dying to slide into that front seat, grip the steering wheel, and let my daydreamy mind take me away on a wild adventure driving Christian's . . . Dangel-mobile.

"Can I sit in it?" I asked him. "In your Dangel-mobile?"

"Don-gelle," Christian corrected my pronunciation. *"Don-gelle.* That is how we say it in France. Dangel is the maker of the vehicle. And, *bien sur,* of course you can sit."

Christian climbed into the driver's seat, reached down, lifted me up, and placed me on his lap. Gazing out over the shiny hood, I was in total rapture. Christian talked me around the various knobs, levers, and pedals, and then he placed my hands on the steering wheel, the part of any vehicle that all kids know and love.

"See, you hold this and turn it this way or that, and that is how you go left, and that how you go right," Christian coached me, as we twisted and turned the steering wheel. "Later, when we have settled in, we will go out for a proper drive."

True to his word, Christian did take me out for a drive. We puttered around the roads in the Umoja neighborhood, with me sitting on his lap and holding tight to the steering wheel. I soon nicknamed it the "Danger-mobile." Once Christian was out on the open road, he loved nothing more than to put his foot down and drive super-fast. Cars were one of his real passions, and that was something he and I—a fortysomething white Frenchman and a six-year-old black Kenyan kid—shared.

The Danger-mobile was Christian's field car, the one he used to visit aid projects all across Kenya. He kept the Range Rover as a city runabout, and the VW camper van was for safaris. Christian worked for something called the European Economic Community (which today is the European Union), and he was often absent for days on end. Whenever he was away, I found myself missing him and longing for him to come home again.

Although he'd been in Kenya for some time, Christian's Swahili was all but nonexistent. I took it upon myself to teach him the basics: *mambo*—hello; *asante sana*—thank you; *kwaheri*—good-bye; and the all-important *hakuna matata*—no problem. They were the kind of words that I thought might be useful to him in his travels. He in turn taught me some basic French: *bonjour*—hello; *merci*—thank you; the French equivalent to *hakuna matata*—*pas de problème*; plus the all-important *voiture à vitesse*—fast car!

We'd hold our makeshift language lessons in the kitchen, while preparing dinner. He'd ask me the Swahili word for something—a frying pan or an onion maybe—and then he'd tell me the French word in exchange. He was into his food and wine, and he used to get me to fetch him the herbs and spices from the cupboards, and to stir the cooking pot when he was busy chopping the salad or preparing vegetables. And once the meal was ready, he'd get me to carry the dishes to and from the dining table.

It wasn't just the way he cooked—throwing alcohol into the hot frying pan so that it burst into a flash of blue flame—that marked Christian out as a real *mzungu*, it was the fact that he cooked at all. He must have been ten years or more my mother's senior, and few African men of his generation would ever dream of cooking. For an

African man to prepare a meal for his wife would be seen as a demeaning role reversal. In the tradition of that generation there was a strict delineation between male and female roles, and the lines were rarely if ever crossed.

Although Christian loved his French cuisine, he seemed happy to eat African. Like mine, my mother's favorite food was *ugali* with fish stew, cooked like my grandma made it back in the village. The *ugali* maize mash was never normally a favorite with foreigners, but Christian appeared to love it. He'd eat in the traditional way, scooping up the *ugali* in one hand, dipping it into the stew, and throwing it all into the back of his mouth. He used to joke around, munching on big hunks of *ugali* dusted with salt and moaning in delight as if it were the most delicious food ever. He'd have my mother and me in fits of laughter, and even little Marvin would gurgle happily.

Whether he genuinely liked *ugali* or pretended for my mother's sake I'm not exactly sure, but it was probably more the latter. It was easy to see how he adored my mother, and it was good to see her with someone who appreciated her charms. Christian also liked baking cakes, but more often than not they were savory. Like most Africans, I like my cake sugary. I didn't care for his salty concoctions, and I refused even to try his cheesecakes. I used to tease him that he loved his cheese too much, drank too much coffee, and smoked like one of Grandma Dorca's cooking fires.

Over time I made a new set of friends in Umoja. Eric became my best buddy. We were age mates, and he lived just a couple of doors down from me. Eric's father was a manager at Kenya Breweries, and on weekdays he'd leave for downtown Nairobi dressed in a smart suit and tie. Eric's parents were middle-class Kenyan professionals, typical of the people who lived in Umoja.

By contrast Christian was the only white man living on the entire Umoja estate (district). Whites living and working in Nairobi lived in the upmarket areas, like Westlands. Umoja was for middle-class black Africans, and Christian would have been earning far more than most. He acted as if our family and Eric's were on the same social level, al-

though he could have afforded to live in one of the far plusher suburbs. He was a down-to-earth kind of guy, and I guess that's why he
chose to live with his adopted family in a place like Umoja.

Eric and I became inseparable. We would spend our time booting
a ball up and down the street, or messing around in the Umoja parkland. Christian wasn't a football man, but he seemed to appreciate the
grip the game had on Kenyan boys our age. He bought me the first
real football that I had ever owned. It was a plain white one, without
any fancy club names on it, but it was still a big step up from our rag
balls tied together with string.

Eric's family were very religious, and in our friendship my mother
saw a perfect way to nurture the Christianity that had taken root in
me via Grandma. While Christian didn't appear to be overly religious, he supported my mother in her desire to keep me grounded in
faith. Every Sunday morning Eric's family and I would dress in our
Sunday best—our smartest clothes, neatly ironed and pressed for the
occasion—and troop down to the local Catholic church.

The priest performed mass either in Swahili or English, and then
we kids would move to a separate part of the church, leaving the
adults to sing their hymns. While the grown-ups took their wafers
and wine, we had Bible lessons, like how to interpret and live by the
Ten Commandments. I enjoyed those Sunday church outings, and
once Marvin was old enough, I made sure we said our prayers together each evening before bed.

> *Our father who art in heaven,*
> *Hallowed be thy name.*
> *Thy kingdom come . . .*

Before meals I would say a short grace—my mother, Christian,
Marvin, and I with our heads bowed, our hands clasped together in
prayer.

> *Father, bless this food before we take it,*
> *And may it work within our bodies to do your good in this world.*
> *Amen.*

Eric and I formed a gang of four, along with two other Umoja boys, Ernest and Daddy. "Daddy" was that boy's nickname, but it was so widely used that few of us knew his real name. When we'd exhausted ourselves at football, we would retire to my house. Ludo, chess, chutes and ladders, Monopoly—we had all the best games at my place. My favorite was Scrabble. When Christian was home we all spoke English, which meant that none of my friends could match me at Scrabble. But I used to argue that this had nothing to do with my winning, for you couldn't practice Scrabble simply by *talking*. I'd argue that I was simply the cleverest in the gang, which drove my buddies wild.

Christian was always up for a Scrabble match, and invariably I would beat him. I don't think he let me win: I just think his written English was poor, and his spelling even worse. Whenever he lost at Scrabble, he'd challenge me to a bout of chess, at which he was assured of victory, and that way honor would be satisfied. My mother liked to play me at ludo, but she almost always won, and that caused a lot of upsets. The bottom line was that I was a bad loser at board games. I didn't care so much in field sports, wherein losing was all part of the game, but I hated losing at board games.

Christian was a keen sportsman. He loved his tennis, golf, and especially rugby. He played rugby for a French expatriate team, and he was big enough to handle himself and to survive a mauling on the field. Neither I nor my football-crazy friends knew the first thing about rugby. It wasn't until Christian took me to a match that I began to understand a little of the rules. I also realized what a hard and physical game it was, as the players went smashing into each other on the hard, sunbaked earth.

Marvin was too young to attend that match, and rugby wasn't my mother's thing, so it was just the two of us. Christian was playing for the better team, and soon the French expatriates had the match going their way. Each time they scored a try, or kicked a conversion, I was cheering quietly from the sidelines. As I watched Christian kick up his heels and make for the touchline, I felt an irrepressible thrill of excitement, and I began to appreciate why he so loved the game. I told myself that one day I would play rugby as well as Christian and make him truly proud of me.

During the school holidays, Christian announced that he was taking us on an adventure. We were going to the seaside. As we loaded up the Danger-mobile with suitcases stuffed full of clothes and beach balls and blow-up toys, my feelings were excitement at being on an adventure, plus a child's apprehension at the new. We headed for the white sands and tropical seas around Malindi, on Kenya's southern coast. It was the first time that I'd been on a proper holiday, and my first ever visit to the seaside.

Christian took us to his favorite beachside hotel. It wasn't common to see mixed-race couples in Kenya at this time, and I had rarely if ever seen any around Nairobi. The hotel staff were all Kenyans, and they seemed to find our turning up there very odd. They stared at Christian and my mother and little Marvin and me as if we were out of a zoo. I had a good idea what they were thinking: *What's that* mzungu *doing with a black Kenyan woman, and with two black, infant children? How on earth does that add up?*

With their eyes upon us, I felt as if we were misfits or frauds or something. As we waited to check in, I felt uncomfortable and embarrassed, and I wished I could melt into the carpet and disappear. I felt as if we shouldn't have come to this smart hotel, one that was mostly full of foreigners. Fortunately, Christian seemed to be known to the hotel management, and soon he had the staff ferrying in our bags from the car.

Once we were in our rooms, I felt as if I could relax a little. Marvin and I had one room, my mother and Christian the other, and each had a balcony overlooking the ocean. By now little Marvin was getting on for two years old, and I was seven going on eight. I was hugely protective of my little brother, and I'd taken it upon myself to be his entertainer whenever my mother wasn't around.

I took him onto the balcony and pointed out the wide expanse of shimmering blue that stretched before us. Seeing the sea was simply amazing. I'd never imagined that anything could exist that was so alien to the hard, sunbaked Kenyan earth, yet here was the ocean rolling out before us, a mass of rippled, pulsating water as far as the eye could see.

"That's the sea," I whispered in little Marvin's ear. "That shiny blue water thing stretches all the way to foreign places that aren't a part of Africa even."

I sat opposite little Marvin, gazing out at the ocean, trying to teach him the thumb-over-thumb game. I gripped his tiny hand in mine and showed him how to trap my thumb under his own. Soon I had him gurgling and chortling in delight, especially when I let him win. And I promised Marvin that on this magical beach we were going to have our first big adventures, and that I'd always be there as his big brother watching over him.

I noticed a swarm of winged termites trying to make their home on our balcony. I reached over and grabbed one and showed it to Marvin. His eyes shone with excitement and curiosity as it crawled about in my palm. It unfurled its wings to escape, but I wasn't about to let it go. I plucked a length of cotton from my shirt and showed Marvin how to tie the thread around the body of the termite, after which it whirred around and around, getting nowhere fast.

I handed over the string that held the termite to my little brother. This was our first big adventure, I announced—a *flying lesson*. We were going to zoom high in the sky in this airplane and send it far over the sea so we could discover just how far the water stretched and where it ended, and who lived on the other side.

Marvin and I spent all that day and the next splashing about in the crystal-clear shallows and kicking a beach ball around with Christian. When we wilted in the midday heat, we had ice creams and chilled sodas beneath palm-thatched sunshades. While my mother loved nothing more than a relaxing doze, Christian was a typical *mzungu*: he was never able to stay still for long. As soon as the afternoon heat had dropped a little, he'd entice me back into the water, so that we could have some swimming lessons.

Unfortunately, it soon became clear that swimming and I were never going to get along. I couldn't bring myself to admit it, but I was scared of the water and of getting out of my depth. But it was very different with little Marvin. While Christian wasn't my brother's real father, for most of Marvin's short life he had been around, and so it was only natural for Marvin to call him "Dada," and to extend to him the kind of trust that existed between a father and a son.

I stood in the shallows and searched for shells, stealing the odd glance at this tall, muscular Frenchman taking my little brother deeper into the sea. Marvin seemed to have no fear when Christian held him, and for a fleeting moment I longed for what he had—a life in which, from his earliest memories, Christian had been around. Then I forced those uncomfortable thoughts to the back of my mind, plucked a shell from the sand, held it aloft, and cried out to the pair of them.

"Look! Christian! Marvin! Look what I've found! We can put it in our shell collection!"

When Marvin and I tired of the beach, Christian chartered a boat that took us out to the reef, where he went snorkeling over the corals, bringing up bright red starfish from the depths. Starfish, jellyfish, and sea urchins—I'd learned about such creatures at school, but I'd never seen anything so outlandish as a dripping wet, bloodred star as big as a dinner plate, one that lived at the bottom of the sea.

We went sightseeing in the Danger-mobile, cycled on the beach, and made a bright collection of seashells in a salty scatter outside our door. In the evenings Christian and my mother would wander hand in hand on the powder white sands, as the sun kissed the bloodred ocean. But in no time our week in paradise was over, and it was time to return to Nairobi. With the holiday done, it felt as if the magic had gone from our lives, but fortunately there were to be many more such adventures with Christian.

For some reason I couldn't bring myself to call Christian Dad. The d-word just wouldn't pass my lips. It was pure childish obstinacy really, for with my Umoja friends I invariably referred to him as "my father." But there was also something deeper and more ingrained than this, and that was the fear of rejection. If I did start to call Christian Dad, what would happen if I lost him, just as I had my birth father? If that happened, I would be hurt once more, only ten times over.

I had never known my real father, Barack Obama Senior, so I had never known what I had lost. Now, I opted to insulate myself from the threat of further pain by not fully embracing Christian as my father.

But it's not so easy to safeguard oneself from the risk of loss and hurt.

CHAPTER 4

Mudfish Madness

A FEW MONTHS after our beach holiday, I found myself heading out in the Danger-mobile on a visit to Nyando and the home village. Christian had already met Grandma and Grandpa during one of his excursions upcountry to visit aid projects. In fact he had to pass that way regularly and had gotten into the habit of dropping by to check and see if everything was all right. But this was the first time that Marvin and I would be going with him.

During the six-hour drive from Nairobi to Nyando, I felt my excitement growing. At last I was going to get the chance to lord it over my cousin Omondi by arriving in the Danger-mobile. Sure enough, as we rumbled and growled along the village's potholed main street, a gaggle of children came out to gawp at the vehicle. Just as soon as they realized that it was a *mzungu* at the wheel, they started yelling, "*Odiero! Odiero!*"—the Luo word for white man.

They broke into a run and came chasing after us, switching to Swahili and crying out in a kind of chanting singsong.

"Mzungu! Mzungu!
How are you, Mzungu?"
"Mzungu! Mzungu!
How are you, Mzungu?"

They started yelling, "White man with a long nose!" "White man with a long nose!" It was very funny and all of us—Christian included—were laughing. I found myself enjoying the attention we were getting. There was a carnival atmosphere as we neared the homestead, and it made me feel special somehow.

I searched the crowd of faces for my cousin Omondi, but I couldn't see him anywhere. It crossed my mind that maybe he was out in the fields herding goats, in which case I would be robbed of my triumphant arrival in front of him. Christian and my mother would be heading on to visit some relatives further upcountry, so unless Omondi turned up in the next hour or so, he wouldn't get to see the Dangermobile. I'd just have to hope that he'd heard all the commotion and would make an appearance sometime soon.

Grandma Dorcas welcomed us into the family compound with a big hug and a warm smile, but she reserved an especially wide embrace for me. A tea-drinking ceremony followed—the traditional Luo welcome—a chance for all to sit and chat and catch up on family news. I didn't detect the slightest trace of resentment or discomfort on my grandparents' part that my mother's partner was a white man. My mother and Christian weren't married, so no dowry had been paid, but he more than compensated for that with his regular visits and the small ways in which he managed to help.

The first I knew of Omondi's arrival was a distant voice crying out, "Hey, City Boy! City Boy's here!"

Omondi was speaking Luo, for he knew only a smattering of Swahili and no English. My Nairobi life was separating me from my rural and tribal roots so much that it was now odd for me to hear someone calling out to me in my native tongue. In my cousin's eyes I was an alien in the village: I wore shoes, I was scared of water snakes and other creepy-crawlies, and I was clumsy and ungainly when we were out in the bush.

Still, it was good to see Omondi again. Before little Marvin's arrival he had been the closest thing to a brother that I had ever had. We'd spent a lot of good times together, and I knew that part of the reason he teased me was envy. In his eyes I had all the prospects that the rural life could never offer. Omondi was going to the village school, but his rudimentary Swahili and his lack of English testified to how basic the education there was.

Omondi presumed that because I lived in the city, I had a pampered life. As he saw it, everything about me cried out privilege—the way I dressed, the way I spoke, my obvious education. To Omondi, and the rest of the village gang, that privilege was grounded in my urban life, my mother's city employment, and my having a white man as my "father." In fact, in their eyes the greatest privilege was having a *mzungu* father. To them, that was the best ever, for with it came amazing things like the Danger-mobile.

But I was hopelessly behind the times. Omondi had seen Christian's car on the previous occasions when he'd visited the village, so when I asked him to come see my dad's amazing vehicle he acted as if he just wasn't interested.

"I've seen it," Omondi remarked. "Your dad's been here loads of times before."

"So, what d'you reckon?" I asked. "Pretty cool, huh?"

"Yeah, it's okay." He shrugged. "But come on, let's go catch some mudfish."

The first time, Omondi had been bowled over by the very sight of such a vehicle, especially as it was driven by my adoptive father, but by now the novelty of the Danger-mobile was beginning to fade.

By the time my mother and Christian were readying themselves to leave, my cousin and I were heading off into the bush. En route to the rice fields we picked up a few of the village gang. We cut ourselves some poles from a grove of bamboo, and improvised fishing line with a length of string. As for the hook, that was a piece of old wire filed to a point at one end and bent into a U shape.

As their name suggests, mudfish live in flooded rice fields, hiding out in the dark, gooey squelch at the bottom of the sun-warmed waters. The best way to entice one out is to dangle a hook with a live worm impaled on it. So first we had to dig out some big, juicy worms from the mud banks that bordered the rice field. We used our bare hands, and before long Omondi and I and the rest of the gang were covered in mud. It was real fun, for I never got to be this messy back in the city.

With a worm wriggling on my hook, I cast my line into the nearest pool and waited. The water was full of sediment, so it was impossible to see any of the fish. All you could do was cast your line and hope. But somehow Omondi seemed to have a sixth sense of where to find the hungriest mudfish—one that just couldn't resist taking a tasty worm. In no time he must have felt the telltale tug on his line, for he gave a triumphant whoop of joy and hauled in his first catch.

I glanced around to see what he'd got, and as I did so I felt a jerk on my own line. No doubt about it—I had a bite! But by the time I'd recovered from my surprise and pulled sharply on my rod to strike, the fish had made its getaway. Line and hook came out of the water without even the shred of a worm left on the end. As I gazed in disappointment at the bare crook of wire, I heard the teasing start up from the rest of the gang.

"Bah! Bare hook!" Omondi exclaimed. "Useless City Boy!"

"Lost your worm! Lost your fish!" exclaimed another. "Typical City Boy!"

"What you trying to catch, City Boy?" a third taunted. "Thin air!"

The thought flashed through my mind that these village idiots wouldn't survive a day in the big city, but I wasn't about to say as much. They outnumbered me five to one, and I didn't fancy my chances if it came to a fight.

There were many different types of mudfish, but we knew them all by the generic Luo word for fish, *rech*. Omondi's catch was a good one, about the length of his foot. We'd each have to hook a similar-sized fish if we were going to have enough for a feast. Luckily, I finally did catch my own, but only with a good deal of coaching from Omondi. Still, I felt deliriously happy. As I unhooked my catch and held it up for all to see, the village boys even gave me a round of applause.

"Hooray! Hooray!"

"Would you believe it!"

"The boy from the city catches a fish!"

I left my mudfish to flap to death on the bank, just as I'd seen the others do. As its writhing and gasping grew weaker and weaker, I told myself that here was proof that I too could be a tough country boy. I took up the dead, slimy fish and drove a sharpened stick through it from end to end. We gathered up a pile of dry wood, and one of the gang hurried off, returning a few minutes later with a burning stick that he'd taken from a cooking fire. He thrust its fiery glow into the wood, threw on some dry grass, and bent down to blow the wisps of smoke into dancing flames.

We gathered around and each of us held our stick fish first in the fire, turning it from time to time as the mudfish sizzled and popped. After five minutes or so Omondi declared that they were ready, and we set about our feast. I gripped the stick in my hand, held the fish to my mouth, and bit off a chunk of hot flesh. In spite of its name, mudfish is firm and meaty and doesn't taste of mud at all.

Sitting there in the bush with the country boys, eating my first catch, I couldn't have been happier. As we picked the bones clean, they asked me all kinds of questions about life in the big city. How tall were the tallest buildings? they demanded. How many cars were there in the city? Did I ever see airplanes swooping in to land? What kind of adventures did we city boys have, if we couldn't go mudfish catching?

Once every scrap of flesh was gone, we threw the remains—the bones, skin, and guts—to the dogs. Most days, after feeding the dogs, we'd take them hunting for rabbits in the bush. And after a day's mudfish catching and rabbiting, I'd start to feel almost at home in the village. But I still didn't quite fit in, and the village boys never let me forget it. I still felt caught between two worlds. Although I looked forward to going to the village, I didn't want to live there anymore. Our family life in Umoja was what I knew best now, and I was happy with my lot in the city.

A couple of days after the fishing expedition, Christian and my mother came to collect me, for it was time to return to Nairobi. En route Christian stopped at a roadside stall to buy water and fruit. All of a sudden a flash Mercedes-type car pulled up alongside us in a cloud of dust, and out got an Indian-looking man. He was short and a bit pudgy, but he was dressed in a smart suit, and the combination of the car and the cut of his clothes spelled power and money.

He rapped on the driver's window, gesturing for Christian to put it down. I wondered what he wanted. I wasn't very keen on the Indians who lived in our country. Mostly they had come to Kenya during colonial times to work for the British, and after the British had left, many had stayed. Often they were smart business people, and many had prospered in post-independence Kenya. But they were intensely tribal and kept very much to themselves. They rarely if ever married outside their community, and they would invariably prefer to employ a fellow Indian as opposed to a black African.

During our holiday in Malindi I had myself been on the receiving end of the Kenyan Indian's brand of racism. A great number believed they were somehow "better" than the black Africans who made up the vast majority of Kenyans. I had tried playing with some of the Indian kids who were staying at the beach hotel, only to be given the cold shoulder. Pretty quickly I'd realized that they didn't want to have anything to do with me. I'd mentioned it to my mother and Christian. They'd tried to explain that many of those Indians wrongly felt they were "higher-class" Kenyans and that we were beneath them.

In response to the Indian man's tapping, Christian wound down his window. "Is there some way I can help?" he asked.

The man at the window gave a wide, flashing smile. "I am indeed sincerely hoping so. My name is Ranjit Asmat, and I would like to buy your most excellent car. It is the first time I am seeing a car like this one, and it is a really most excellent one."

"Well, I appreciate the offer," Christian replied. "But it is not for sale, I am afraid."

Ranjit frowned. "The car is not for the selling?"

Christian shook his head. "*Pas du tout.* Not at all."

"But why?" Ranjit asked. "You can please name your price. I am very serious about this." He put his hand into his back pocket and pulled out a checkbook. "I am ready to pay whatever price you are asking. I will write you the check right now, at this very moment."

Christian shrugged. "Maybe, but it is still not for sale."

"Not at any price?" Ranjit insisted. "Surely, there must be—"

"*Non.* Not at any price," Christian cut in. "And we must be getting on; we have a long drive ahead of us."

Ranjit looked crestfallen. "Yes, of course, of course, I have been too presuming." He stood back and took a lingering glance at the Danger-mobile. "Dangel four-by-four," he pronounced, reading off the decal on the side. "Such a terrible shame not to have reached a deal to both our happiness, but perhaps you might tell me where I can buy such a machine?"

"It is from *la France*," Christian replied. "I imported it directly, and I am afraid you cannot get one like this here in Kenya. *Au revoir*, Mr. Asmat, and *bonne chance*."

I knew both those phrases from Christian's kitchen French lessons: he was wishing the Indian man good-bye and good luck. As far as I was concerned, it was just fantastic that Christian had stuck to his guns and refused the Indian man's offer to "name his price." To my way of thinking the Danger-mobile was priceless, and Christian seemed to agree. He'd stood up to Ranjit Asmat, and even refused a blank check. No doubt about it, Christian Bertrand was my hero.

As the Danger-mobile issued a low, throaty growl and we pulled away from the parked car, I felt like cheering Christian. Instead, I sat there in the back and allowed myself a quiet smile. For a moment I had feared that the Danger-mobile was about to be sold off, but how could I ever have doubted Christian?

In a way I was still confused and trying to anchor my fractured identity. Christian was my hero, but I still couldn't quite embrace him fully as the father that he had become. My friends and I would talk about him as my dad, but then they'd see me address him as "Christian" to his face. Eric and the others would stare at me. I could tell what they were thinking: *Why don't you just call him Dad?*

At one time or another all my friends had asked me why I had a white father. I used to shrug and say that I didn't know. It was a hard question for a young child to answer, *Why does your dad have a different skin color from your own?* But in a way I was growing to like being the odd one out. I was starting to relish it, for I didn't want to be like everyone else. "The kid who lives with the *mzungu*"—that's how I was known, and it made me a local celebrity.

In any case, the discomfort I felt was far outweighed by the advantages. Christian was proving to be a good father, and his presence in our lives gifted us privileges that few others could dream of—our smart vehicles and our holidays, for starters. Then there were the toys. The old, push-around Tonka toys had been replaced by a radio-controlled racing car with go-faster stripes, plus a big red fire truck that I could sit on. No one else had toys like those, and in the eyes of the others, they made me special.

And in the eyes of the girls in Umoja I was the kid with the exotic life, the one who was always doing exciting things. At eight years of age I was too young to have a girlfriend, but I did notice the shy glances from the girls whenever they saw me driving by in the Danger-mobile, and I liked the admiration.

I had gotten into the habit of popping into Christian's office on the way home from school, so that he and I could travel the downtown-Nairobi-to-Umoja leg together, in his car. While I was waiting for him, he'd sit me at his office desk so I could play computer games. I loved zapping the aliens in Space Invaders and playing Pacman.

On the drive home Christian would tell me stories from his life before he'd come to Kenya—of his military service at the age of eighteen, and how he'd fared in the French army. He'd gone on to work in Brussels before discovering his passion in life, which was running aid projects in the developing world.

Back in the Umoja house he'd show me pictures of the French

town in which he grew up, parts of which seemed to me fantastically old, with winding streets and grand buildings like ancient castles. I hoped that one day he would take me there, for it looked like a magical place to visit. But I didn't dare ask, for that wasn't the sort of thing a Kenyan child could ask of his real father, let alone his adoptive one.

Toward the end of that first year Christian left for what was to become his annual visit to France. He was away for a month, and I missed him badly and counted the days until his return. A part of me was uncomfortable with the way his absence had affected me, for it meant that almost without noticing I had become dependent on him. His going away served to remind me that he wasn't actually my father; perhaps he wouldn't always be around. Subconsciously at least I decided to try to distance myself from him.

There was another factor that sowed doubt in my young mind. Christian had a previous family. I wondered if he'd gone back to be with them and if he would simply forget about us. He rarely if ever spoke about that family, and I saw no photos of them around our home. That side of his life remained closed to me, and I was happy for it to be so. I didn't want to know about it. I didn't want there to be any complications. I just wanted us to be the happy family that every child craves.

Christian returned from France laden with gifts. His flight had taken him via Paris, and he'd made the most of the shopping opportunities. There were beautiful clothes and exotic French perfumes for my mother, and toys for little Marvin, plus something extra special for me. Christian presented me with a Swatch watch. I gazed at it in awe. The casing was completely see-through, and as I turned it over and over in my hands, I could see the working parts whirring away inside.

"Go on, you can open it," Christian urged. "Then I will show you how to wear it."

With Christian's help I levered open the plastic container, and then I was holding the watch in my eager hands. I just knew how my friends were going to react to this: it was without doubt the most amazing thing that any of us had ever owned.

"So, you wear it like this," Christian continued, strapping it around my left wrist. "*Voilà!* Very grown-up looking!"

I gazed at the fantastic gift that he'd brought me. "Thanks . . . Christian," I murmured. "It's really, really *cool.*"

Christian laughed. "I knew you would like it. Now, you need not worry about taking it off in the water even, for it is completely, how do you say, *waterproof.*"

"Really? Even if we go in the sea?"

"*Bien sur.* Even when you go in the sea."

Even the name itself—Swatch—was cool. As soon as I was able, I raced over to Eric's place to show off my prized possession.

"Wow!" Eric marveled, as he held the Swatch in the palm of his hand. "*Wow.* Can I try it on?"

I smiled. "Go on. Try it. It comes all the way from France."

Eric wrapped the transparent skin of the watch around his own earth-brown arm and held it up in the light to admire it.

"Where could you get such a thing in Kenya?" he remarked. "You can't, that's what." He glanced at me, a little enviously. "You know something, you're dead lucky having that *mzungu* for a father."

Every kid in Umoja was jealous of that Swatch, as were all my friends at school. One day one of the older boys asked if he could borrow it, just for a few minutes. As soon as I'd handed it to him, he made himself scarce. The next day I managed to track him down and I asked to have it back, but he told me that he'd lost it. I knew that he was lying, yet he was bigger than I, and there was no way that I was going to challenge or to fight him.

I didn't know what to say to Christian or my mother about the loss of my watch. I reckoned Christian would be pretty relaxed about it, but not my mum. She'd be angry, and she'd demand to know why I'd been so stupidly trusting with that older boy. She might even go around to his parents' place and demand that he return it, which would likely cause me trouble with the older boy's gang. Eventually, I decided to tell them a white lie. I said that I'd been playing with Eric in the bush and that's where I'd lost it.

My mother scolded me for being so careless with my possessions. Christian tried to soften the blow by promising to get me another one when next he traveled overseas. But he did counsel me to be more careful with my things in the future. Some of the older boys, including the one who'd stolen my watch, reckoned that I was a softie and a pushover because I had a *mzungu* for a father. They presumed that because he could buy me such fine things, I must be spoiled and cosseted.

I'd lent that boy the watch partly in an effort to curry favor with him and the rest of his gang. But my plan had backfired, for rather than impressing them with my fine things, I'd ended up looking like someone who was weak and naive. And in truth, I didn't yet know whether those boys might be right about me. I'd only had one chance to test my boyhood mettle, and even that incident hadn't actually come to blows.

A few months back, one of the boys in my class had started picking on me. He was bigger than I was and a known bully. On the day that he came to attack me, I threatened to beat him with a *ngomongo*. He didn't know what I meant, for Ngomongo is the name of a marketplace on the outskirts of Nairobi. The market is set amid a rocky landscape, which is why I'd coined the nickname *ngomongo* for a rock.

The bullyboy ignored my warning and came at me, so I grabbed a rock off the ground.

"This is a *ngomongo*!" I warned. "So d'you want to know what it feels like?"

He backed off, and never again did he try to pick on me. But I wasn't certain whether that one near-fight proved that I wasn't a pushover and a softie. Would I really have bashed that bullyboy with the *ngomongo*, if he had tried to hit me? I didn't know for sure. Only time would tell if I had it in me to defend myself against the real bullyboys.

After his trip to France I asked Christian what it was like to fly all that way in an airliner. I was fascinated to know how it felt to sit in an airplane and be lifted into the clouds. Eric and I used to watch the sleek, gleaming shapes gliding through the skies above Nairobi as they came in to land. Of course, I'd never been inside an airplane, but I knew the theory of how they kept themselves aloft in the air. We'd learned all about it in our science lessons, and about the men and women who flew the aircraft.

Christian described to me the power of the jet engines as the aircraft accelerated down the runway. He explained how the g-forces at takeoff had thrust him down hard into his seat. He related how he'd killed time on the flight to Paris by watching the in-flight movies and enjoying some good food and wine. I was fascinated by airplanes and by the lifestyle of those who flew them, and to me that seemed like a dream career.

"You know, that's what I want to do when I grow up," I told Christian. "I'd like to be a pilot and fly an airplane just like the one you were in."

"Well, it is not such a bad idea," he replied. "But you will have to study hard. Many people want to be pilots, but if you want it badly enough, Georgie, then, *pas de problème,* you will make it!"

I shared my dream with Eric, and he in turn confided in me that he wanted to do the same. In fact, "airline pilot" was the most common answer whenever teachers asked the boys in class what they wanted to be when they grew up. It was seen as being a way to travel the world and earn good money, with a degree of glamour attached. I knew the competition was going to be fierce, but if I studied hard and kept doing well at school, I stood as good a chance as anyone.

I had my heart set on it, so why on earth should I fail?

CHAPTER 5

For Jennifer

My mother and Christian took my aspirations seriously. They made inquiries as to which high schools taught aeronautical engineering, the kind of course that would give me a real head start in qualifying to be a pilot. It turned out that there was only one, the Nairobi-based National School, that taught the subject. That was where we decided that I would be going, although we knew getting a place wouldn't be so easy.

In Kenya, the crucial hurdle for all schoolchildren is the Kenya Certificate of Primary Education (KCPE), a series of nationwide exams taken in the last year of primary school. Those who pass the KCPE with distinction are offered a place at a handful of Kenyan National Schools—the elite academies. Although there were many good high schools, there was only the one National School that taught "aeronautical engineering"—which to me simply meant flying—and I was determined to win a place there.

In a way there was an odd disconnect in having Christian so closely involved in my education. In our history lessons we were taught about the white colonizers who had come to our country and taken the best land and the best resources, while treating the indigenous blacks terribly. The bad guys were the whites, and in Kenya, at least, the colonizers had been British. The whites had brought a degree of development in terms of roads, railways, schools, and hospitals, but that in no way compensated for what they had taken in terms of agricultural land, timber, and minerals, and worse still for how they had treated the black Africans.

In the war for independence the British had carried out heinous acts, while the Kenyan freedom fighters—the Mau Mau—fought heroically to throw off the shackles of oppression. In our geography lessons we were shown a map of the world and learned where Britain was—this far-off nation that had so exploited us. And we were taught that the British had justified their oppression on the basis of differences in race and national identity.

The fact that the British had colonized us allowed me a kind of get-out-of-jail-free card as far as Christian was concerned. He was a white man, but he was French and the bad guys had been British, and that made Christian *not one of them*. It was a relief, for I didn't have it in me to resent or to blame him. He had taken us in, provided us a home, and loved my mother, Marvin, and me as his own family. The last thing he deserved was my resentment or my bile.

When we were taught the wider history of the colonization of Africa, I learned that the French had occupied much of West Africa. I had to console myself with the thought that West Africa was a very long way from Kenya, and I only really cared about what had been done to our country. Ergo, Christian was still pretty much all right.

One evening my mother decided to have a little chat with me about the roots of my identity and my birth father. She had decided that I was mature enough to know a little about him. She told me that he had been a very clever and professional kind of man—the sort of man who would have been a role model for me if he were still alive. He'd earned a PhD and had worked for the Kenyan government, and right until his death he had been a believer that our country could become a leading light in Africa. She remarked what a tragic loss his death had been for her and the wider family, if not the country as a whole.

My mother told me this with the best of intentions, but I wasn't really listening. I couldn't even visualize my father, and I'd had little contact with his side of the family. In short, he didn't figure in my life. When she told me that I had older brothers and sisters, both here in Kenya and overseas, there was a vague flicker of interest. But apart from the momentary acquaintance I'd made with my Kenyan sister and my American brother, I didn't know them at all. They didn't feel like a part of my family or a part of me, just as my blood father didn't feel like my father anymore.

As a nine-year-old boy bursting with energy, I'd prefer to be out playing with my buddies, rather than listening to stories about a side of the family that was dead to me. Playtime was precious, for my mother had set a strict curfew of six o'clock in the evening. By then I had to be scrubbed clean and ready to eat a family supper. In Kenya the day length varies little, with the sun rising and setting at the same time throughout the year. It would remain light until seven o'clock, and I knew that my friends would be out playing until then, but I would have to be in for curfew.

My mother was both strict and soft. As long as I behaved myself, I was lavished in love, but if I stepped out of line—coming home late, for example—she would beat me with the stick that she kept in the corner of her bedroom. She'd order me to lie on the floor, so she could whack me across the bottom. She'd beat me until the pain brought tears to my eyes, but it was a matter of pride that I never cried.

After she'd finished she would start to feel bad about it, which was typical of my mother.

"I'm sorry, Georgie," she'd tell me, as she smothered me in guilty hugs. "But you made me do it. If only you wouldn't misbehave."

"All the other kids are allowed out till seven," I'd object. "So why not me?"

"Because we like to have a family meal sitting around the table together," she'd reply. "And we eat at six, don't we? It makes us close, like a real family."

My mother seemed desperate to build that family closeness, something we'd never had with my real father. That was why suppertime was so precious to her—this sitting around the dining table and eating together as one big happy family.

If I was really naughty, my mother would ground me, which meant no going out to play. But as soon as she left the house, I'd sneak into the bedroom she shared with Christian and take her stick. I'd jump over the wall of our compound, throw the stick into the bush, and be gone. When she came home and discovered me missing she'd be furious, but with her stick nowhere to be found, I might just escape another beating.

It was over this aspect of our upbringing that Christian and my mother had one of their few differences. While my mother was a strict disciplinarian, Christian was dead against either of us children getting beaten. Whenever he caught her using the stick, he'd immediately tell her to stop. I'd be sent to my room, while he tried to convince her to let him do the disciplining. More often than not Christian's admonishment came too late, for she'd already have beaten us soundly.

Nearly all the kids in our community got a beating. That was how Kenyan parents maintained discipline. When I was out with Eric and the others, we'd swap stories about how we'd been beaten, and we'd have a good laugh about it. Christian was the odd one out in being so against it, but strangely enough I used to think that his method of dealing with bad behavior was the better way. We kids had reached the point where we were so used to getting beaten that we expected it, and once the punishment became predictable, it lost its effectiveness.

By contrast, whenever Christian caught me misbehaving, his way was to sit me down and give me a serious talking-to—explaining why something was wrong and not particularly smart. He'd talk to me for twenty minutes or more, and I never knew quite what he was going to say. After one of his disciplinary lectures I'd end up in tears. The way he reasoned things through made me feel guilty for what I'd done, and in truth it hurt more than being caned. I far preferred a caning from my mother to one of Christian's talking-tos.

Christian seemed remarkably at ease in Africa. He'd made Kenya his home and he'd made us his life. Our family was his family, and in the same spirit that he embraced us, we embraced him as a father, as the head of the household, and as someone to look up to and admire.

Marvin had yet to start school. He was five years younger than me, but the gap in our ages felt even wider, for I'd commenced my schooling almost a year early. He was a soft and gentle child and we rarely if ever fought. I felt like his protector, for I sensed from early on that he was going to grow up to be vulnerable. But that didn't stop him from ratting on me if ever he caught me doing something wrong.

One day I brought a girl home to the house. Her name was Mary and she was my age mate, and I had a wild crush on her. It was all very innocent—a bit of sitting close together on the sofa and holding hands as we watched TV—but Marvin didn't see it that way. He promised he wouldn't say anything, but just as soon as Mother came home, he blurted it all out. As far as my mother was concerned, bringing home a "girlfriend" was one of the worst possible transgressions. She ordered me to lie on the floor for the beating of my life. And unfortunately, there was no Christian around to save me.

I was approaching my tenth birthday by now, and girls were just starting to figure as a factor in my life, especially one called Jennifer. Jennifer was from one of the biggest tribes in Kenya, the Kikuyu, and as with many Kikuyu girls she was strikingly beautiful, with a heart-shaped face and enormous doe eyes. There was rarely a chance to talk to girls at school, for it was forbidden to do so even during break time. But Jennifer shared the same *matatu* route home as me, and that meant the chance to catch some time together at the bus stop or on the road home.

I used to try to chat her up in the shy, clumsy way of nine-year-olds. I hadn't even kissed her, or any other girl for that matter, but I used to dream of doing so. Every day I used to tell myself that I would rustle up the courage to hold her hand on the bus, but when the time came I never quite managed to go through with it. I'd leave my hand open on the seat where she could easily place hers in mine, but whenever our fingers touched, a bolt of fiery electricity would shoot through me—and her, I reckoned—and our hands would be swiftly withdrawn.

One afternoon I was traveling home from school and I got off one *matatu* to catch another, which would take me all the way to Umoja. Just as I alighted, I spotted the unmistakably alluring figure of Jennifer standing on the far side of the road. Without checking I went to dash across the busy road to join her, my heart booming with excitement.

Just as I took a step off the curb, the *matatu* that I had been traveling on began to reverse. It drove over my foot and I fell to the ground, twisting my shin. Jennifer had seen the whole thing and was horrified, but there was little she could do. I was in such pain that I couldn't stand. I also felt like a complete idiot and was consumed by embarrassment. Whether it was from the shock or the pain I'm not sure, but I was also in tears.

The *matatu* tout—the young boy whose job it was to rustle up passengers by calling out the *matatu* number—had seen it all happen, and he could tell that I was in a bad way. Together with the driver he kicked all the passengers off the *matatu* and lifted me onto one of the seats. They offered to drive me to the nearest clinic, where I could get myself some painkillers and some bandages. Choking back her own tears, Jennifer said that she couldn't accompany me, for if she was late in she'd be in real trouble with her parents.

After the medic at the clinic had seen me, the *matatu* driver dropped me at home. I managed to hobble inside, but the ankle had swollen up to double its normal size. Christian and my mother had just gotten home from work. They took one look at me and declared that I was going straight to a proper hospital. They rushed me to Nairobi's private Aga Khan Hospital, where the doctors took a series of X-rays, which showed that the ankle was broken. They put me in a cast from my foot to just below my knee and sent me home with orders to rest the leg until it healed.

On the drive home I pretended that I was in too much pain to talk, which got me out of having to explain what had happened. But my mother wasn't to be put off so easily. She tracked down the *matatu* driver and got the full story out of him. Needless to say, she wasn't very happy that my injury was owing to my being sweet on a girl.

It was in the moments after that accident that my mother decided to send me away to boarding school. I guess Christian must have gone along with it, for when they announced the plan, they put up a united front. No one told me that this was my punishment for being sweet on Jennifer, but that's what it amounted to. I knew that there was little point in trying to object: in Kenya, young children don't defy their parents. In any case, they did a good job of sweetening the pill for me.

The school that they had chosen for me—Busara Forest View Academy—is one of Kenya's top private establishments. It sits in the lush and forested foothills of Mount Kenya, some four hours' drive north of Nairobi. My mother and Christian sold the idea to me by stressing how outstanding the school was and how pupils from the Academy regularly topped the Kenyan exams league. Going to the Academy would really boost my chances of making it into the National School to study aeronautics, a big step toward becoming a pilot.

Christian and my mother went about buying me my new kit, from a list provided by the Academy: blanket, mattress, bucket, smart uniform, books, plus a fantastic sports kit, including a hockey stick, which I had no idea how to use. Seeing all of this smart new stuff, I couldn't help but feel as if I was pretty special, and that going to the Academy would not be a bad thing. And I let myself believe that my mother, Christian, and Marvin would be visiting the school on a daily basis, so I wouldn't be alone.

The first day of my new school Christian loaded a green tin trunk crammed full of my things into the back of the Danger-mobile, and the four of us set off for Mount Kenya. The mountain itself creates its own microclimate. I had learned all about it in my previous school. The mountain is the largest in Kenya. The summit rises so high above

Kenya's baking-hot plains that it carries a permanent ice cap. Normally it's visible from many miles away, but on that day there was only a towering mass of thick, dark cloud, the mountain invisible in the gloom. It was a forbidding apparition—Mount Doom.

By the time I was formally booked in for my first day of term, Christian, my mum, and Marvin were preparing to say their good-byes. I couldn't quite believe that this was happening, that they would be leaving me here alone for days and days on end. Via a big dose of dreamy wishful thinking I had somehow convinced myself that boarding school and separation from my family weren't one and the same thing. Now I was waking up to the harsh reality.

I wanted to ask my mother and Christian either to stay or to take me with them, but all the other boys were saying good-bye to their parents, and I didn't want to make a scene or to look like a fool. Yet as I stood at the school gates watching the Danger-mobile take the road back to Nairobi, I felt myself start to cry. Eventually, the gleaming speck in the distance was completely gone.

I wasn't alone in my grief: a lot of the other boys and girls were in tears. But just as soon as the last of the parents had disappeared, the new boys matron started to show her true colors. Matron had acted kind and motherly in front of the adults, reassuring worried mothers that she would look after each and every one of us as if we were her own, but in reality she was the harridan from hell.

"You, *new boys*! Stop that crying!" she thundered. "You're to form a line and follow me to your dorm. I want everything tidied away by suppertime. That leaves you less than an hour! So get moving!"

"Yes, Matron," came the sniveling reply.

"*Not Matron!*" she thundered. "*Madame!* From now on you address me as *madame*. Now stop your blubbering and follow me."

We trooped after Matron in a sorry line of weeping, downcast boys. She took us from the front gate past the enormous sports field and the classroom blocks to the single-sex dorms. The two girls' dorms and the two boys' dorms were segregated from each other by a high barbed-wire fence, the meaning of which was blindingly obvious— no fraternizing between the sexes.

In the new boys' dorm Matron allocated each of us a place among the serried ranks of bunk beds. You took what you were given; there was no arguing with Matron. She looked to be in her late forties, with graying hair pulled back in a tight bun. She was tall and fat and fearsome, and her face looked as if it would crack open if she were ever forced to smile. Worst of all, she had a big stick that she kept always at her side, and she was more than happy to wield it if anyone so much as thought of misbehaving.

I was lucky in that I got allocated a top bunk, but it was a lottery, pure and simple. I shoved my metal trunk under the lower bed alongside that of my bunkmate, and we stood to attention wondering what came next. As I stole a glance at the boy who shared my bunk, I wondered if I looked as scared and as worried as he did. Matron began to address us in what we were soon to realize was her one and only way of speaking—a staccato stream of barked orders at top volume.

"Listen up, new boys! All possessions to be kept in your tin trunks. All trunks to be kept well under your beds. All beds to be kept neat and tidy at all times. Understood?"

"Yes, Matron."

"Not *Matron*!" she exploded. "You address me as *madame. Madame!*"

"Yes, madame."

"Better. Now, toilet blocks are to your rear, as are the shower blocks. You will wash each morning, before breakfast. No washing, no breakfast! Understood?"

"Yes, madame."

"Tonight I will be sleeping at one end of the dorm, and so there will be no larking around. Heaven forbid if I hear anyone talking after lights out. Lights out, no fights. Understood?"

"Yes, madame."

And so it went. The boys in my dorm were about my age, but of course I knew not a soul among them. That evening I couldn't bring myself to eat any supper, for my stomach was all knotted up with anxiety. Most of the new boys were unable to manage any food, but

Matron didn't appear to care in the slightest. "If you don't eat, you go hungry" was her attitude.

That first night I lay awake in the pitch-dark dorm, listening to the other boys sniveling into their pillows. I wondered where on earth it was that my mother and Christian had sent me. I didn't have a single toy to comfort me. My tin trunk was crammed full of books, kit, and more books, and that was all.

I stared at the invisible ceiling, feeling as if I had been banished to a place close to hell. I told myself that I hated this life. I hated my new school. I hated Matron, just for being Matron. I hated my mother and Christian, for having sent me to such a place. But most of all I hated myself, for being gullible enough to allow myself to be sent here.

I barely slept at all that first night, and at some stage I had to venture out to use the loo. It was dark as the grave and freezing cold in the dorm, and I had to stumble about until I found the door handle, after which it was only marginally lighter outside. I made my way to the toilet block by heading for the one bare lightbulb on the outside wall. The light was a magnet for all sorts of enormous flying insects of the night, and the nearer I got, the more they kept crashing into the side of my head and my ears.

After I'd had my pee I still couldn't manage to sleep. My mind was a whirl of thoughts. I lay there thinking about what Eric and my other Umoja buddies would have been doing that day, and I ended up feeling very sorry for myself. It seemed like a lifetime before I heard the dawn bell. It was still dark, but there was no sleeping through Matron's wake-up call. She marched along the line of bunks rapping on the wooden bedposts with her stick.

"New boys!" she cried. "Everyone up! Out of your beds! Now!"

There was a sleepy muttering of "Yes, madame."

"Get up! Get up!" she barked. "In line with your buckets at the ablution block in five minutes flat."

I grabbed my plastic bucket from under the lower bunk and made my way to the shower block in bare feet and my polka-dot pajamas. A crowd of other pajama-clad boys were shuffling forward like a sea of ghosts in the milky half-light of dawn. Before the sun burned off the worst of the mist, the foothills of Mount Kenya were cold and foggy, the grass glistening with thick dew. I joined a line of boys hunched and shivering against the cold.

At the front of the queue Matron warmed herself over a blazing fire, a huge cauldron balanced over the flames. Each boy held out his bucket, as Matron doled out the one jugful of hot water that was our daily ration. I in turn drew level with Matron. I found myself staring into the depths of the cauldron, which was bubbling away fiercely, throwing out a thick cloud of steam.

"Bucket, boy!" Matron demanded, jerking me back to my senses. "And quick about it—or do you want to go to the back?"

I held out my bucket and she poured in my scalding-hot water ration. It made the bucket a miserly one-quarter full. I carried it over to the shower block, careful not to spill a drop. Inside, boys were already dousing themselves, trying to scrub the sleep from their eyes and to warm their frozen bones. There were rows of cubicles all without doors, and only one boy was allowed in each at any one time.

The wait seemed never-ending, and I was soon to learn that if I didn't make the front of that first queue, by the time a space came free in the shower block, my water would be stone cold. I gazed up at the massive bulk of the mountain above us and cursed it for its altitude and bitter climate, which were doing so much to make a misery of our lives.

As I strained my eyes to see the uppermost reaches of the mountain, I fancied I could just make out a flash of snowy brightness, but I didn't make the observation with any joy. I glanced at the cloud of steam issuing forth from my bucket and berated the greedy mountain for sucking all my water's heat away. By the time a cubicle was free, my water was lukewarm, but even that was better than freezing.

I ripped off my pajamas, splashed a little of the bucket's contents over myself, and grabbed my bar of soap—one of several pristine white ones that my mother had packed for me. As I worked up a thick lather, I was aware of the eerie silence of the place. It was barely 5:30 a.m. and not a word was being spoken. Apart from the noise of the scrubbing and splashing, the shower block was utterly silent, and that suffocating quiet weighed on us all like a thick cloud.

Back in the dorm, I changed into my school uniform—a white collared shirt, plus matching chocolate brown tie, sweater, and shorts. Even the socks had to be regulation-issue caramel brown with chocolate brown stripes, and the shoes a glossy black. Once dressed, I joined the third queue of the morning, for breakfast in the dining hall.

Matron was on our backs again. The dining hall served meals in shifts, and each year had a ten-minute time slot in which everyone had to get fed or go hungry. We shuffled forward to the hatches, each holding out the tin bowl that our mothers had bought for us back in whatever towns and cities we hailed from. Breakfast was a ladleful of porridge, a hunk of bread and butter, and a mug of sweet milky tea.

At least the porridge was still warm by the time I got my ration. The slower boys at the back of the queue would be getting a congealed lump as cold and hard as iron. We new boys crammed ourselves onto the wooden benches at an enormous communal table. We were just about to start cramming the food into our mouths when Matron intervened.

"*Grace!*" she thundered. "*G-R-A-C-E.* What about grace?"

A row of boys—myself included—froze, spoons piled high with porridge suspended halfway to our mouths.

Matron pointed at one of the smaller boys toward my end of the table. "You there, say the grace. Now!" She turned on the rest of us. "And no one eats so much as a morsel until he is done."

"Thank you, Father, for this food that you have blessed us with today—"

Matron smashed her wooden baton down on the tabletop barely inches from that boy.

"*Stand up!*" she roared. "Don't you know you stand when you say your grace at the Academy!"

The boy struggled to his feet, almost falling over the bench as he did so. He was visibly shaking, and he began stumbling over his words.

"Thank you, Father, for t-t-this f-f-food . . ."

Under the baleful eye of Matron, not a soul among us dared to touch our food until he was done.

After breakfast Matron had us herded into a classroom for our first lesson of the day. At eight sharp the door flew open and the teacher strode in. As one we rose to our feet with a scraping of chairs. The teacher surveyed the room to make sure everyone was standing smartly to attention. In Kenya teachers are seen as having a prominent position in society. Those at the Academy were the very elite, and they demanded a level of respect from us that reflected their status.

"Hello, class," the teacher announced. "I am Mr. Ouma."

"Hello, Mr. Ouma," we responded as one.

"Please sit. When I call out your name, respond with a simple 'present' to indicate you are here."

"Yes, Mr. Ouma."

"Kimani?"

"Present."

"Otieno?"

"Present."

My mind drifted as the teacher ran through the list of students. I had barely managed to speak to another pupil since arriving at the Academy, what with Matron's barked orders and her regimented discipline. I knew that my bunkmate's name was Henry and that he came from Mombasa, but that was all. He seemed as cowed and dispirited as the rest of us.

"Odongo?" the teacher continued.

"Present."

"Mwikali?"

"Present."

"Obama?"

"Present," I replied, reluctantly.

The Academy was just about the last place on earth that I wanted to be.

CHAPTER 6

In the Shadow of Mount Kenya

AT THE ACADEMY, each of us new boys had eleven compulsory subjects: English, Swahili, math, geography, history and civics (H & C), Christian religious education (CRE), science, music, agriculture, arts and crafts, and home science. Monday to Friday our routine was one of regimented timekeeping, from the five a.m. wake-up call to the ten p.m. lights-out in the dorms, after which there was no talking allowed.

Shoes had to be kept mirror-shiny all the time. You had to polish them at night before bed, and first thing in the morning you'd buff them up. Skin was to be moistened with Vaseline after every shower; otherwise it would go dry and flaky in the cold. Hair had to be kept razor short, and every two weeks we boys were supposed to have our heads shaved by our mothers. If you did something wrong, you'd get caned by the teachers—boys on the bottom, girls across their palms. Over time I would learn to shove a book down my underwear, to insulate myself from the blows.

After the first few days I knew that I had to toughen up, for no one was coming to rescue me. Either I got used to it, or I wasn't going to survive. I was tempted to try running away, especially when I allowed myself fleeting thoughts of home. The school was enclosed by a thick thorn hedge, with barbed wire around that, but it would have been easy enough for a determined boy to climb over. Yet how would I ever make it back to Nairobi? I had no money for the bus fare and I didn't have a clue what route to take.

Even if I had found my way to Umoja, I knew what would happen when I got there: my mother would send me back again. And then there would be the wrath of Matron and the headmaster to face. One of the Academy's rules was that parents had to visit every two weeks during term. It was better to knuckle down and count the days until my mother came to see me.

I found myself a tiny slice of privacy—a place where I could sit by myself and dream sunny dreams of home. Just to the right of the front gate and adjacent to the school playing field was the "tortoise hole." It was a kind of grassy amphitheater sunk into the ground, at the bottom of which lived three giant tortoises. Each was about the size of a sheep and completely harmless. It was the job of the school groundsman to keep them well fed with clover and dandelion, plus any waste lettuce or greens from the school vegetable gardens.

Some of the schoolboys would do the inevitable and try to ride the tortoises, but in my first few days at the Academy I discovered something else about those gentle, ponderous beasts. They made the perfect silent companions, demanding neither to be fed, petted, nor talked to. I found a place of peace sitting in the quiet of the tortoise hole, waiting for one of them to move or poke its head out from its mottled gray shell. Down there I was rendered completely invisible, and it was an ideal place in which to daydream.

During those first few days boys did escape—invariably ones whose folks lived near the school. Their parents reacted with anger that their child could squander the hard-earned cash that they had paid to cover a year's fees. The Academy wasn't cheap by anyone's standards, and so the runaways would end up falling out with the school and their parents. While in a way I admired the runaways, I also wondered at their apparent stupidity. Just as soon as they got home, they were returned to the school, where they faced a beating or worse, and so their escape was no escape at all.

As the days went by I started to get used to life at the Academy. It was very different from the life I had lived in Umoja, but there was a small part of me that was actually beginning to enjoy it. Apart from mealtimes, the strict regime of the weekdays was abandoned at weekends, and that was fun time. Saturdays were free and so was Sunday after morning mass, and for us new boys free time meant football time.

The facilities at the Academy were far superior to anything at my former school. The playing field was vast, and at either end there were goals. The pitch was carpeted in green, as opposed to the bare dustbowl at my old school, and while it was still a bit bumpity-bumpity, it was far flatter than what I was used to. I could race across the grass, feet skimming, making maximum use of my speed, and slam the ball into the back of the net.

Goal!

But even our football games were constrained by rules, rules, rules. As no one was allowed toys at the Academy, we didn't have our own football. We'd have to go ask the school storekeeper to unlock his storeroom and lend us one of the Academy's balls, and woe betide anyone who didn't return it.

When we tired of playing football, there was the school cowherd to go keep an eye on, which was really just an excuse for girl watching. The single-sex dorms were segregated by barbed wire and baton-wielding matrons. Our classes were mixed boys and girls, but no talking between the sexes was allowed. And so it was at the school vegetable garden, and the adjacent meadow where the cows were tethered, that we tried our best to mix with the fairer sex and impress them.

The school garden was planted with the kind of crops that grew well in the shadow of Mount Kenya—kale, cabbages, and lettuce. It served a double purpose: it was an integral part of our agriculture lessons, plus it was a source of salad and vegetables for the school kitch-ens. Each class had its own set of crops to look after, and during agriculture lessons we took off our shoes and socks and tended the plants in our bare feet. Any leafy leftovers were fed to my friends, the giant tortoises.

The gardens were a favorite hangout for the girls, and so "cow watching" rapidly became a favorite pastime for the boys. None of the girls could quite compare to Jennifer, I reckoned, the girl for whom I had gotten run over by the *matatu*. But some of them were definitely cute; if only I could pluck up the courage to talk to them.

The culture at the Academy was unforgiving, and it punished any sign of weakness. We started doing cross-country runs through the bush around the school, which for some reason always seemed to be scheduled for the heat of the afternoon. I had a typical Luo physique—tall and lean—and I was the best 200-meter runner at the school, but I loathed cross-country.

A handful of the new boys were seriously overweight, and for them cross-country was pure torture—both physically and psycho-logically. They'd end up crawling through the school gates, exhausted and soaked in perspiration, hours after the rest of us had returned, at which point the verbal abuse would begin.

"Hey! Fatty!"

"Lard-ass!"

"Blubber-bucket!"

"Porky Pig!"

The relentless teasing created a cringing self-loathing among the fat boys. Their self-esteem was never the highest anyway, but the ver-bal abuse—and the bullying that inevitably followed—destroyed what little self-respect those boys may have had. For the older boys especially, those overweight new boys made for easy pickings. And for the victims of such bullying there was no easy way out. If they reported the bullying, then they were "snitches," and that was the worst thing of all.

A couple of those older bullyboys tried to pick on me, as they did with all the newcomers. The bullying always seemed to follow a similar pattern: it began with verbal abuse and moved on to physical abuse if the kid didn't resist or defend himself. For me it started when an older boy tried to make me polish his shoes. That was when the stubborn, argumentative side of me that my mother had hinted at came to the fore.

The call came out of nowhere. "Hey! You! Obama! Clean these shoes."

I glanced at the scuffed, dust-covered shoes thrust in front of me, then at the face of the older boy, who was far bulkier than I was. For an instant I almost gave in, but then the obstinate, rebellious side of me took over.

"You think my parents paid for me to come here to shine your shoes?"

"I'm warning you," the bullyboy retorted, "you'd better do it, or else."

"Or else what?"

"Or else I'll be forced to teach you some respect," he blustered.

A crowd gathered to watch the confrontation.

"This guy thinks a shoeshine is worth getting in a fight over," I remarked to the others. "Why don't you find something serious if you want to fight me?"

"Well then, do my math homework!" the bullyboy demanded. "I hear you're hot at math."

I glanced at the notebook he was shoving in my direction. "What, you're not clever enough to do it for yourself? It isn't difficult; it's just a few sums. Surely you can manage that?"

The bullyboy realized that he was being made to look foolish. He stomped off, but not before issuing a final threat.

"I'll be back, Obama." He brandished his fists. "And maybe next time I'll smash that smug smile off that face of yours." Like most bullies he was a coward, and he had hated being made to look small. And as most bullies will, he moved on to an easier target.

There was rarely a serious punch-up between pupils, for that would mean a caning from the headmaster. Anyone caught repeatedly fighting would be expelled, which would mean big trouble at home. So the bullying was more underhanded and spiteful than it was physically violent. It was the kind of thing that left no physical scars but must have caused deep psychological ones.

I started to make new friends at the Academy, yet in my heart I remained loyal to my buddies in Umoja. There I had chosen my friends: here, we were thrown together, and we were friends of circumstance. In Umoja everyone knew my background and my family, and the friendships I formed there seemed more real. At the Academy our comradeship would only ever extend as far as the school gates.

Most pupils at the Academy were black Africans, plus a few Arab-looking ones. They hailed from the Kenyan middle and upper classes, and the fees were certainly too high for poorer families. Needless to say I was the only kid with a white father. Part of me worried that having Christian for a dad might draw unwelcome attention, or get me picked on by the older boys.

On the Saturday two weeks after I had enrolled, the Dangermobile pulled up at the school gates. I was relieved to see that the monster vehicle drew the boys' attention far more than my *mzungu* father. I got in and we headed for the Thomson Falls Lodge, a smart hotel complex situated at the foot of a waterfall that tumbles 243 feet off the Aberdare Ranges.

Situated at an altitude over 7,700 feet, the brick cottages of the lodge were built at the turn of the twentieth century. The cool climate reminded the colonials of life back home in Britain, and the place had retained a distinctly colonial air. It was a regular hangout for white expatriates and rich Kenyans alike, but not, it seemed, for mixed-race couples—and especially not one with a young boy in tow, one dressed in shiny black shoes and a chocolate brown school uniform.

At first we received some very strange glances, but it turned out that some of the staff here knew Christian. The lodge was one of his regular stopovers during his trips upcountry to visit aid projects, and so they knew he was a professional living and working in Kenya, and that he had money. That in turn conferred on us a certain status and bankability, which enabled the staff to overlook the "odd" racial makeup of our family. This was especially so because Christian tipped generously.

A fire had been lit in the lounge to ward off the chill. We ate a lunch of fried tilapia fish, then wandered up to see the Thomson Falls. A wall of white water roared down a sheer rock face like polished ebony, the whole enclosed within a bowl of lush forest thick with creepers and vines. There was a kind of secret garden feel to the place, and a romantic atmosphere that made me wonder for a moment if my mother and Christian mightn't have preferred to come here alone.

On the stroll back my mother voiced the subject that was on everyone's mind. "You are enjoying it, aren't you?" she ventured.

I glanced around me, feigning ignorance. "This place? Yes, it's kind of pretty, kind of nice."

"Not here, George, your new school. The Academy."

I shrugged, then gave a slight, awkward grin. "Don't worry, Mum. It's fine."

"You're getting enough to eat?"

"Yes, Mum."

"You're sure you're eating well? You look thin to me."

"Well, it's hardly Christian's cooking," I joked. "But I'm not starving."

"You're making new friends?"

"Of course."

I knew there was no point in telling her the truth—that I pretty much detested it and wanted to come home. Whatever I said, my mother wasn't going to change her mind. She was the disciplinarian of the family, and with its rigid rules and iron regime the Academy was her kind of place entirely.

As for Christian, while I was sure he would listen to my concerns, I was equally sure that he'd find powerful arguments to back up my mother and convince me to stick it out. And in truth, they were probably right. The Academy was the kind of place where I could thrive academically, and that in turn would help me achieve my dream. If I was serious about becoming an airline pilot, then the Academy was the place for me.

We were back at the school by early evening. A line of cars was parked along the road leading to the gates. A part of me wanted Christian to stop as far away as possible, so that few people would set eyes on my *mzungu* father. But another part of me wanted Christian to bring the Danger-mobile right to the front, so that all the boys could see what a cool car he drove. In fact, it was such an eye turner that I reckoned it might draw the odd glance from the girls, which would be no bad thing—as long as my mother didn't notice.

After all the parents were gone, there were several comments about my being "the kid the with *mzungu* father," but just as many boys came up to ask me about the Danger-mobile. In fact the two subjects were inseparable in their minds—for only with a father who was a foreigner could I possibly have ended up riding in such a cool vehicle.

I had gotten used to such notoriety in Umoja. I had learned that to do anything but play up to it would invite attack. Here at the Academy I had to act as if I thrived on the difference, just as I'd learned to do before. *Yeah, I am the kid with the* mzungu *father, and just look what a cool car he drives!*

After years of playing that act, I had started to live it for real. In fact, it had become an indelible part of me. For years I had forced myself to rejoice in that difference, but now being different was what I craved.

Yeah, I am the kid with the mzungu *father: and you should see the kind of adventures that guy takes me on!*

By the end of my first term I was coming within the top five in my class. In the end-of-term exams I took fourth place out of the forty-odd students in my year. In a way, I hadn't expected anything less. I expected to do well. And my mother and Christian saw in my achievement a ringing endorsement of their sending me to the Academy.

I was pretty much a model pupil, my only real misdemeanor being my talkativeness. I'd earned the reputation of being something of a noisemaker during our evening preps. I found preps pretty easy, and once I was finished I got bored. As no one was allowed to leave early, all I could do was chat, but we were supposed to keep quiet and read. Every week someone was appointed class monitor, and it was his job to keep a noisemaker list. My name was always on it.

I used to threaten the class monitor with dire consequences if he put me on the list. But at the end of preps, if my name wasn't on it, the teacher would become suspicious. Two or three evenings with my name missing and the class monitor would get into trouble for not doing his job properly. I was made class monitor once and once only, for the system was totally unworkable when the class monitor was the one making all the noise!

If I was on the list too often, the teacher in charge of preps would punish me. I'd get a caning in front of the class, a rap on the knuckles with a ruler, or a few whacks with a stick. The really vicious teachers made me hold a pen between each of my fingers while they thumped my hand sideways, crushing it into the desk and all but breaking my fingers. But I was used to beatings from home, and so this just seemed to be a somewhat more vicious extension of that punishment system.

At the end of first term the parents of the Nairobi kids clubbed together and hired a *matatu* to bring us home. Just as soon as it had nosed its way through the school gates, Matron started calling out the names of those who were supposed to be on it. With a surge of excitement we grabbed our few possessions and piled aboard.

The sense of sweet anticipation as the minibus neared the big city was tangible, and I couldn't wait to set foot in Umoja and see my family and my home. I still felt as if my real friends were here, and just as soon as I laid my eyes on Eric and the gang, I knew that I wasn't wrong. Eric ran to grab a football from his place—no asking a storeman's permission this time—and before I could even greet my parents, we ran out onto the nearest patch of open ground for a celebratory kick-around.

We challenged a bunch of other kids to a match, and in no time I had thumped the ball past their goalie and between the goalposts made of two piles of scrunched-up T-shirts.

Goal!

Eric, Daddy, and Ernest grabbed me and we danced around in delight. It felt as if I had never been away at all.

After dinner Christian spread out the Scrabble pieces facedown on the coffee table, and he, my mother, and I prepared to do battle as Marvin watched from the sidelines. I guess they must have been glad to have me home, for Christian even let me get away with cheating. I was always trying to put down words that didn't exist, and I would argue until I was blue in the face that they were for real.

In tonight's game I tried to use the word *snoob*.

"A *snoob*?" my mother challenged. "What's a *snoob*?"

"It's like when you snub someone," I replied, with as serious a look as I could muster.

"Then why not put down the letters *s–n–u–b*?" my mother queried. "Or is that because you don't have them?"

"*Snoob*'s a past tense of *snub*," I countered, trying to keep a straight face.

Christian let out a chuckle. He knew I was bluffing.

"What's so funny?" my mum asked, trying not to laugh herself.

Christian gave a Gallic shrug. "I am not sure . . . I am a Frenchman. Of course I do not know all the English words."

"So where's the dictionary?" my mum demanded.

"But maybe this—this *snoob*—maybe this is one of the new words he learns at that fancy school of his," Christian continued, ignoring my mother's question. "He did come fourth in his year, after all."

"Oh, go on then," my mother relented. "We'll allow you your *snoob*."

After my questionable win at Scrabble my mother took Marvin off to bed. She'd rented a video for the evening, and it was a family favorite—one of the classic Eddie Murphy movies. While she read Marvin a story, Christian and I were left at the table. He poured himself another glass of wine.

"You want another soda?" he asked me. "Go fetch one from the fridge."

"Thanks. I'd love one."

I came back with an ice-cold Coke.

"Not too many luxuries you have at that Academy, eh?" Christian queried.

I grinned. "No sodas, that's for sure."

Christian raised his glass. *"Salut."*

"Salut." Cheers. I clinked my Coke bottle against his wineglass.

Christian took a long sip, savored the wine for a moment, then swallowed. "You know, experiencing hardship isn't always a bad thing. You know why I say that?"

I shook my head. "No."

"Because that way, we learn a little about how most of the world are forced to live. Most people in this country are very, very poor, you know that, *n'est-ce pas?*"

"Kind of, yeah."

"But you have never really *felt* it."

"I guess not."

"In my work I see it all the time. I don't experience it directly maybe, but I feel it. I feel it here," he added, thumping his heart. "We try to help by building them schools and clinics and putting in water wells and finding small ways for them to earn some extra money. But it does not alter the fact that most have never even tasted a soda. Imagine that. Imagine not having the money to even buy yourself a Coke."

I thought about it for a second. "I can't. I can't imagine what that must be like."

"Exactement! But that, George, is how most of the people in Africa live. To them, an education such as you are getting is a precious gift beyond their wildest dreams. Do not forget that. With such an education you can do anything you want in your life. You know this. I know this. But it is something most Africans can only ever dream of."

It was rare that Christian talked to me about his work, but I knew that for him it was far more than just a job. He truly cared about what he did; for him it was a vocation. And tonight I sensed perhaps that he was trying to show me something. Perhaps a part of him wanted me, his adopted Kenyan son, to follow in his footsteps.

By showing me just a little of the passion he felt for the work he did in Africa, was he trying to influence me to follow in the path that he had taken? I suspected that he might be. It was a far cry from the jet-set life that I had imagined for myself—that of an international airline pilot—but I went to bed that night ruminating on all that he had said.

I hadn't forgotten Jennifer—my original Nairobi sweetheart—and hoped that I might see her around Umoja. But there was a girl at the Academy who had somewhat taken her place in my affections, although it was never easy to get any time with her. If a boy was caught in the girls' dorm, there were no second chances: he was instantly expelled. The only way was to meet somewhere outside the school buildings, or even outside the school grounds.

By the time I was into my second year at the Academy, I had developed a real crush on this girl, Judith. As with Jennifer it was all very innocent, and would never amount to more than a bit of holding hands in a secret corner of the vegetable garden. The teachers found a way to turn a blind eye to that kind of thing, but it was when I decided to take her out of school for a stroll into the forbidden bush that things took a turn for the worse.

I was ten years old pushing eleven, and all was going swimmingly at the Academy. But one evening a teacher spotted Judith and me sneaking out of school via a hole in the hedge and climbing through the wire. He followed us, and it didn't take him long to realize that we were sweethearts. We were apprehended on our return and marched before the headmaster. My "crime" on this occasion was twofold: I had been caught out of school without permission, and I had been in the company of a girl.

I tried to take the bulk of the blame by saying that it was all my idea, but even so I knew that this was serious and that Judith and I were in big trouble. My mother was summoned to the Academy, whereupon she was called into the headmaster's office and told everything. I didn't get to say a word in my defense, for I was made to sit in disgrace outside the office. And that was pretty much that. I was kicked out of the Academy. I guess the same fate awaited Judith too.

It was the only blot on an otherwise excellent record at the Academy, and I didn't see why I should feel guilty. In fact, I was pretty angry about the whole thing. I knew the Academy's rules, and mostly I accepted them, for I could see the reasons behind them. But the outright ban on boys having contact with girls—that was downright stupid. We shared the same earth, breathed the same air, and at school we sat together in the same lessons, yet we weren't supposed to talk to each other. It made no sense, and the stubborn side of me—the Obama side perhaps—rebelled against it.

I was unrepentant. Yes, I had been thrown out, but I hadn't done anything bad or wrong. Yet in my mother's eyes I had really stepped out of line, and so she sought a way to get me back on the straight and narrow. The course of action she hit upon was to send me to the Mosocho Academy, a school to the far west of Kenya, not far from Lake Victoria. As before, this was a boarding school, but the key difference was that it was all boys.

I guess my mother thought that by removing temptation, she could solve the "problem." However, putting a large number of prepubescent and teenage boys together in a single-sex school appeared to have the opposite effect.

It just seemed to drive us all the more wild.

CHAPTER 7

The Drinking Den

THE MOSOCHO ACADEMY was an expensive school beset with draconian rules and regulations, but I was used to all that by now. Mosocho was further still from Nairobi, so in a sense I felt more cut off than ever from my family and my Umoja friends. The one good thing about Mosocho was that it was set in a gently undulating landscape and at a much lower altitude: it was never as cold as it had been in the shadow of Mount Kenya.

While my mother was quick to anger, she was equally quick to forgive, and my "illegal fraternizations" with Judith were quickly forgotten. She had read up on Mosocho and was well acquainted with the school regime. In some ways it was more relaxed, for at least we were allowed to bring our own foodstuffs to school. She had stuffed my green trunk full of my favorite things—raspberry jam, peanut butter, margarine, ketchup, and chili. Plus she'd packed two tubs of hot chocolate, so that I could make a bedtime drink before lights-out, and—joy of joys—some chocolate bars.

But the day of my arrival at Mosocho someone forced open my tin trunk and raided my goodies. All the best things were gone—my hot chocolate, my sugar, and the chocolate bars. One of the older boys must have noticed my disquiet, for he came to have a word. He'd seen me arrive that morning, and he had a special reason to want to talk to me.

"What's up, kid?" he asked, with what looked like a friendly smile. "You lost or something?"

I shrugged, feigning indifference. "Nothing much. Someone just stole all my best stuff, that's all."

"Where did they steal it from?"

"My tin trunk under my bed."

"What's missing? Tell me. I reckon I can get it back for you."

I glanced up at him, warily. Why was he trying to help me? I wondered.

"Just some cocoa, sugar, chocolate bars—that kind of thing."

"Right, I'm on it. Don't you worry about a thing. I'll get your stuff back, okay?"

"Yeah. Thanks."

"No problem. Oh, and the name's Henry, by the way. Henry Maina. Nice to meet you . . ."

"George. George Obama. And thanks again."

Sure enough Henry came and found me later in the dorm.

"Look what I got!" he announced, dumping most of my stolen goodies on the bed. "What have we here? Two tins of hot chocolate, a couple of bags of sugar, and five chocolate bars. I reckon he may have eaten a couple of those."

"Wow! Thanks."

Henry shrugged off my gratitude. "It was one of the older kids stole it, over on our side. But I reckon he won't be troubling you again."

"Thanks, Henry. Would you like something—you know, a chocolate bar maybe?"

"No. Nothing like that. But there is one thing you can do for me."

So here it was. I knew it couldn't have been all for nothing.

"Like what?" I asked, warily.

"That chick you turned up with this morning—is that your sister or something? I mean, she is hot. Hot, hot, hot, man . . ."

My sister? What did he mean, my sister? I didn't have a sister. As Henry continued going on about this "hot chick," I suddenly realized that he could only mean my mother.

"Er . . . She's, er . . ."

"She's spoken for, is that what you're trying to tell me?"

"Um, not exactly."

"Right, so I want you to put in a good word for me, okay? Just tell her what a nice guy I am, and that I really like her. Okay?"

I shrugged, then smiled. "Sure. I'll tell her. Nothing guaranteed, but I'll let her know. I mean there's a lot of guys like her, but . . ."

"No harm trying, eh?" Henry grinned. "That's my kid. I like you, George. And I sure as hell like your sister."

I decided to let Henry believe that my mother really was my sister. It would have been cruel not to. And anyway, as a new arrival at Mosocho I could use a protector of Henry's imposing size and bulk. In fact, I reckoned I should string Henry along for as long as I could. The only danger was if he ever got to speak to my mother and realized she wasn't actually my sister. But when all was said and done, I reckoned that was a risk worth taking.

Once I'd repacked my goodies, I went to see if I might borrow a padlock from the school stores. The thief must have picked the lock on my trunk, for it wasn't even broken. There were obviously some streetwise kids in the school, if that was the kind of thing they were up to. Having Henry as a protector looked as if it might be no bad thing.

My favorite master at Mosocho was Mr. Nyango. He was a tough cookie, but he was also a brilliant math teacher, and math remained the one subject above all others at which I truly excelled. But in Mr. Nyango's math lessons mistakes were punished immediately, and with precious little mercy. If a boy answered a question incorrectly, Mr. Nyango would stand over him and order him to puff his cheeks full of air. He'd then slap his hands together on the kid's face, forcing a massive explosion of air.

Fairly quickly Mr. Nyango realized that he had a star pupil in me. The first time I made a mistake, he came and ordered me to do the cheek-puffing-out routine. He drew back his hands and I closed my eyes, dreading what was coming. He brought them crashing in toward my face, and I steeled myself for the blow, but none came. He'd stopped just short of hitting me.

The other kids were trying to hide their smiles behind their hands. If you were caught laughing, then you'd get punished.

"Next time, it'll be different," Mr. Nyango warned me, quietly. "You're too smart to make such a stupid mistake, George. Now do the calculation again."

"Yes, Mr. Nyango," I replied.

I glanced at the blackboard and started working on the equation in my head, all the while thanking my lucky stars that he hadn't actually whacked me. The next couple of times that I made a mistake, I got the same mock slap. I reckoned he was going easy on me because I was the new kid on the block, yet already I was at the top of the class.

Then I got a fairly simple sum wrong because I wasn't concentrating. This time he really did whack me. The blow left me stunned, and with a ringing in my ears that sounded as if a TV inside my head had been left on. It was a horrible, high-pitched whine. There was no hope of my answering any other questions in that lesson, for I couldn't hear a thing.

The friends that I made in those first few weeks became my closest buddies. There were three guys from Umoja—Elvis and Mark, who were in my year, and Joseph, Mark's younger brother. Together with a couple of other city boys we formed a close-knit gang of Nairobi kids. We prided ourselves on being the bad boys who always got away with it. Although we never studied hard, we'd do well in our exams. We thought we were pretty cool, but pride, they say, comes before a fall.

At Busara Forest View Academy the presence of female pupils had helped keep the boys in line. No one had wanted to look stupid or immature in front of the girls. But at Mosocho we were a bunch of boys on the cusp of puberty, and in the absence of mellowing feminine influences, our hormones were free to run riot.

The first time I sneaked out of Mosocho, I must have been nearly twelve. I was in the company of Elvis, Mark, and Joseph, but it was actually one of the older Nairobi boys who led the way. His name was Julius, but everyone called him "Professor." It was a Friday night, and Professor had planned the breakout something like a military operation.

It was a still, hot night lit by a bare sliver of a moon. After lights-out we sneaked out of our dorm one by one, climbed the school perimeter fence, and made for a rendezvous at the Big Tree, a place in the bush not far from the school boundary. We each carried with us a bag of casual clothes. We weren't really allowed to have them at Mosocho, but we had sneaked them in. We changed out of our school uniforms under the Big Tree and followed our leader, Professor, into the night.

We took a narrow, dusty track. Such paths crisscrossed the Kenyan bush, leading from mud-hut villages to farmers' fields and back again. We walked in single file and in silence until we were a safe distance from the school. Our way was lit only by the faint moonlight, and the scene reminded me somehow of my rural home and of the adventures I'd had with Cousin Omondi. Yet tonight we were seeking adventure of a very different kind.

After some twenty minutes we reached a shack made of wooden poles and thatched in grass, one that was illuminated faintly by a couple of oil lanterns. The shack was in the middle of nowhere, and I first knew of it when music from the place drifted to us on the muggy air. It was here that we intended to get our first taste of *changa'a*.

Changa'a is an illegal knockout brew available just about anywhere in Kenya. More often than not it's made from fermented maize and sorghum flour, and laced with methanol. *Changa'a* is poisonous, but that doesn't stop Kenya's poor from drinking it—the main attraction being how cheap it is to make. Even the tiniest rural settlement boasts a *changa'a* den, and this was the one nearest to our school.

The den was so deep in the bush and so far from any road that if

Professor hadn't known it was there, we wouldn't have been able to find it. There was little chance of the cops ever managing to raid it. According to our leader, it had the added bonus that no one seemed inclined to ask too many questions about a group of young lads turning up for a drinking session. The owner didn't care what age we were; he was only after our money.

I followed the others inside, ducking under the low roof. A few chairs were strewn about on the bare earth floor, each made from a rough wooden frame, the seat strung with a crisscross latticework of tough rope. Apart from us, the place was deserted, and the only noise was from the transistor radio sitting on one of the tables. Each of us grabbed a chair, as Professor went to order our first *changa'a*.

We waited in a tense silence, one punctuated by the Afrobeat playing on the radio. I could feel my heart pounding. I was excited because I knew this was forbidden, but also nervous because I wondered how I would handle my first taste of *changa'a*. Professor returned, a wicked smile on his broad features.

"It is coming," he announced, with quiet satisfaction.

He glanced at Elvis, Joseph, Mark, and I. "You guys ready?" A beat. "Ready to have your heads blown off?"

We grunted a series of nervous replies.

The owner's daughter emerged from out of the shadows. She plonked the drink down before us on a rough-hewn table, without even the barest hint of a smile. It was a plastic mineral water bottle full to the brim with a colorless liquid that slopped back and forth as it settled. I stared at it with mixed fascination and dread. How was I going to handle this? Messing up wouldn't look good in front of the others.

"Sixty shillings," the girl announced, without looking at anyone in particular.

Professor had sorted this out back at the Big Tree. Each of us had given him two ten-shilling coins, the equivalent of about thirty U.S. cents. That, he had assured us, was more than enough to get us all totally slammed. There was a clinking of metal as he handed the girl the coins. She glanced at them without interest, turned silently, and retreated to her place out the back. We were her only customers, and it was hardly a warm welcome. But we hadn't come for that: we'd come for the *changa'a*.

Professor unscrewed the bottle, tilted it, and poured himself a measure in the upturned lid. He glanced at the rest of us, licked his lips, and threw the liquid into the back of his throat.

"Damn!" he announced. "Burns like fire! Now, who's for the next one?"

"Over here. Me."

I had spoken those words almost without thinking, and almost against my will. I was drawn to that stuff, to the irresistible badness it represented.

Professor smiled. "Hussein. Got to be you. Good on you, brother."

"Hussein" was the name that the gang had chosen for me. It was my second name, and there was something exotic and different about it that I liked. Again, it was the difference that drew me. There were plenty of Georges at school, but no other Husseins. It wasn't a regular Kenyan name, that was for sure. In fact the only guy I'd ever heard of called Hussein was Saddam Hussein, so maybe it hailed from Iraq.

Professor handed me my tot. All eyes were upon me. I raised it to my lips. I threw it into the rear of my mouth, just as he had done. I forced myself to swallow hard, a fiery, burning sensation racing down my throat and churning like a red-hot furnace in my gut.

"D-d-damn!" I just managed to choke out. "Damn!"

Professor gave a whistle of appreciation. "Down in one! Hussein, you the man!"

I felt as if I'd had the skin peeled off my mouth and throat and replaced by fire, but I managed to give Professor a smile. He raised his fist, reached across the table, and we cracked knuckles in a sign of the brotherhood. Professor poured another shot and glanced around at the rest, inquiringly.

"Over here!" Elvis called. "I want a try."

Ten minutes later that first bottle was done. This wasn't drinking for the fun of it; this was drinking to get slammed. And sure enough I'd pretty much forgotten the burning pain in my throat and stomach by now. Instead, there was a warm, woozy feeling in my head, and I was gripped by a sense that I could do anything. Anything was possible. *Anything*. Put Judith before me now and I'd chat her up in an instant; put Jennifer next to me and I'd laugh and talk to her like there was no tomorrow.

Damn. If this was what *changa'a* was like, I could well understand what Professor had been going on about. It was fine. It was more than fine. It was the best. Fantastic.

"How you guys doing?" Professor queried, his eyes gleaming. "Another bottle?"

"You bet." I smiled euphorically. "Bring it on."

Elvis, Joseph, and Mark nodded their acquiescence, grinning drunkenly.

"But first the test!" Professor announced. He got to his feet. "You all got to do as I do. If any of you falls, there's no more *changa'a* for him."

Professor proceeded to stand on one leg and stretch his arms out horizontally, so that he made a kind of crucifix. He held relatively steady like that, doing his best not to crack up laughing.

"One, two, three . . . eight, nine, ten," he counted. He sat down, a big grin on his face. "Now, let's see the rest of you do it."

One by one Elvis, Joseph, and Mark followed suit. Each seemed noticeably more unstable than our leader, but they managed to hold the pose for ten seconds before collapsing into their seats. For each there was a round of drunken applause. It came to my turn. As I swayed about on one leg, I figured I could see the floor swimming up to greet me, but somehow I managed to hold a wobbly, one-legged crucifix until I reached ten. I slumped into my seat, the cheers ringing in my ears.

Professor laughed. "You guys, I tell you, you're naturals. This rate, we'll drink this place dry. Hey! Lady! Over here! A half bottle . . ."

Those one and a half bottles were more than enough for the five of us. By the time the last tot was downed, we were all smashed. Not drunk enough to fall over, but drunk enough to have trouble standing and to not really remember the journey home. But the real problem was the following morning. I awoke late feeling as if my head were on fire. There was a throbbing, pulsating pain behind my eyes that just wouldn't go away. I lay in bed feeling sick as a dog, and I vowed never to touch another drop of *changa'a* for as long as I might live.

Of course, we'd heard the rumors about the dangers of *changa'a*—that it could blind and kill—but we told ourselves that it was probably just talk. In any case, we were young and we thought that we were indestructible. We told ourselves that the bad *changa'a* was the stuff made in the big cities, where they had all kinds of nasty chemicals that they tipped into it. Here in the rural areas it was a purer kind of *changa'a,* and it wouldn't hurt us at all.

The Friday after my first *changa'a* binge, all the pain and suffering had been forgotten. I seemed to have a highly selective memory: I thought only of the good times we'd had in the *changa'a* den, not the bad times that had come after. Friday night became a regular drinking night, and perhaps predictably I had to prove myself to be the hardest drinker of all. I was always drinking the extra tot, always the last to call a halt, and once again my aim was to make myself stand out, to be *different.*

Being different was no longer a means to an end, as it had been in the early days of having a *mzungu* for a father. Being different and being noticed had become the end in itself. No matter what the cost, I craved difference. It had become my drug.

At the end of my first year at Mosocho, we had to take our exams. In spite of the drinking I was still ranking in the top five of my year, and my confidence was unshakable. Just for the sheer thrill of it my buddies and I decided to go for a *changa'a* session on the Sunday night before our first exam.

After a couple of bottles we did the standing-on-one-leg test. Most of the others fell over, ending up in a heap of hysterical laughter. But I managed to count to ten without collapsing, although it wasn't easy. Professor and I called for a half bottle. We plowed through a few more shots, with myself matching the older boy tot for tot, and then we decided we had to leave, or else we were never going to make it out of there.

The next thing I knew I awoke to the most horrific hangover ever. I was back in my bed in the school dorm with no idea of how I had got there. I had never in my life felt so awful—not even when the *matatu* had run me over as I was trying to speak to my sweetheart, Jennifer. I couldn't open my eyes; it was too painful to move; I felt as if there was a jackhammer pounding away inside my skull. It was then that I remembered that it was Monday, the day of my first exam.

As soon as word got out that I was awake, Elvis, Joseph, and Mark gathered around. I could see the worry on their faces. It would have been laughable if I hadn't been feeling so unbelievably bad. Bit by bit, in half whispers and sniggers, the story of what had happened to me the night before emerged.

During the walk home my condition had quickly worsened. I'd been slurring my words and incoherent, and at one stage I'd wandered off the path and gotten hopelessly lost. The rest of the gang had been forced to search the bush, trying to call out my name without alerting anyone at the school, which wasn't so far away. When they did locate me, I was slumped against a tree, fast asleep. They had to half carry and half drag me back to the dorm.

Being out of school without permission was an offense that warranted a suspension; being comatose drunk on top of it would mean instant expulsion. But if anything, I almost liked what had happened and the effect it had had on my gang. Sure, I felt like hell. But if it was difference that I craved, a certain notoriety, then this was it: I was Hussein, the *changa'a* drinker, and I could drink the rest of them under the table.

Luckily, Monday was the day of our math exam, and in spite of the state I was in, I managed to muddle my way through.

Difference and identity. Difference and identity. On the one hand I reveled in my differences: my white father, my drinking prowess, my stubborn willfulness, my exotic-sounding name, Hussein. On the surface, these were the things that I craved. Yet deep down I had started to ask myself why. I was old enough now to question the way things were in my life. There were certain things that didn't add up, and I was curious and increasingly troubled.

The Mosocho Academy is in Nyanza Province, a district that abuts that of my mother's home village. It was only natural that I was expected to pay the odd visit to the homestead to see Grandma Dorcas, Cousin Omondi, and the rest of the clan. By now Grandma's Christianity had become even more rigorous, and she had built a church in between the compound and the road. In theory the church was open to anyone, but it was still very much a family affair.

It was a very basic structure—a grass thatch roof on tree-branch rafters, the whole raised upon posts and with open sides. One of my uncles was a self-taught priest, and the entire clan was expected to attend Grandma's church at least once a week, on Sunday, to hear him preach. And if Grandma could drag some of the family along for a few evenings during the week, so much the better, as far as she was concerned.

During my first visit to the homestead, I refused to go to Grandma's church. I didn't want to hurt her feelings, so I made the excuse that I wanted to be out fishing with Omondi. Cousin Omondi was equally unenthusiastic, so no one paid my refusal too much mind. But in reality I was troubled, and on a far deeper level than anyone realized.

I had chosen the "street name" Hussein, and that was now the name by which all my buddies knew me. And of course, I knew full well that Hussein wasn't a Christian name. My birth father had given me a middle name that was Muslim, and I guessed there had to be a Muslim connection from the Obama side of the family. It didn't escape me that it was from one's birth father that we Luo traditionally inherited our identity, including our religious leanings.

This was a side of my identity that remained closed to me, yet my choosing to be known by the name Hussein had to signify something. Did I feel an innate affinity with the Obama side? Was I drawn to it somehow? Did I feel incomplete as I was, as if I were only half a son, with only half a father? Or was it simple curiosity that drew me? I wasn't sure. I was confused, and it was that confusion that drove me to ask questions of myself for which I had no answers.

Christian had been a fantastic father to me. He was, I knew, generous to a fault. I was well aware that it was his wage that had to be paying my school fees, for neither Mosocho nor my previous school were bargain-basement affairs. Yet it wasn't Christian who had named me Hussein, or given me my ink-black skin and rangy stature. And while both Christian and my mother were keen to see me get a Christian education, neither of them were churchgoers.

They thought a Christian education would be good for me—good for my moral fortitude, good for my values, good for my sense of right and wrong. Yet if they had belief themselves, they didn't wear it on their sleeves. It was at this moment in my life that I decided I would stop going to church completely. I didn't say anything to anyone. There was no violent or vocal rebellion. I just decided to let it go.

My birth father had named me Hussein, and now, more than a decade later, I had christened myself with that same name on the streets. I was Hussein, and for better or for worse I didn't think that church was a place for me. Likewise, saying grace, my bedtime prayers—I let all of it go. I might sit in the dining hall at Mosocho and mouth the words along with the other boys, but I didn't own them anymore.

I was Hussein, and no longer was this house of Christ a place for me.

CHAPTER 8

No Second Chance

I WAS BECOMING less and less rigidly defined by tribal, racial, or religious identity. In fact, we children of the city had many layers of belonging that could be unpeeled, like the skin of an onion. Back in the home village I'd have gone to an all-Luo school, and all my friends would have been Luo. But in Nairobi tribe was irrelevant. I spoke Luo with my mother and Marvin, Swahili at school, and English mixed with a smattering of French at home, which served to further obfuscate tribal and racial loyalties.

In response to the fracturing of age-old certainties, the city youth had begun to forge a citywide identity rooted in our own street language, called Sheng. Sheng is basically a mixture of Swahili and English, with extra words culled from Kenya's tribal languages. But the very essence of Sheng is that it eschews tribal identity by blending the spoken words of all the city tribes into one. And because it was the language of the city youth, you either learned it as a young person or you'd never be able to master it.

Sheng had a certain delicious exclusivity. If I was speaking Sheng with my Mosocho buddies, no grown-ups would be able to understand us. It was a secret language, and that was the real attraction of it, and that was the reason why our use of it infuriated the adults. If the teachers overheard us using Sheng at school, we'd get beaten with a cane.

In fact, there were further subtle layers of exclusivity embodied in Sheng. Each Nairobi neighborhood had its own blend of Sheng, and no two Shengs were the same. Loyalty lay less in one's tribal identity and more in one's Sheng. So if someone from Huruma came to Umoja and caused trouble, we Umoja kids would close ranks to protect our own against an "outsider." We mightn't even know the tribe of the kid we were defending; all we would know was that he spoke our brand of Sheng, and that would be enough to make him "one of us."

Sheng was forever evolving and changing, and that's what kept it rooted in the day-to-day lives of the kids who spoke it. For some reason a lot of the Umoja Sheng was Luo-based. The Sheng word for chicken was *ngueno*, from the Luo word for chicken, *gueno*. The overall effect of the emergence of Sheng was that it broke down tribal differences. And considering how tribalism had divided Africa and caused untold strife, to me this had to be a good thing.

Our Mosocho gang would use Nairobi Sheng to communicate whenever we weren't in class, which gave us a secret language with which to plan the bad stuff that we were doing. For example, *changa'a* was *water* in Sheng, *beste* was a good mate, *pareh* was a party, and *mtiaji* was the Sheng word for a school sneak. We needed this secret language, for many boys would have snitched on us if they had realized what we were up to.

I didn't underestimate the risks of getting caught. My least favorite master at Mosocho was the school head, Mr. Magazete. Anyone caught sneaking out of school would get an automatic two-week suspension. At the end of the two weeks the miscreant would have to return to the school in the company of his parents. Mr. Magazete would then explain exactly what the pupil had done, after which he'd deliver a caning right there and then.

One Friday we were getting ready for a drinking night when the school lighting failed. We decided we could sneak out of the main gate under the cover of darkness and come back via the same route. It was four o'clock in the morning by the time we were done drinking. But our luck didn't hold, for just at that moment there must have been a surge of power in the grid, and the lights came on.

I'm unsure who spotted whom first in the blinding glare, but in an instant we were running for our lives as a figure yelled out for us to stop. I recognized that voice instantly: Mr. Mageto, the deputy head. I was in the lead as we streaked through the gate, my pace outstripping that of my fellow gang members. Suddenly, there was a curse from behind and I risked a glance over my shoulder. Mr. Mageto had sprinted after us but fallen, and was now sprawled facedown on the ground.

Fortunately for us he had been wearing slick, moccasin-type shoes, while we were all wearing running shoes. We sprinted for our dorms, Mr. Mageto's curses ringing in our ears. Each of us dived under our blankets fully clothed, and in an instant we acted as if we were fast asleep. The combination of a belly full of *changa'a*, the adrenaline rush of the chase, and the sight of Mr. Mageto sprawled in the dust made me want to laugh fit to burst. It was such a *blast*. But I knew that I had to keep absolutely silent. Anything else, and he was bound to catch me.

Over time our gang attracted new members, foremost amongst them Vaud, Jack, and Isaac. Isaac was my best buddy at Mosocho and we were pretty much inseparable. He hailed from a fairly wealthy Nairobi family, and I guess we shared a lot in common.

We were pushing fourteen when we decided to strike out for the nearest big town, Kisii. The main attraction of Kisii was the disco, and the main attraction of the disco, as opposed to the *changa'a* den, was the chance to meet some *supuu*, Sheng for pretty girls. And the thing to be avoided at all costs was the *ombwakning*—the tough, working girls, who'd be out hoping to catch a guy from whom to earn a little cash. We were starved of female company, so this was an exciting adventure.

Disco night in Kisii was Saturday, but the problem facing us was how to get to town. The local *matatus* that plied the route into Kisii stopped at six o'clock sharp. It was possible to sneak out of school only after dark, and by then the *matatus* had ceased running. Kisii is surrounded by rolling hills, and the fifteen-mile route into town was all uphill, and so the solution we hit upon was to hitch a ride on a passing truck.

That first night we hid in a roadside ditch until we spotted the lights of a heavily laden vehicle crawling toward us. We let it pass, thick black diesel fumes billowing out the exhaust, then sprinted after and jumped aboard. I had to haul myself up onto the trailer, feet perched on the rear fender, and I clung on for dear life as the truck snorted onward. There was just about room for the six of us, and with the hot smell of diesel fumes in our nostrils we were on our way!

Kisii was a medium-sized place, with half a dozen discos in the town center. After a truck ride of fifteen minutes, we jumped off and dusted ourselves down. The most well-known disco was the Backyard, but it was also one of the most expensive. One bottle of Kenyan beer—Tusker and Pilsner Ice being our favorites—was around 100 Kenyan shillings. By contrast, for 120 shillings we could get two bottles of *changa'a* in the drinking den, which was enough to get all of us smashed.

But tonight wasn't about drinking; it was all about getting to meet some girls. We headed for one of the cheaper joints, the kind of place where we could afford to buy a beer. I was tall for my age, and I could just about pass for eighteen, the legal drinking age in Kenya. By the time I'd finished my first bottle of Tusker, I'd started talking to a sweet girl. She was a couple of years older than me, though I didn't let on, and she could tell by my accent and the way I talked that I was a Nairobi lad.

She found it pretty cool the way my friends and I peppered our speech with Sheng. She kept asking me to teach her the words. Kisii was a rural place, and to the local girls there was something exotic about meeting boys from the big city. It gave us a real advantage over the locals, the only problem being that I was fast running out of money to buy the drinks. My girl presumed that as a city boy I had to be loaded. And there was no way I could confess to being a schoolboy out spending my pocket money!

It was 4:30 a.m. by the time we left the disco. We had a kiss and a cuddle good-bye, and I promised to see her again the following Saturday. It was black as pitch as the six of us headed out of town in the direction of Mosocho. The trouble was that the route back was all downhill, and most of the trucks were leaving Kisii empty. We couldn't jump one downtown, for people were bound to see us and alert the driver.

By the time a truck reached the outskirts, it was roaring and snorting at full speed, but somehow we managed to catch one and clamber aboard, reaching down to pull up the slower runners. But now we faced a new problem: what were we to do when the truck reached Mosocho? There was no way we could get it to slow down, for the driver didn't know he had the six of us clinging to the back of his vehicle.

Mosocho was approaching fast and there was no other option; we were going to have to jump. I hit the road with my feet flying, and the momentum of the truck all but threw me forward onto the tarmac. Somehow I managed to run with the forward movement and stay on my feet, but only just. Behind me in the dark there was a chorus of loud curses as some of the others wiped out on the road. Luckily, there were no serious injuries. A couple of the boys had bad grazes, but that was about all.

We sneaked into the darkened dorm, and as I lay in my bed, I reflected on the night that we'd had in town. It had been costly, and I wouldn't be able to afford to do it every Saturday, but at least I had gotten to meet a real *supuu*—a sexy girl. There was no doing that in our bush drinking den, that was for sure. Admittedly, the truck ride back had been a bit of a challenge, but my speed had made it easier for me than the others. It was mission accomplished, as far as I was concerned.

Soon there were eight of us hitting the drinking den of a Friday night, and the disco on a Saturday whenever we could afford it. Each of us had his own speciality in the gang. Professor was the *changa'a* head par excellence, and no one could compete with him. Isaac was something of a drinker-philosopher. On most evenings in the *changa'a* den we'd sit around reminiscing about the city and all the things we missed there, but Isaac would invariably take the talk somewhere new and unexpected.

As for me, I was the crazy guy, the one who could always be relied on for any drunken misadventures that might be in the offing. And I had the most fanatical tastes in music, which in turn made me something of an entertainer. Music was a big thing for us, and some of the others were hip-hop crazy. But for me there was only one type of music worth listening to, and that was reggae.

My favorite band of all was Bob Marley and the Wailers. Marley had died from cancer the year before my birth, but I still loved his songs. For me, the fact of his death made him something of a martyr for his art and his beliefs. I loved the beat and the melodies, but most of all I loved the words. Bob Marley's lyrics were all about love, peace, and racial harmony, and for some reason they spoke to me.

My favorite song was "Who the Cap Fit." Whenever we were in the drinking den and it came on the radio, I'd force the others to stop talking. I'd be singing gently to the words, and Isaac, Professor, and the rest couldn't help but tap along to the beat. I'd get to my feet and start shuffling around the dirt floor, shoulders hunched up, arms bent at my sides, legs swaying long and elastic below me, a child's smile on my drunken, dancing face as I lost myself in the words.

Man to man is so unjust, children:
Ya don't know who to trust.

There was a truth to these lyrics, though after several shots of *changa'a* I was never quick to put my finger on what exactly it was. It took Isaac's philosopher's mind to take us there, and he never missed an opportunity to meld my love of Marley with his love of *changa'a*-fueled debate.

" 'Who the cap fit, let him wear it,'" Isaac would muse. "What exactly does it mean, Hussein?"

"It means it's the best damn music in the world." I'd smile. "It means Marley's a hero, man. It means he lives. Here in my heart he lives, and yours too when you hear him."

Isaac would roll his eyes. "Yeah, fine words, but what does it really *mean*? Get under the skin of the words, Hussein, and tell me what he's really trying to say to us."

I tried to focus my *changa'a*-frazzled mind on what Isaac was getting at. "Color is skin-deep? Is that it, bro?"

"Maybe. Or maybe he means whatever place we come from—whatever race, country, social class, whatever—we're all equal. We all can wear the cap."

There was a pause in the conversation as Professor lined up a round of *changa'a* tots.

"Talking of all being equal, you heard that crap we were fed in history today?" Isaac asked of no one in particular. "Who writes those history books? Do they think we're idiots? If we believed that crap, we'd believe the whites are to blame for all the problems in this country. Can you believe it? Do they really think we are that stupid?"

I nodded my agreement. "So why not tell the teacher what you think?"

Isaac snorted. "Because if I did, I'd get hauled before the headmaster and caned, that's what. We have to sit and write down everything teacher says, even when we know it's a heap of bullshit, because who are we to challenge anyone, right? We're just school kids. We don't write the history books, so what do we know? And no questions allowed."

I glanced around the gang. "Let's have a show of hands," I suggested, with a smile. "Who blames the whites for all the shit that's happening in our country?"

Not a hand went up.

"I know I'm biased," I continued, "'cause I got a white man for a father and all that, but Isaac's got a point. Anyone who swallows the bullshit and blames the whites for the shit state of this country needs their head examined."

"So who do you blame?" Professor asked, as he toyed with the half-empty *changa'a* bottle.

I thought for a moment. "I'm not sure. But no one ever teaches us about the good things the whites did when they came here: building roads, schools, railways, and drafting the law. They did a lot of bad shit, but they did some good stuff too. And who ever talks about the fact that it's over sixty years ago now? *Sixty years.* That's a damn long time for us to have got our shit together."

"So if we've failed to get our shit together, we only got ourselves to blame," Isaac added. "I mean, who even *remembers* colonialism? I don't; my father doesn't; Grandpa does, but he'll be dead soon. And then it'll be long gone. In the past. Time to move on."

The gang made grunts of approval to what Isaac was saying. We were bad boys, and largely we were out for kicks, but a maverick, rebel spirit united us. Different members of the gang exhibited that spirit to a greater or lesser degree, and I guess it was embodied most in me. For a moment I thought about Christian, and the passion he felt for the aid work he did across Kenya.

"And another thing," I announced. "Who in this country ever talks about the sixty years of aid the whites have poured into Kenya since colonial times? And who ever talks about how much of that aid the big men at the top have siphoned off into their foreign bank accounts? Do we read about that in the history books? Do we, hell!"

Professor let out a yelp of approval. "Yo! Hussein. Now he's talking!"

"Yeah, I am, and this is serious shit." I'd found a place of clarity in my *changa'a*-addled thoughts, and I was on a roll. "You ever checked where Kenya stands in the world league table of corruption? We're at or near the top. That's not something to be proud of. It rots the country from within. And it sure as hell isn't taught us in our history books."

"So how do you *know* all this stuff?" Professor queried. "I mean, this world corruption index, that kind of shit?"

"My white father talks about it at home. I listen." I paused for a second. "You heard about the Golden Bank scandal? You must have read about it, or seen it on the news?"

"Some, yeah," Professor replied.

"It's *Goldenberg*, not Golden Bank," Isaac corrected. "Goldenberg."

"Goldenberg, Golden Bank, whatever," I continued. "The point is, there's so much money gone missing at the top that no one knows how much. It's billions and billions of Kenyan shillings. *Billions and billions.* Like my father says, most people in this country can't afford to even buy a soda. Not once. Not ever in their life can they afford to drink a Coke. But those at the top are stealing hundreds of millions of shillings."

Professor whistled. "That's one hell of a lot of *dough*, brother, one hell of a lot of *dough*."

"And what has the theft of all those billions got to do with the whites?" Isaac continued, picking up on the theme of our discussion. "Nothing. *Nothing.* Absolutely nothing. This is a homegrown disaster, one manufactured by those at the top—by our fellow brother Kenyans. And the point is, when do we ever get to read anything about that in our history books? Look up the chapter on Goldenberg: there isn't one. Next lesson, ask our history teacher about Goldenberg," Isaac suggested, bitterly. "Ask if we can study the Goldenberg scandal. Ask if we can spend just one lesson trying to solve who did it. Ask if we can study a bit of real, relevant, modern Kenyan history for once, not the myths they like to perpetuate about colonialism being the cause of all our ills. And you know what will happen? You'll get a good caning, that's what."

"People are scared even to talk about this shit," I added. "The people at the top are creaming off billions and those at the bottom have nothing, and everyone's too scared even to talk about it. I listen to my parents at home. They talk about Goldenberg some, but even they do so quietly, when the doors are shut and when no one can hear. It's the same with us. We can drink *changa'a* and rage about it in a drinking den hidden in the bush, but raise it at school? No way. *No way.* No way can we do that at all."

"Talking of *changa'a*, who's for another tot?" Professor announced. "Time to lighten the mood a little."

I smiled. "Sure, time to lighten the mood. *Changa'a* is good. But imagine it, bro. All they mention at school is colonialism and how the British took everything, but in real life, now, it's Kenyans taking everything. That's why the gap between rich and poor is so huge. It's got nothing to do with colonialism; it's got to do with those at the top stealing the country. Colonialism wasn't good, that's for sure. But it isn't the issue anymore."

Professor handed me a tot. "All you can do is drink, ain't it, bro?"

I threw the tot down my neck. "Damn! You the man, Professor. All you can do is drink."

The following morning I had little or no memory of the night before. It was only when chatting to the others that I'd start to remember the drinking and the talk. *Changa'a* did that to you; it blew your mind away. And long term, it could really mess with your head.

Whenever we were asked what we wanted to be when we grew up, the answer Mosocho pupils gave was always a lawyer, doctor, accountant, or pilot. Everyone sought a professional career or to go into business. No one ever said they wanted to be a politician, for politics was almost a dirty word in Kenya. Everyone knew that politics and corruption went hand in hand, and no one wanted to go there.

I was nearly fourteen by now, and with the November exams fast approaching, I should have reined in my excess. But of course, being the wild one, I did no such thing. In spite of the *changa'a* binges and the disco nights, I was still doing well at Mosocho. I was still at the top of my year in math and somewhere in the top five in our regular exams. I was convinced that I could mess around and still excel. I had always gotten away with it, so why should things be any different now?

But this end-of-year exam was different. It was my KCPE, the nationwide examination that would determine whether I made it into the elite, Nairobi-based National School that I had my heart set on. No amount of wild excess had detracted from my aim—to get into that school and get a head start to qualify as an airline pilot. That remained my dream, and it had the added attraction of offering an escape route out of the malaise that had taken hold in Kenya. Never for one moment had I imagined that I might *not* achieve that dream. As far as I was concerned, I already had my place booked at that National School.

The night before our first exam was a Sunday, and out of sheer bedevilment I and a couple of the other lads decided to make it a special drinking night. I had always gotten better grades than my drinking buddies, and I believed that our fellowship was pretty much over. They would be moving on to the secondary school at Mosocho, while I would be heading for Nairobi, and the National School. It was the last time that we'd be together as a gang, and so we would drink to the end of an era.

We'd finished the first bottle of *changa'a* and a second, and then Professor suggested a third. I was determined to keep pace with him, tot for tot. We ordered another, and now it was just the two of us. When there were just the dregs left, we decided we had to call a halt. Otherwise I'd fail to make it for my first day of exams. I got to my feet and went to move toward the door, but all of a sudden my world went black, and the floor was rushing up to meet me at great speed.

The next thing I knew someone was shaking me awake and warning me to get the hell up, for it was exam time. I felt as close to death as it is possible to feel without actually having died. Somehow I managed to crawl my way out of bed and into the exam hall, but I was still drunk from the night before and I could barely speak, let alone concentrate on the paper before me. I managed to scrawl a signature and get through the morning without throwing up, but I didn't kid myself that I had done well.

Later that day the others told me exactly what had happened. I had hit the floor of the drinking den with a horrible, hollow-sounding thwack, my head bouncing off the table. I lay there white as a sheet, and for a moment everyone feared that I was dead. It wasn't until Professor had thought to check my breathing that he knew for sure I was alive. They knew they had to get me back to school, for otherwise disaster loomed.

Professor had hoisted me onto his shoulders, and somehow he had managed to carry me all the way back through the bush and dump me in my bunk. Seeing me in such a bad way had sobered everyone up, and most of the gang had yet to get over it. But as I hadn't actually seen myself in that state, or gone through the horror and the shock of thinking that I was dead, the incident hadn't left such a lasting impression on me.

There was even a part of me that felt it was pretty cool, pretty damn *different*. I was Hussein, the hardened drinker, and I had come back from the dead before their very eyes.

A few weeks later the results of the KCPE exams were posted. Pupils are graded Excellent, Good, Average, Below Average, Poor. I could barely believe my eyes. I had flunked. I had scored only a Good, and in that instant I knew that I wasn't going to make it into that National School. Only those who scored Excellent were offered a place at the elite academies, and I would be getting no second chance.

I knew then that I wasn't invincible. I wasn't unbeatable. I was only human, and I had been living a lie.

CHAPTER 9

The Gulf Between Us

ODDLY ENOUGH, NEITHER my mother nor Christian seemed that angry at my failure to get a top mark. If anything, they appeared to feel sorry for me. They knew how much I had had my heart set on that National School, and how hard my failure to win a place had hit me. To them, my failure was inexplicable. In my three years at the Mosocho Academy I had never once been caught misbehaving, so they had no idea how much I had been messing around.

But I knew. I knew why I had messed up. My dream to work for Kenya Airways, or British Airways, or any other world-class airline, had taken a big hit. It wasn't over yet, but my confidence had taken a real pounding. I had failed, and failure wasn't exactly something that I was accustomed to. I had always been seen as the brainiest of the bunch, and no one could fathom how I had messed up so badly.

As I reflected upon what had happened, I wished I hadn't been so foolish. I wished I hadn't been so arrogant as to think that I was above it all. My regret was made all the worse by the fact that some of my old friends from Umoja had scored an Excellent mark, and of course they were looking forward to going to the National Schools of their choice.

Eric had attained the same mark as I had, but we'd always known that I was the smarter of the two of us. Yet just like Eric, I would now have to settle for second best—a provincial school. All I could hope was that I would do well, and so secure myself a place at university. It should be well within my capabilities, and from there I could still go on to qualify as a pilot. I wouldn't get the head start the National School would have given me, but it was all still doable.

After completing your KCPE, you're given an extra-long holiday, and so I had time at home in which to contemplate my failure. My mother and Christian made a real effort to console me. When was it, they asked, that things had started to go so wrong? Part of me wanted to confess, to tell them all the bad stuff that I had been up to, but I felt too ashamed to do so. I told myself that I should face it like a man. I told myself that from now on I would stop the drinking and the partying. After all, there was still everything to play for.

Christian and my mother went about finding a new school for me. They settled upon Dagoretti High, situated in a smart Nairobi suburb. For pupils that hadn't made it into a National School, this was the next best thing. It was one of the best high schools in Nairobi, and one of the few in the city that would take boarders.

They told me that if I studied hard enough, I could still make it. If I applied myself, my dream of becoming an airline pilot was still there for the taking. I vowed to myself that I would turn over a new leaf. At my next school I would make sure that I excelled. I owed it to my mother and to Christian, after all that they had done for me.

Yet in spite of their support, I couldn't shake off the feeling of failure that hung over me. I had failed where only success had beckoned. The KCPE was the vital examination at which all Kenyan school students were divided, and I couldn't help but conclude that I had been placed in the category of the failures. I had always sought to be different, and to do the unexpected, but this wasn't the kind of difference that I craved.

Having time on my hands to dwell on all this wasn't healthy.

More and more I was wondering why I had this name, Hussein. Hussein Onyango—just like my paternal grandfather. Hussein, and yet I'd spent all these years going to church as if I were a good Christian. I knew that some of my cousins on my father's side were Muslim, and I guessed my grandfather must have been a follower of Islam. So why had I been brought up a Christian? The religion of my birth might just as easily have been Islam, had my father not died when I was so young.

I wasn't my usual self; I wasn't out playing football the whole time, or larking around with my friends. My mother seemed worried at my introspection and my disquiet. When in an effort to cheer me up she suggested I go to church with Eric, I point-blank refused. I didn't say why. I couldn't tell her that I didn't believe anymore that the Christian church was a place for me, for I knew it would hurt her feelings. But I guess my mother must have sensed something. In her heart I think she recognized and understood some of the turmoil that her teenage son was going through.

My mother had never tried to prevent me from learning about my father's side of the family. In fact, she had made several efforts to interest me in who he was, but I had always rebuffed her. As a young kid I just hadn't been that interested. She'd tried to get me to spend time with my aunts Sarah and Zeituni, my birth father's sisters, but the prospect hadn't excited me much as a young and headstrong child.

Now, seeing how I was troubled, my mother suggested that we pay a visit to Auntie Sarah, my father's oldest sister, as if rediscovering my roots might help ground me. My mother harbored little resentment toward the Obama clan, in spite of the lack of financial support she'd received for my schooling. In reality it hadn't mattered much, for with Christian's help I had received the best education that Kenya had to offer. It was only thanks to my stubborn willfulness that I had made such a mess of it all.

On my mother's urging we took a drive into Huruma, where Auntie Sarah lived. We used the Danger-mobile, and I think Christian hoped the ride might cheer me up a little. We headed into the downtown crush, edging along streets teeming with cars and *matatus*,

and people on foot or riding bicycles or heaving heavily laden handcarts. Hemmed in by the towering buildings, somehow the seething
mass of humans and machines continued to function, in spite of the
absolute chaos.

I stared out the window, barely noticing the crowded streets, for
this scene was normal to a city boy like me. I wondered, absentmind-
edly, if a visit to Auntie Sarah's really would cheer my spirits. The
paved road gave way to a dirt track, the Danger-mobile kicking up a
trail of dust in its wake. To either side the city had changed. Barely
minutes from Nairobi center the concrete and glass office blocks and
plush hotels had given way to a low-rise vista of rickety wooden
shacks and stalls.

To either side of us people squatted on the dusty verges, hawking
their wares: a glistening pile of blood red tomatoes; onions, beetroot
puce in color; heaps of dried fish, shimmering golden brown in the
morning sun. A cobbler hawked an avalanche of dusty, worn-out
shoes; a man wielded a welding gun, sparking star-bright in the shadows, crafting tin trunks of the kind that I had taken to my first boarding school. I knew this place. We were approaching Mathare, the vast
sink of the Nairobi slums.

We overtook a man pulling a cart, half running to speed its load,
the wooden shafts worn smooth by the passage of a thousand hands.
The cart was empty, and I figured he had to be returning from the city
to collect another load. I glanced at the man's face, glistening in the
heat. For a second he grabbed at the front of his shirt, and pulled it
up to wipe the sweat from his brow.

In that instant his eyes met mine, and I sensed the gulf between
us—I a child of privilege gazing out from behind polished glass; he
one of the teeming hordes of the uneducated underclass who are little
better than beasts of burden, feeding the insatiable hunger of the city.

A view opened before us—a wide, shallow valley filled with the
smoke-blue haze of cooking stoves and smoldering refuse fires. Here
and there was a bright patchwork slash of color—lines of washing
hung to dry amid the universal smudge of dull, stinking gray. Tin and
plastic shacks piled on top of each other in hopeless confusion, pencil-

thin alleyways snaking amid the littered and predatory chaos. I had seen this place before, and somehow it never ceased to fascinate me, to unsettle me even. How did people survive its lawless and anarchic deprivation? How did they resist the ghetto's insatiable maw?

Somehow the ghetto drew me to it. We thought we had been so cool and edgy in our Mosocho gang. With our drinking nights and our partying we thought we were invincible, but this place— this ghettoland—this was the place of true survivors. If you could live here, with the ghetto's guns and gangs and drugs and shacks and *changa'a* dens and open sewers, you could survive anywhere. *Anywhere.*

As I gazed out over the sprawling wasteland of Mathare, I knew that I wouldn't last a minute in there. I felt soft and fearful and cosseted before the raw ebb and pulse of the ghetto. What was I doing here? I wondered. What were *we* doing here? Affluent Kenyans were never seen in this part of Nairobi. The ghetto was a place the average Kenyan would prefer didn't exist; a place of shame, one to be kept strictly hidden; a place of abuse, brutality, and despair.

As for white people, what would ever bring the foreign tourists and the businessmen here? Down here, in the ghetto, a person with white skin wouldn't stand a chance. Even for me with my blue-black skin, my clothes and my accent and my bearing would mark me as not being of the ghetto, as being an outsider.

There were unspoken rules here, unwritten formulas, informal hierarchies—and all directed toward safeguarding the ghetto's own and rejecting outsiders. The law in the ghetto was its own, and if an outsider was foolish enough to stray into its midst, he would fall victim to its predations. This we all knew. All Kenyans knew this, and instinctively we steered clear of the secret, stinking, smog-filled city of the dispossessed that lay at the heart of the wider capital.

We drew to a halt near Auntie Sarah's place. Of course, the ghetto dwellers stared. They stared at the vehicle that looked as if it had fallen from a far-off planet. They stared at the white driver, this money-eyed *mzungu* who dared stray into this part of town, their part of town, their territory. And they stared at the black kid who dismounted from the *mzungu's* spaceship vehicle, the kid with the clean clothes and the shiny shoes and the scrubbed nails and the neat hair, the kid who stank of privilege—of privilege, easy living, and money.

I felt different now, more different perhaps than I had ever felt before, but this was not—*this definitely was not*—the kind of difference that I craved. I wished the dirt road would swallow me up. I wished we hadn't come, at least not in the way that we had. But then Auntie Sarah rushed out to greet us, and in her smiles and waves and cries of welcome and her ushering us toward her home, the crowd of onlookers knew; they knew that somehow, despite the gulf between us, we were also of their tribe—that in some way we too were people of the ghetto.

I had to duck my head to enter through the gate leading into Auntie Sarah's compound. Inside, a wall of wood and corrugated iron surrounded us on four sides, fencing off her living space from the chaos outside and hiding us from prying eyes. I welcomed its embrace, and the fact that it shielded our brazen difference from the ghetto dwellers' curiosity, and their need.

Auntie Sarah had had a tough life. I saw it in the lines on her face and the smoky yellowing around her eyes. I felt it in the hard, calloused hands that gripped me as she welcomed me to her home. Auntie Sarah was a survivor. She had to be, to make a life for herself in the ghetto. And the one thing she had never eschewed was her differences, her desire to make her own way in the world. Fiercely independent, she had the same stubborn streak that my mother said ran through me.

In the past Auntie Sarah had gone through several marriages, for she had refused to accept the kind of laziness and abuse that Kenyan men are sometimes wont to visit on the woman of the household. She lived without a man now, an unapologetic single woman making her own way in the world, with a coterie of her children around her. Auntie Sarah would take no abuse from anyone, and on the few occasions that I'd visited before, that's what had drawn me to her.

The area where she lived, Huruma, butted up against the slums of

Mathare. Huruma was a little more upmarket than the neighboring ghetto, but not by much. There was a tap with running water in Auntie Sarah's compound; there was a tin shack toilet in one corner, plus a bucket of water; there were a couple of cramped, brick-built rooms, one doubling as a kitchen and the women's bedroom, the other serving as the living room, complete with electricity and a TV. There was a jumble of tin-sheet huts along one fence for the men and the boys.

Like most people living in Huruma, Auntie Sarah owned the land on which she had built her compound. By contrast, the tiny tin, plastic, and wooden shacks in Mathare were mostly illegal squats, and few if any had the "luxuries" found in Huruma.

Auntie Sarah worked hard to make a living. She sold snacks at her own little roadside stall. She'd squat on a wooden stool behind the counter with a charcoal-fired iron stove at her feet, deep-frying fish in a golden crescent of bubbling oil. I'd visited her a couple of times in recent years and she'd taken me out to help her on her stall. I'd sat behind the counter gazing out at the riot of life all around me and feeling very much as if I didn't belong. How did people survive here? I used to wonder. How did they *survive*?

Auntie Sarah had six of her own children, but most had grown up and moved on and made for themselves a life of their own. Only two remained living in Huruma, and that meant that she had room in her life for me. She was warm and welcoming, and I sensed the strong pull of an instinctive bond between us. Whatever she cooked for the family meal, there was a plate for me too, and she seemed easygoing and relaxed at the occasional appearance of another Obama child— myself—within her clan.

Christian and my mother stopped for tea, and then they left me at Auntie Sarah's place. They would return to pick me up that evening, so I had a whole day with her. Once they were gone, Auntie Sarah glanced at me with her strong, piercing eyes that had seen so much in this world.

"I hear you didn't get the result you were after. So, are you going to persevere, or are you giving up on your education?"

Auntie Sarah didn't beat around the bush.

"No, Auntie, I'll keep trying," I told her. "But I wasn't expect-ing it—"

"Stuff happens in life that we don't expect," she cut in. "Look at me: whoever would have thought I'd end up here? But I deal with it; it's not so bad; a good life can be made almost anywhere."

I smiled. "I guess."

"You persevere with your studies," she encouraged me. "You keep trying. A good life can be built anywhere, of course it can. But a good education is a rare blessing, and it will certainly help."

I nodded my agreement. They were wise words, and the kind of piths of wisdom I expected from her.

She stared at me hard for an instant. "You been misbehaving, Georgie? Is that why you didn't do so well?"

I shrugged. "Some . . . I was pretty stupid, really—"

She cut me off again. "I don't want to know the details. But you know what your father would say, if he was alive? He'd tell you you're wasting your abilities, and that those abilities are vast, and you'd be a fool to squander them. A fool. You do know that, don't you? You're one clever boy, Georgie. Don't mess it up. Don't throw it all away."

"Thanks, Auntie. I appreciate what you said."

I liked it when Auntie Sarah talked to me like this, telling me it like it was. I needed that kind of blunt and direct approach. I needed it to pull me up short and jolt me out of my self-belief or self-delusion, call it what you will. Auntie Sarah was different from anyone else I knew, for she had no problem talking to people and giving it to them straight. She was too old and had seen too much to care what anyone thought of her.

She got to her feet. "Now come along, or d'you think you're grown too big to help your auntie on her stall?"

When we had exhausted Auntie's supplies of dried fish, selling all that she had available, we returned to the compound. Auntie set about cooking the evening meal, and I fell into conversation with one of her sons—like me, named Hussein. He was four or five years my senior, so he was practically a grown man. I was curious to discover if he had any insight into this name that seemed to dominate the male lineage of our clan, this Hussein.

I didn't know my cousin Hussein at all well, and I didn't quite know how to broach the subject.

"There was something I wanted to ask you," I ventured.

"What is it?" Hussein replied. "You want me to lend you some cash, is that it?" He laughed at his joke. "A rich kid like you asking for a loan. Well, you know what the answer's going to be—"

"No, no, nothing like that. It's just . . . well, all the Obama kids, the males that is, seem to share this name—this *Hussein*. We've all got different first names and stuff, but Hussein's still in there somewhere. I just kind of wondered why."

"You a Hussein?" he queried. "Everyone calls you Georgie."

"George Hussein Onyango," I confirmed. "I use Hussein as my street name. That's what all my buddies call me."

"So you want to know why Hussein?"

"Yeah."

"Well, what d'you think might be the reason?"

"Well, it's kind of a Muslim name, isn't it? All the Husseins I've ever heard of are Muslim."

"It is. You were called Hussein because your dad was a Muslim and his father before that—"

"There's three generations of Muslims in the family," Auntie Sarah interjected, from the kitchen. She wiped her hands and came over to join us. "The religion of your birth is Islam, George, because that is the religion on your father's side of the family. You know, you're a third-generation Muslim in our eyes."

"I did wonder," I said.

"You were brought up a Christian, George," she continued, "and that's no bad thing. Your mother's a Christian and your *mzungu* father I guess is one too. They're good people and they've seen you get the best in this world. But by birth and by rights you're a Muslim. If you want to know any more about that, or what a Muslim believes, then you only have to ask. You know that, don't you?"

"Thanks," I replied. "I learned a bit about Islam at school. But it's the first anyone's actually told me that I was born a Muslim."

Hussein eyed me for a moment. "Hussein Onyango. You must be named after Grandpa. I guess there is something of Grandpa about you." He turned to Auntie Sarah. "Hey, you reckon Georgie here—sorry, Hussein—has got Grandpa's ears?"

Auntie Sarah guffawed. "He's got Grandpa's ears, eyes, and nose, plus he's got Grandpa's mind! He's like Grandpa come back to live amongst us." She stared at me for a moment. "Coming to think of it, he's the spitting image of his father too."

Auntie Sarah shuffled about and pulled out a cardboard box from somewhere. She leaned across and handed me a photo.

"Your father," she announced. "That's him during his university days. And no doubt about it, you and him have exactly the same ears!"

I gazed at that photo, and into the eyes of my birth father, and for an instant I wondered what life would have been like had he lived. Would *difference* have come to mean so much to me with a black man as my father? Would courting notoriety have been so important in my life, if I had never had a *mzungu* "dad"? Auntie Sarah pulled out another dog-eared photo.

"And look!" she declared triumphantly. "Here's one of him carrying you as a baby. That proves it: even at that tender age you can tell you're your father's son."

As I held that photo in my hand, I felt a mixture of emotions. There was pain at the fact of losing him, and losing all the love so clearly shown in the way he was holding me and in the light in his eyes. And there was confusion too, for this man cradling me with such tenderness was an utter stranger to me. If he had lived, would I have called him Father, as I was unable to do with Christian? How then might my life have been different?

"You know, Georgie, you've lived a life of privilege," Auntie Sarah remarked, her words drawing me back to myself. "And let's not pretend it isn't because of that *mzungu* father you have. There's a lot of Kenyans would give their right arm for the kind of chances you've been given. Stick with it, get yourself a good education, and there'll be plenty of time to explore all of this—your father, your religion—in the future."

"I guess so, Auntie." I smiled. "I guess so."

I liked Auntie Sarah. I liked the mellow depths that existed beneath the spiky surface of her exterior. Instinctively I felt close to her, and I guess that our bond had to be rooted in blood. I was too old to be cuddled or to fall into her arms as I used to do with Grandma Dorcas, but I felt drawn into an intimacy with her—especially when she was sharing with me her wisdom and her memories of the past.

I felt more grounded after this visit with Auntie Sarah. I'm sure my mother noticed and sensed it had been good for me, something that I needed to do. She had always wanted me to feel connected with my Obama side, a generous and open-hearted wish on her part.

A few days later it was my fourteenth birthday. I was lucky that the month of my birth was nearly always a time of school holidays, and so I got to celebrate the passing of each year at home. This time my mother had ordered a sponge cake, and it arrived with the number 14 piped upon it in icing. My Umoja friends came around to celebrate. We had sodas and snacks while everyone sang happy birthday and I blew out my candles.

I had to make a wish. I wished for something connected with my long-lost father, but no way was I telling anyone about it, for to do so would mean that the wish would never come true. My mother was a genius at finding wonderful birthday presents for little Marvin and me. She never once asked us what we wanted, and yet she seemed able to look into our minds and see what we longed for. This year she thrilled me with the pile of carefully selected gifts, the best of which was a shiny new skateboard.

Time to start my new school was fast approaching. I felt happier in myself. Home life was near-perfect, and I would be boarding at a Nairobi school, so I could visit more often. Auntie Sarah's words had hit home—those that had warned me to appreciate my life of privilege. I also felt more centered in myself, as I learned about my Obama roots and the nature of the religion that I had been born into. I knew belief was a matter of personal choice, but by inheritance and birth I should be leaning toward Islam.

Marvin was still a regular churchgoer, and there was no reason that he shouldn't be. We didn't share the same father, and there was every likelihood that his father might be Christian. I hadn't started going to a mosque, but I had stopped going to church. I hadn't started to read the Koran yet, but I had stopped reading my Bible. My mother wasn't pleased, but she accepted that it was my choice to believe as I wanted.

I felt ready to open a new chapter in my life, at Dagoretti High.

CHAPTER 10

Dagoretti High

BUILT DURING COLONIAL times, Dagoretti High was made up of a set of old-style, grand buildings situated in a wide expanse of grounds. None of my friends from Mosocho or Umoja were here, so it was the perfect opportunity to turn over a new leaf. I was determined to do well. I was also determined to make a good account of myself in the new sport they played here, rugby—largely because rugby was one of Christian's main passions in life.

In spite of my newfound interest in the Obama side of my family, I still saw Christian as my father and, as most teenage boys do, I craved his affection and approval. I hoped to earn it by doing well academically and by proving my fleetness of foot and my bravery on the rugby field. I had never played rugby before, for I had been too young to do so at Mosocho, but I dreamed of being an ace player and basking in Christian's praises and his pride.

In the center of Dagoretti High was the school parade ground, a beaten-flat area where all pupils had to gather first thing in the morning, standing to attention as we sang the national anthem. After that the school head would give a lecture, typically on a theme of moral fortitude or national pride and patriotism and invariably rounded off with a religious lesson.

On my first morning that parade ground was an impressive sight. The members of the school band were perfectly turned out in the Dagoretti High uniform—white shirt, gray trousers, maroon tie, maroon pullover, gray socks with maroon stripes, and a blue blazer over it all. They struck up the stirring tune of the Kenyan national anthem, and I had to admit they were good. I felt a surge of pride in my heart as we belted out those verses.

Oh God of all creation,
Bless this our land and nation.
Justice be our shield and defender,
May we dwell in unity,
Peace and liberty.

The headmaster then gave us a talk on what was expected of the new arrivals at the school. There was to be no spitting, no fighting, and no arriving late in class. Pupils were to be polite to teachers and smart in their dress at all times. Discipline and obedience to authority were clearly big things at Dagoretti High, and I sensed that I was going to have to toe the line here. I was going to have to kick my habit of being different, of seeking notoriety, and do my best to blend in.

That evening I was doing my preps along with the other boys from my class. I had a habit of reading with my chair tilted back and balanced on two legs. We were in one of a set of laboratories newly built at the school, and all around us were solid laboratory benches, Bunsen burners, racks of test tubes, and shelves piled high with scientific glassware. As I swung back in my chair, I all but banged into one of those shelves. I moved my chair slightly and accidentally bumped the leg of the boy next to me.

He turned on me. "Hey! You! Watch it!"

I didn't want any trouble, not here, not on day one at my new school.

I shrugged, apologetically. "Sorry."

"Yeah, well, just watch it, all right?"

I dragged my chair a little farther away from him, being careful to avoid the racks of glass. But no sooner had I done so than he moved over and deliberately placed himself in my way. As I went to lean back in my chair, it knocked into him again.

"I told you to watch it!" the guy snapped. "Or weren't you listening?"

I sighed and gritted my teeth. "Okay, I'll move the chair again."

I moved it slightly farther, but now I was boxed in against the wall. As I leaned back, he stuck his leg out again. I had a bad feeling about how this was going to end.

"I'm warning you," the boy grated. "Don't do that again."

I stared at him. "Then get your leg out of my way."

I leaned back for a fourth time, and the guy rammed his leg under my chair, nearly knocking me over.

"One more time and I'll fucking smash you," the boy snarled. "One more time."

The only answer I gave was to lean my chair back a fifth time, all the while staring at my tormentor. The eyes of the class were upon us now. I had done nothing wrong and no way was I about to back down.

This time the guy kicked as hard as he could, and the legs of my chair flew out from under me. An instant later I was on the floor with my tormentor on top of me, pounding my head into the tiled floor. The guy was heavier than me, and the floor was rock hard, and each time he smashed my head down, it hurt like hell. But he was nowhere near as wiry or as wild as I was, and using all the strength that I could muster, I flipped him off me.

An instant later I was on top of him, punching him hard. By the time the prefects had arrived to break it up—drawn to the fight by the wild chanting of our classmates—my attacker was bruised and bloodied. The prefects dragged me off and held us apart. My tormentor got to his feet a little groggily, and then we were face to face and glaring at each other.

I knew what the rules were about fighting at Dagoretti High: it warranted an instant suspension. I couldn't believe that after all the promises I had made to myself I had gotten into this much trouble on my very first day. I cursed the boy who had attacked me. Why the hell couldn't he have picked on someone else?

"Fighting, is it?" the lead prefect sneered. "Think you're real tough nuts, do you? Real hard nuts, eh?" He turned to his fellow prefects. "Real bloody little Rambos."

They laughed.

"You know what the punishment is for fighting?" the lead prefect demanded. "Maybe you won't feel so smart when they kick you out of school."

He stared at us, and we glared back at him, my tormentor and I now united against a common enemy. There was no point denying anything. We'd been caught red-handed, and apologizing would only make us look weak and vulnerable.

"You've got two choices," the prefect continued, feigning boredom. "It's either the headmaster for you, and let me tell you he's a mean bastard who doesn't approve of little boys fighting. Or there are some chores we need doing in our dorm. Up to you. You choose."

He stared at the two of us, but neither my tormentor nor I wanted to make the decision. If we chose to do the prefect's chores, the rest of the class were sure to accuse us of being chicken. If we chose to go before the headmaster, it would mean an automatic suspension. I could just imagine how Christian and my mother would react if I were thrown out—albeit temporarily—on my first day at Dagoretti High.

We were damned, whatever choice we made.

"Come on, get moving," the prefect ordered, finally breaking the impasse. "It's punishment time."

Without another word he marched us over to the older boys' dorm, whereupon he and his fellow prefects presented us with a huge basket of dirty laundry.

"Here's your punishment, Rambos," he sneered. "Over there's the washroom. And don't stop till you've scrubbed every shirt and sock pristine clean. One speck of dirt, and it'll be up before the headmaster from hell for both of you."

I hesitated for a moment, my mind a mass of indecision. He and his fellow prefects were eighteen-year-olds, practically grown men, but if I let them bully me like this, there was no knowing where it would end. On the other hand, if I stood up to them I would be suspended, and all my vows of good behavior would have come to nothing. Yet I couldn't take this kind of crap. The stubborn part of me just wouldn't accept it.

"I'm not doing it," I stated bluntly. "My dad didn't pay my school fees so I can do your dirty laundry."

"What the fuck did you say?" the prefect snarled. He lifted me by the scruff of the neck and slammed me against the wall, bringing his face close to mine, his breath in my nostrils. "Listen, Rambo," he hissed, "you're really asking to have your head kicked in, you know that? Now me and the other boys will be happy to oblige. But I'm a nice guy, Rambo, and because of that I'm going to give you a second chance."

He shoved me in the back and sent me flying. "That's the direction of the washroom. Now get going!"

Inside the washroom my tormentor and I set about our task in a sullen silence. We filled two bowls with water, worked up some soapsuds, and threw in the pile of washing to soak. As at Mosocho, all the boys at Dagoretti had to do their own laundry, and so the prefects were trying to make us their servants or their slaves. I hated it, and I could feel the anger and rebellion rising up inside me, like an unstoppable wave.

I glanced at the boy I'd been fighting. I'd beaten him soundly, but it was small consolation for the situation in which we now found ourselves.

"Smart move that, picking a fight," I remarked, my voice laced with sarcasm. "But next time, Rambo, why not pick on someone you can beat?"

He shrugged, keeping his eyes on the washing. "Shit happens."

"Yeah, it does, but there's some shit that just isn't worth the taking."

He shot me a look. "What's that supposed to mean?"

"It means I'm out of here." I glanced at the door to make sure none of the prefects were listening. "You do what you want, but I'm leaving."

"You can't just bugger off," he objected. "You heard what that mean bastard said. It's either this or the headmaster."

I shrugged. "I don't give a shit. You stay here and do their dirty laundry if you like. I'm leaving."

I turned and walked to the door. I stuck my head out to check that the coast was clear. The prefects hadn't posted a guard, and it clearly hadn't entered their heads that one of us might try to get away. Without another word I sneaked out and made my way across to our dorm. I didn't give a thought for what the consequences might be. Christian hadn't paid my school fees so I could do anyone's dirty laundry.

The following morning I was in the first lesson of the day when the head prefect appeared. He exchanged a few words with the teacher, who nodded his understanding. I knew exactly what was coming.

"Otieno! Obama!" the teacher called out. "Collect your things and go with the prefect."

"Yes, sir," we replied, pretty much in unison.

I glanced at Otieno as he gathered up his rulers and pencils. He tried to avoid my gaze, but I stared at him long enough to force a response. He shrugged almost imperceptibly, as if to say, *It's you who got us into this, so you'd better think of something.* I had no idea how long he'd remained behind the previous evening, or how much of the prefect's laundry he'd ended up doing. But it couldn't have been all of it, or we wouldn't now have the head prefect at our door with a face like murder.

"Big trouble, Rambos," the head prefect snarled, just as soon as he had us outside the classroom. "I thought we had a deal, but you welched on it. So now it's trouble fucking big-time."

We were marched directly to the headmaster's office. He was a short, stout, pompous man who was never seen wearing anything but a stiff business suit. We stood to attention shoulder to shoulder, as the head prefect related our crimes.

"Sir, these two new boys were caught fighting in one of the new laboratories," he announced. "I'm sorry to report that they could have smashed up valuable equipment, had myself and the other prefects not arrived and put a stop to it. We got there just in time, sir."

The headmaster nodded somberly. He turned to stare at us.

"The punishment for fighting is a two-week suspension from school," he announced, with quiet menace. "At the end of those two weeks your parents will bring you back, and your misdemeanors will be laid before them in detail, and we will administer further punishment as appropriate. Make no mistake, fighting will not be tolerated at Dagoretti High. I'll be contacting your parents right away, so they can arrange for your collection."

He dismissed us with a wave of his hand.

"I'd like to say something, sir," I ventured.

He dragged his eyes up from his desk until he was staring right at me.

"You'd like to speak, would you? Well, what can you possibly have to say? I'm sure the head prefect isn't making this up. You were caught fighting, *ergo*, you face the consequences."

"Sir, we were caught fighting, but—"

"But what? *What?* What more is there to say, boy?"

I plowed on. "We were fighting and I accept that we should be punished. But before bringing us here, the prefects forced us to do their laundry. That isn't right, sir. That's bullying, and if the head prefect's going to tell his side of the story, you should also hear ours."

He flicked his eyes across to Otieno. "Is there any truth in this?"

Otieno nodded. "Yes, sir. Obama's right, sir."

"And, sir," I added, pressing home my attack, "if our parents are to be told about our fighting, then surely they should also be told about us being forced to do the prefects' laundry. If we're to be punished, that should be taken into account as part of the—"

"Yes, yes, Obama," the headmaster snapped. "That's quite enough."

He got to his feet. "Head prefect, would you step outside my office for a moment." Then, to us, "You two, stay exactly where you are."

There was a hurried murmuring from outside the headmaster's door, and it sounded as if the prefect was getting an earful. Otieno hadn't said much in our defense, but at least he'd confirmed the basics of the story.

"Otieno," I hissed out of the corner of my mouth. "Back me up on this, okay?"

"Fine," he hissed back. "But what are you up to, Obama?"

"The headmaster can't be seen to allow bullying. Maybe he'll let us off. It's worth a try."

Otieno shook his head. "I dunno, but I'll back you up. It's the truth, anyway."

I grinned. "You're the man. Say, what do people call you, anyway?"

"James," he replied.

"I'm George. But my mates call me Hussein."

The headmaster came back in, with a red-faced prefect following behind. He sat at his desk, then glanced at us, his anger and annoyance showing in the slight twitching of one eye.

"I have decided that you will be caned instead," he announced stiffly. "Obama, you first. Bend over, and face the desk."

I did as I was ordered. I didn't give a damn about a caning. I'd had enough beatings before. In fact I was quietly jubilant, for at least now we weren't going to be kicked out of school.

"Head prefect, hand me my cane," the headmaster demanded.

I gritted my teeth as I heard a piggy grunt of exertion, followed by the swish of the cane through the air. No doubt about it, the headmaster knew how to give a good beating. He was taking out the anger he was feeling on me, and it hurt like hell. But I didn't let out a sound. Just one cry and I'd have shown myself up in front of Otieno and the head prefect, and I couldn't allow that.

It was crucial that I come out of this with my honor and my courage intact, for only in that way would the head prefect and his cronies be deterred from taking their revenge. Likewise, Otieno took his beating like a man and without making a sound. We were dismissed from the headmaster's office with a final, dire warning never to be caught fighting again.

In Kenya we have a saying that once you have fought a man, you have his measure, and then you will become friends. Sure enough, James Otieno and I went on to become good buddies. And from that day onward I was never again bullied by any of the prefects. After my performance in front of the headmaster, they must have concluded that I wasn't afraid to speak my mind and that I was best avoided.

My behavior couldn't have endeared me to the headmaster much. By threatening to expose the level of bullying at the school, I had struck at his Achilles' heel. New boys were regularly bullied at Dagoretti. In fact there was an informal system of servitude at the school, which resulted in younger and weaker boys having to slave for the older, tougher pupils.

I had gone to Dagoretti promising to hide my differences and to fit in, but in practice it wasn't proving easy. There was a regular Sunday church service at the school, but from the very first I refused to attend. For the first time in my life I actually told people that I was a Muslim and that I couldn't be expected to attend any Christian worship. There was no mosque at the school, and fewer than five percent of the pupils were Muslims, but the masters had to respect our wishes.

During the first months of school the Muslim festival of Ramadan was declared, whereupon all Muslims are expected to fast and to cleanse themselves. From my fellow Muslim students I learned what was expected of me—how no food or drink should pass my lips from dawn to dusk. In the evenings we handful of Muslim students would break fast, cook our meals together, and eat a celebratory feast. I was feeling my way into this thing—this faith of my father's—gradually, as if I were trying on a new suit of clothes.

In spite of my run-in with the headmaster and the otherness of my faith, I did well academically, and I put in maximum effort at sports. Gradually rugby took over as my favorite game, and somehow it even eclipsed my passion for soccer. It was my natural prowess at the game that drew me to it—my ability to run, to dodge and dummy and jink and sidestep, and to score dramatic tries. My best position was on the wing, where I could take the ball and use the width of the field to outrun my opponents.

Rugby is an extremely tough game. It is a little like American football, but with different rules and with no protective padding or facemasks or helmets for the players. As a consequence injuries are common, and I had my share of sprains, bruises, and breaks. Dagoretti was a fine school by Kenyan standards, yet still we didn't have our own personal rugby kit. Each match we had to draw our boots and uniform from the school kit room and play as best we could with whatever we were given.

The rugby coach really supported me and nurtured my talent. He proved to me how much better I was at rugby than soccer and he convinced me that I could do something truly special with my speed and footwork on the rugby field. He taught me the real secret of success. If I could just stay out of the opposing players' reach and avoid being tackled, then no one could catch me.

Toward the end of that first year the coach put me onto the Dagoretti High rugby team. I was the youngest player on the squad, all the other boys being four years or so my senior. I played in a couple of games against rival schools but never for a full match, and mostly I sat on the benches and waited for my chance to shine. But it was still an extraordinary achievement for a boy of fifteen to be representing a school such as ours at rugby, and I thrilled at the thought of how Christian would react when he first got to see me play.

My opportunity came sooner than I had hoped. The climax of the rugby season was the tournament played between the top Kenyan schools. Each year the tournament was hosted by a different school, and this year it was to be held at St. Mary's, an elite fee-paying school in Nairobi. In fact, St. Mary's schooled the elite of the elite, following a curriculum of GCSEs, which is a British-led examination system. St. Mary's was populated mostly by white kids, plus the children of other expatriates, and to them, Dagoretti was a school for the Kenyan masses.

St. Mary's, Upper Hill, St. Christopher's, and the Nairobi National School shared the reputation of being the best rugby schools in Kenya. Dagoretti High came after, and we knew we would have our work cut out if we were to do well. There was one other aspect that sharpened our hunger to win. St. Mary's was a mixed school, so there would be girls galore in the audience. The girls loved watching rugby matches, and for us this was a golden opportunity to show off our muscles and our bravado.

With the day of the tournament fast approaching, I redoubled my efforts to get selected. A few days before the big day itself, the coach sat me down for a quiet chat. He pointed out all my obvious shortcomings—that I was young and not as experienced or physically robust as the older lads on the team. But he did have a couple of injured players, and that was why he was tempted to make me an offer.

"I'd like you on the reserve bench for St. Mary's," he told me. "There's five matches we have to play that day, and I can guarantee you'll be picked for one of them. But George, it's your call. We're up against the toughest teams in Kenya, and it will be hard, fast, and brutal. You're three years junior to the rest of the players, and I want you going into this with your eyes wide open."

"I want to play." I grinned. "I know I'm the youngest, Coach, but you said yourself, once I start to fly, there's no one can catch me. If they can't catch me, they can't smash me, so what's the harm?"

Coach smiled. "Fair point, Obama. I think you'll do great. You're our secret weapon. If you're up for it, I'd love to put you on the field that day and see you run."

"I'm up for it, Coach," I cut in, before he could change his mind. "I'm totally up for it. I won't let you down."

He gave me a playful punch on the shoulder. "Great. I believe in you. But don't do anything stupid and get stretchered off the pitch. I don't want to be explaining to any angry parents why I put their weedy fifteen-year-old kid on the field to face a pack of eighteen-year-old ruffians."

The coach's remarks brought a quiet smile to my face. I could just see it now: Christian screaming wildly from the sidelines and uttering French exhortations—*Mon Dieu! Vite! Vite!*—as I made a dash for the line to score the winning try. I couldn't wait to let him know that I was on the school team—and for the St. Mary's tournament, of all things. Coach had guaranteed me a game, which meant that Christian could see me run like the wind, dance like a butterfly, and pounce like a leopard for an ace try.

The day of the tournament we were up early to select our boots and kit. Coach told us that we could do this, that we could win this thing. He reminded us that the teams we were up against had the best of everything—kit, trainers, practice machines, the works—but that they were only human. We had something they could never match, and that was our team spirit. He told us the story of David and Goliath, wherein a simple shepherd boy had beaten a giant warrior in battle. Those rich-kid schools were the Goliaths of Kenyan rugby, but we were like David, and like him we could overcome.

Thus fired-up, we boarded the coach to St. Mary's. I felt sick with anxiety as we pulled out of our school gates, and I wondered if I really could perform at this level. And then the incantations began, as a sonorous chant of "DA-GO-RE-TTI! DA-GO-RE-TTI! DA-GO-RE-TTI!" rose up from the team veterans, a chant that was taken up in turn by all down to the very youngest player, me. The chanting fired my spirits and settled my nerves. By the time we reached the rolled-grass expanse of St. Mary's, I was ready.

St. Mary's was a place of such wealth and status that there were five pitches within the school grounds. This meant that several matches could take place at once, with all the teams able to play each other over the duration of the day. It would be a little confusing for the supporters, who mightn't know at first which match was which, but I felt certain Christian would find us. I had left a message at home alerting him to my debut performance, and I felt sure he would be there, for this was the moment when he would feel real pride and admiration for me, his adopted son.

Midway through the afternoon I still hadn't got a game. Dagoretti was trailing behind the leaders, but there was still all to play for in our last match, against St. Christopher's. Coach had given me a hint that this was the game that he had me pegged for, and in my message to Christian I'd said that the afternoon was the best time to come. I'd been on the bench all morning, willing my teammates to win, and by now I was dying to get out onto the field and to have the chance to test my mettle.

I saw the familiar figure of Coach approaching along the touchline.

"Okay, George, you're on," he announced. "St. Christopher's. Go get 'em, George! Run like the wind, and whatever you do, avoid getting tackled!"

I felt an odd mixture of panic and pride as I ran out onto the pitch. I did a quick scan of the supporters, checking the white faces, but still I couldn't see Christian. I tried to put him to the back of my mind. I had to play now. For my teammates and myself, I had to perform. We lined up facing the opposing team. My eyes sought out my opposite number, the wing on St. Christopher's side. He was a white kid with a jutting jaw and a flash of blond hair, and he looked bigger and heavier than me. But I told myself that if I could just keep out of his grasp, then I could beat him.

The whistle blew and the torpedo shape of the ball looped high into the sunlit sky. There was the thundering vibration of studded boots slamming into turf, as both sides charged forward, and then the thudding, grunting impact of flesh on flesh and bone on bone. Battle had been joined. For the first ten minutes the ebb and flow of the match was pretty much equal and I was forced to stand on my lonely wing and watch the furious struggle unfold. As so often happens to the winger, the ball had yet to reach me, but I had to remain one hundred percent focused for the moment when I could shine.

All of a sudden our side made a surging break, and I saw the gray streak of the ball arcing down the line of players. I took it in outstretched fingers, tucked the ball into my side, and suddenly my feet were flashing across the turf toward the try line, barely thirty yards in front of me. My opposite number lunged, but his intention was far too obvious, and as he went to crush me, I sidestepped his diving tackle. I lifted my feet and kicked out for the try line. An instant later the thin line of white chalk flashed beneath my boots, and I dropped with the ball, slamming it onto the hallowed earth.

Try! Touchdown! Goal!

I rose to my feet. My teammates were dancing around wildly and grabbing me in bear hugs, as a roar went up from our supporters.

I strode back to our half, scanning the crowd for the one person I had really needed to see me score that try. I searched and searched, but I couldn't see him.

I couldn't see Christian, my adoptive father, anywhere.

CHAPTER 11

Crash and Burn

By halftime we were eleven points up. My try had been converted, so I had brought seven of those points onto the scoreboard. I should have been overjoyed, and I was pretty damn ecstatic, but there was still no sign of Christian. I couldn't kid myself anymore: it looked as if he wasn't coming. Perhaps he had failed to get the message, but I doubted it, and that meant that something had to be wrong.

This wasn't like him. He knew how much this meant to me and would have done everything possible to be here. And if for some reason he couldn't have made it—perhaps an aid visit upcountry—he at least would have sent me a message of *bonne chance*. As we sat in the changing room at halftime, sucking on orange slices and listening to Coach's words of encouragement, I told myself that I couldn't let it bother me; I couldn't let it ruin my game.

But deep inside I was hurt and angry. I had dreamed of this moment for years—the moment when my adoptive father and I might truly bond on a level that I longed for. Now the chance was upon us, but Christian was nowhere to be seen. I tried to channel that anger toward something positive, to direct it against the opposing team.

And the target I chose was the *mzungu* kid who was my opposite wing.

That second half I ran rings around him. It was almost as if my anger had given me wings. When I took a pass with a third of the field to cover, I told myself that I would do this, I would run faster than the wind and I would hit the try line. I raced ahead like a thing possessed, eyes wide with anger, feet flashing with fury, muscles fueled by the hurt inside me, and I left that winger in the dust. The try was an ace, and it brought our score to twenty-six points, leaving St. Christopher's on a miserly seven.

So be it. In spite of their money and their privilege and their white skins, we had beaten them.

On the journey home our team was wild with the elation of our victory. The chants of *Da-Go-Re-Tti* were thunderous and all-consuming. Of all the players, I had perhaps performed most remarkably, for I was the new guy and the rookie who had run rings around the opposition. But I felt distant and uninvolved, dislocated and untouched by it all, my smiles and chanting a hollow act to hide my hurt. My mind was clouded, beset by confused and bitter thoughts.

Where was Christian? Why did he fail to show? Where was Christian? Where was he in my hour of glory? Where was Christian? Where was he in my hour of need?

Just like my previous boarding schools, at Dagoretti we were allowed no phone calls home. Of course, none of the students had anything like a mobile phone, so it would have been difficult to call anyway. I thought of writing a letter home asking what had happened, but when I tried to put pen to paper, the words just wouldn't come.

What was I going to say? If Christian had cared for me like a father would a son, he would have been there. More to the point, if he'd been prevented from coming, he would have written me to explain why. He only lived on the other side of the city; he could even have popped by the school. It was his silence that cut me the deepest.

A few weeks later it was half term. I took a *matatu* home to Umoja. I went with mixed emotions. On the one hand I was keen to see my friends and my family, and to have some chill-out time. On the other, I was anxious about seeing Christian. Part of me wanted to rage at him for missing the match. Another part of me wanted to tell him all about it, to relate in detail my heroic dash across a third of the field to score the winning try.

But when I reached home I stood there dumbfounded, staring at the parking lot at the front of our house. It was empty. *Completely empty.* Not one of Christian's three vehicles was there. How could it be? How could the jeep, the camper van, and the Danger-mobile all be in use at the same time? It didn't make sense. He couldn't be driving all three of them at once, so what the hell was going on?

With a mounting sense of panic, I hurried inside.

"The cars?" I blurted out, just as soon as I caught sight of my mum. "Where are they?"

She bit her lip and shook her head almost imperceptibly.

"But—"

She shook her head again, more fiercely this time.

"But Christian—"

"Gone," my mother whispered. "Just gone."

I stared at her for a moment, trying to make sense out of what she was saying. How could he be gone? He couldn't just have disappeared like that. After all, he was my father and he'd been my father for the last ten years. I'd sometimes had trouble accepting it, but in truth that's who he had been to me. He'd brought me up. Nurtured me. Guided me through the storm. *Gone?* He couldn't just be gone.

I shook my head, confusedly. "But . . . but gone where?"

My mother gave a weary shrug. "I don't know. Just gone. Gone for good, I think. Gone."

She half closed her eyes as if trying to shut out the memory of it all, her sorrow and her pain. I stared at her, not knowing what to say. She looked tired, so tired, and part of me wanted to run to her and to hold her, but I was too old and too manly to do things like that. After all, I had just earned my spurs on the rugby field. I couldn't go hugging my mother anymore.

I sat in my room for hours, staring blankly at the wall. I had to accept that my mother was telling me the truth, for the house screamed it out at me whenever I cared to listen. One glance around was enough to prove it. His cars were gone; his stuff was gone; his mess was gone; his ambience was gone; even his smell—strong cigarettes, rich aftershave, and fine red wine—was gone, gone, gone. I knew it was true, yet I couldn't bring myself to accept it. In my heart I couldn't bear to think that he was gone.

Over the next few days I sank into a dark depression. It was like living inside a skeleton, being in that house in Umoja. It just didn't seem like we were a family anymore. I tried to spend as much time as possible at my friends' houses, but I couldn't hide from them that something was wrong. They could see it in my eyes and tell there was a dull, pulsing ache that made everything listless and dead to me.

I didn't speak to anyone about what had happened. My pain and anger were so great that I locked it all away in a place of fire and hurt. If I went into that place, I knew it would consume me. But in the quiet, lonely moments waiting for sleep that wouldn't come, that place kept breaking open to me, and my mind was tortured by painful thoughts.

How could he have left like that, without a word? How could he have disappeared so completely, such that there was no contact at all? There was no note for me, no phone number by which to call him, no letter, no way in which to get in touch. He had cut himself off so completely that it was as if he had never existed in our lives.

Word got around Umoja pretty quickly that there was no Christian anymore. There was no kid with the *mzungu* father now. The only thing that made me different now was that *I had no father at all*. It was my mother and Marvin and me now—just the three of us. My long-dead birth father was all but forgotten and my adoptive father was gone. I didn't blame my mother. After all, she was still there for me, for us. But I did blame Christian. I blamed him with a vengeance that seared my soul.

Christian's leaving was the switch that flipped me out, and there seemed to be no flipping me back again. As the blame and pain consumed me, I crashed and I burned. My breakdown was rapid and brutal, and the darkness washed over me. I didn't care how anyone else—my mother, nine-year-old Marvin—was dealing with it. I cared about me, and I was alone in a place of empty, howling darkness.

From that moment on I rebelled and went seriously off the rails. When I went back to school I really hit it—drinking *changa'a*, smoking weed when I could get my hands on it, anything to dull the anger and the pain. I started blowing off lessons. I had my first, second, and third suspensions, and I didn't give a damn.

Dagoretti was a place of regimented discipline and of punishment for those who stepped out of line. No one sat me down and tried to talk me through what was happening. No teacher took me to one side and asked me what the hell was going on. I stopped playing rugby, yet not even Coach tried to fathom what was happening to his star player. In short, no one wanted to know.

At times my mother was furious with me, but by now I was too big for her to give me a beating. In any case, I guess she had her own upset and troubles to contend with, not least of which was losing Christian. The headmaster told my mother that I had to become a day pupil, as if that might help stop me from cutting school. It didn't make the slightest difference. I'd become hardheaded and uncontrollable, and my mother knew that she had little influence over me.

She tried sending me to Auntie Sarah, to see if she could talk some sense into me. But no matter who was doing the talking, I wasn't hearing. Had Christian still been at home, I might have listened to him. In fact, I'm certain that I would have. Like many a teenage boy, I craved the presence of a father figure. But there was no contact with him; he was just gone. I felt angry and abandoned, and all twisted up inside.

Halfway through my second year at school the inevitable happened: I was expelled. My mother was devastated. She tried to get me to go back to school—to any school that would have me. But I thought that I knew better. There were some older kids in Umoja who'd already quit school, and I started hanging out with them. I was not yet sixteen, and they were two years or more my senior. Those kids became my new gang.

At first we did stuff that was pretty innocuous to fill the emptiness of our days. We'd go to the Nairobi clubs for the big jamming sessions and dance the night away to reggae and soul music. I got into the new beat that was making the rounds—dance bands like Sizzlar, soul artist Turbulence, and Banuwela. And we'd kill time by smoking pot—*stoot* in Umoja Sheng—whenever we could get hold of it, and drinking.

I told myself that I was old enough to make my own decisions in life. I had no plan for what I was going to do, but I wasn't about to admit that I was lost. I was masquerading as a cool gang member; I had the clothes, the walk, the talk, and the attitude; I was drinking and smoking weed like it was going out of fashion. But it was all a complete sham, and beneath the mask I was falling apart inside.

Pretty quickly I found myself a girlfriend, a girl from Umoja called Stacey. She was drawn to me by my difference, I guess, but now that difference manifested itself in streetwise attitude and rebellion. When I wasn't going clubbing, I was big into gangster movies like *Pulp Fiction* and *Gone in Sixty Seconds*. In that latter movie the star is a gangster who steals fifty cars in one day. These guys were my new heroes. It wasn't rugby players that I wanted to be like now; I'd no desire to be an airline pilot; I wanted to be a hard and angry badass gangster.

Never for one moment did my mother give up on me, regardless of how my life had fallen apart. I was still living at home, and she was still providing me with a little pocket money, the amount that she had been giving me at Dagoretti. But it was nowhere near enough. For the kind of lifestyle that the gang was leading, I needed a lot of money, and we found ways to get it.

In the evenings we'd go to the Stage, a *matatu* park local to Umoja. This was the busiest time of day, and we'd act as *matatu* touts—the callers who hustle people into the vehicles. If we worked from seven to ten o'clock at night, the drivers would pay us around two hundred shillings—about three dollars—or thirty shillings for each *matatu* that we managed to fill. On a weekday we'd use the money to go buy ourselves a meal, but on the weekend we'd spend it clubbing and drinking. If we'd done especially well, we might treat ourselves to beer, but normally we'd only have enough to go drinking *changa'a*.

This was Nairobi *changa'a*, city *changa'a*. Maybe it was worse than the stuff we used to get in the Mosocho drinking den. It would completely blow you away. It would wipe you out and leave you comatose—a state we called *KO* in Sheng, short for a knockout, as in boxing. You'd wake up hours later sprawled on a piece of ground, a rock for your pillow and covered in dust. Your pockets would have been emptied of any money, and you would feel like the walking dead. But I drank *changa'a* to forget and I drank it to feel good, and the aftereffects came with the territory.

Our Umoja gang worked like an informal democracy. We'd talk among ourselves and decide what we wanted to do for the day. Invariably, it depended on whether we had money, and there was never enough of that. What we really needed was *maganji*, our Sheng word for "real money." And working as *matatu* touts was never going to earn us *maganji*. There was only one route to getting real money and that was crime, and so we resorted to pickpocketing and to mugging.

The best place to pickpocket someone was inside a *matatu*. Passengers were crammed in so tight that some would be left clinging to the outside, gripping the open door. It was easy to squeeze in alongside someone and lift their wallet or their handbag in the sweaty, suffocating crush. Once I'd got my hands on a wallet I'd wait for the bus to slow a little—for a tight corner or a set of traffic lights—and I'd jump off and be gone.

Downtown Nairobi had the richest pickings, but the risks were far higher. We'd operate in a larger group, usually seven or more, and we'd run snatch operations against affluent-looking Kenyans or foreigners. The city center was crawling with cops, so we had to be doubly careful. The seven of us would select likely victims and tail them on the streets, trying to work out exactly where they had their cash. Telltale signs were a man who kept patting his back pocket to make sure his wallet was there or a woman who kept fidgeting inside her handbag, feeling for her purse.

We might pick up a victim at a cash machine, having observed where he put his money. One person in our team would make the robbery, while the rest provided diversion and backup. Three would move ahead of the target, to provide some kind of distraction, maybe acting as if a fight had broken out. While the target was distracted, the three behind would guide the lone robber in, warning him of any potential trouble—like a police van coming down the street. The lone robber would make a grab for the victim's money, and we'd run in our separate directions.

We knew that foreigners often carried serious amounts of cash on them. Generally they didn't have a clue about the risks of walking the city streets, and so they were easy pickings, but the risk of robbing a foreigner was still immense. They were found only in downtown Nairobi, so the robbery had to take place under the coppers' noses.

If the coppers came after you, speed was the essence of escape. The safest option was to head for an area where I knew there would be hordes of street children. Nairobi is teeming with such street kids. Most are orphans or utterly estranged from their families and have ended up living on the streets. If I could lose myself within their number, I could rely on the street kids to hide me, for the police were our common enemy.

I always had to make my way back to our emergency rendezvous. If it was a downtown snatch operation, the pickings would have to be split seven ways, among the seven of us involved. If I had lifted a *mzungu*'s wallet, more often than not there was more than enough cash to go around. And whenever the street kids had hidden me, I'd show my gratitude by sharing some of my ill-gotten gains. I'd buy the kids a plate of rice and lentils from a roadside stall, or some clothing from one of the secondhand vendors.

As time went on, my relationship with the street kids became more and more central to my life. I was still living at home, but on occasion I might be away all weekend, partying and drinking around the city. If it reached the stage that I needed a bolt-hole, I'd head for a patch of waste ground in Umoja where the street kids had made their home. In among the piles of rubble and refuse were the scattered humps of plastic and cardboard—the street kids' makeshift homes. It was there that I'd be given space in a hovel-shelter to sleep things off.

What I most liked about those street kids was that they never judged anyone. You couldn't sink lower than the life of a street child, and yet they welcomed me in as their brother. But if it reached the stage where I didn't go home for days on end, my mother would go wild with worry. She'd threaten my old buddies that she would call the police unless they found me. Eric knew where I was hanging out, and so he would come and fetch me home. When my mother saw the state I was in, she was embarrassed and appalled. She was despairing of me and what my life had become.

I was approaching my sixteenth birthday when my grandfather died, leaving Grandma Dorcas and the other wives widowed. My mother and Marvin were going to the funeral, but I didn't want to leave the city. I was sad that Grandpa had died, but the very idea of spending time in the homestead bored me to tears. I had no interest in the rural life or the traditional ways of the village, but my mother persuaded me that I had to go.

With Christian gone there was no car, so we had to use public transport. We made a seven-hour journey by two different *matatus* before finally we reached the home village. I was saddened by Grandma Dorca's distress—all three of his wives seemed to have taken Grandpa's death very badly—yet at the same time I just didn't want to be there. As for my cousin Omondi, his life and mine had gone in opposite directions, and we had nothing to say to each other.

As would happen with any traditional Luo funeral, animals were slaughtered with a knife cut to the throat, and days of feasting and mourning followed. I sat in glum and sullen silence, surrounded by the rich and vibrant music and traditions of my culture, yet blind to it all.

Grandpa's body lay in the main house—the same house in which I had listened to Grandma's stories and slept so soundly as an infant. I was obliged to pay my last respects, but as I gazed down on Grandpa's pale face, I felt nothing. Grandpa was an old man and it struck me that he looked to be at peace, so what was all the fuss about?

An old man had died and gone to wherever we went when we died—to dust and ashes, for all I knew, for I certainly didn't believe in an afterlife anymore. I didn't believe in anything anymore. My credo was that of the city gangster I was becoming: easy money, drink and drugs, and partying with the hard city girls. The ways of the countryside, and the traditions of my tribe, had become closed to me.

When it came time to leave, I said a heartfelt farewell to Grandma Dorcas, for the ties that bound us couldn't be broken that easily. But I was far from sad to be going. The village seemed to be stuck in the dark ages, whereas I was a son of the fast and angry city.

CHAPTER 12

They Call Me
the Mamba

WE STARTED MUGGING people in and around Umoja, but there was always the danger of being recognized, and then someone might report it to my mother or the police. We got around this problem by operating in teams of three. Invariably we mugged men, because they were likely to be carrying the most money. Two of us would distract the victim, while the third would come up behind, grab him in a headlock, and fleece him of his money. In that way the victim never got to see exactly who it was who had robbed him.

Invariably, I was given the job of being the robber, because I was tall, wiry and strong, and very fast. That was fine by me. I didn't give a damn. In my mind I was a mean and badass gangster, and my deep pain and anger made me the wildest of the bunch. We operated at night, when the victim had often been drinking, so it was pretty easy. Just as soon as I had his wallet, we'd run our separate ways. Before the mugging we'd have arranged a meeting point—normally a club or a bar where we'd gather to divide the cash.

As my behavior became more and more extreme, a core of gang members coalesced around me, the kind of guys who could handle the bad stuff that I was getting into. We were a hard core of seven. My closest gang buddy was Ramjo, whose name was a play on Rambo, the macho U.S. movie character. Ramjo was two years my senior, and he was a hard man. Before resorting to gang life, Ramjo had trained as a boxer. He and I were inseparable. Ramjo was a real joker, a funny guy who was forever charming the girls, but he was a dangerous man to cross.

Then there was Nicky, who was closest to me in age. He was tall and wiry like me, and he was also the handsome one of the bunch. We were all lucky enough with the girls, but Nicky really turned heads. He didn't have an ounce of fat on him, and when the going got tough, he would prove to be the one with real guts.

Tin Tin was our third member. He was a useful guy to have around. He got his gang name from the cartoon character, and like him he was diminutive in stature. Tin Tin may have been the smallest of the lot, but he was fast, being short and stocky like a sprinter. Whenever we needed a runner, Tin Tin would volunteer, in part to take some of the pressure off me.

Ndule was the fourth member. He wasn't as tough as the rest of us. Ndule and I had once had an argument in a bar, and I'd had to teach him a lesson. Gang member number five, Maleh, was another of the softer guys. And Nito, gang member number six, was something of a gangster-intellectual. I guess he was like Isaac had been, back in Mosocho, a kind of street philosopher who was always trying to get the rest of us thinking.

And then there was me. Ramjo had chosen for me the gang name the *Mamba*, which is "crocodile" in Swahili. I was charming like a crocodile, and if we had to talk our way out of anything, I was the one who had to do it. But the main reasons Ramjo had named me the Mamba were that I was fast and I liked fighting. And like a crocodile, when I attacked, my prey never got away.

Together, we were the Magnificent Seven of Umoja. Others came and went, but we were the hard-core group. We had a formal gang structure and anyone who wanted to join had to prove themselves. Our gang initiation centered on *war*, the Sheng word for "fighting," and invariably it involved proving oneself in battle against a rival gang. The initiate had to prove his *jam*—his aggression—by giving the other side a *pano*, a real beating.

The gang wars were all about turf. The *matatu* touting was controlled by gangs, and if we wanted to take over a new patch, the only way to do it was to fight. These gang fights were vicious, and we'd utilize whatever weapons came to hand—sticks, iron bars, machetes, even rocks. Ndule and Maleh were good at "backing up"—carrying the weapons to support those of us who might get into serious trouble—but they never led from the front. The one person who led us into battle more than anyone else was me.

I have to confess that I liked fighting. I was forever picking a *war* with a rival gang. In no time I earned a reputation amongst my enemies of being bad trouble, and with my friends of being a good guy to have on their side. The repute of the Mamba went before me, and in fighting I found a way to vent all my anger. I was good with my fists and quick like a crocodile, and each time we fought a *war* I felt satiated. For a while at least I felt as if the painful mess of betrayal and loss that my life had become was put to one side, as all things were subsumed under the golden rush of the battle.

In my status as the Mamba—the foremost warrior of our gang—I had claimed my territory, I had staked my claim on being *different*. Deprived of the difference that came with having a *mzungu* father, I had acquired a new notoriety. Locked out of the distinction of academic success I had become the Mamba—the angriest, meanest son of a bitch on the streets. But only my gang buddies recognized and looked up to that difference, and increasingly they became my brothers and my family.

The credo of our gang was all for one and one for all. If a rival gang member tried to pick on one of us, I'd strike fast and hard without asking questions. I'd use the element of surprise and go all out to defend my fellow gang member. I can't remember a fight I lost, so I guess there weren't many. My speciality was a "start and stop" fight.

One punch, no delaying, and the other guy would be on the ground, and the fight would be over. No week seemed to pass without a fight: fighting had become my life now.

I was sixteen years old, fueled by the elixir of youth and feeling indestructible. I had been gouged by broken bottles, cut by machetes, and smashed by stones, but getting injured was part of the life of the gang and we dealt with it in our own way. We treated whatever wounds we suffered within the milieu of the gang, for to do anything else would raise difficult questions. We never went to a hospital, and none of us could go home with our injuries, for we knew our parents would be horrified.

We'd hang out with the Umoja street kids, nursing our injuries and smoking hash, rubbing the ash from the cannabis joints into our wounds. After being passed the joint, I'd take the inch or so of gray ash and crumble it hot from the glowing end into the bloodiest of injuries—the machete cuts and the gashes from rocks. I'd press the ash deep and hard into the wound—so hard that it caused a stab of pain to shoot up my arm or leg, or wherever I was hurt. The more pain, the more I told myself that the ash was doing its work. And the more hash I smoked, the more it dulled the hurt.

We told ourselves that the cannabis ash was a kind of "medicine," that it was better than the chemicals and pills that came from the hospitals because it was "organic." In Kenya's hot and humid climate, cannabis grows abundantly, and getting hold of some was never hard, as long as you had money. In our adolescent minds we believed that the ash would seal up and heal our worst wounds. I suffered deep cuts that I "treated" in this way, and strangely enough they did seem to mend.

I never had any stitches or bandages, and I wore those wounds for all to see like a badge of respect—to show how I had been bloodied in battle. Soon, the ash gray scab would fade to a silver scar on my blue-black skin. Each new scar was like a battle honor, and I wore them on my arms and back with pride.

But a year into the gang life the inevitable happened. One afternoon I was hanging out in Umoja with the street kids, smoking hash

My father, Barack Hussein Obama Senior. His legacy as the first educated Obama has cast a long shadow over the entire clan. He was killed in a road accident before I was a year old. Right until his untimely death, he believed that Kenya could become a leading light in Africa, an aspiration that has largely been frustrated by the corruption that plagues the country.

As an infant in my mother's arms, at our Nairobi home. Jael Atieno Onyango was a typical Luo woman—tall, slender, and strikingly beautiful. The fourth wife of Barack Obama Senior, she was widowed at an early age. Jael was the disciplinarian in the family, and she used to beat me if I misbehaved. Yet I always thought of her as gentle but strong.

With my brother Marvin (left), at home in Umoja, a middle-class suburb of Nairobi. I was hugely protective of him. But during my late teens, my lost and wild years of drink, drugs, and crime, I lost touch with my family, and Marvin moved to the United States with my mother. I haven't seen them for over a decade.

Proudly showing off my legs in my All Saints Cathedral Nursery School uniform. In Kenya, short trousers are obligatory until you reach high school. Like many Luo, I'm tall and rangy in stature, and I was tall even as a four-year-old. I'm standing on a wall in Uhuru Park, in Central Nairobi, a green and well-tended part of the city, and a world away from the Huruma ghetto where I live today.

My adoptive father, Christian Bertrand, with my mother in the family home in Umoja. For the first sixteen years of my life, Christian, a French aid worker, was my de facto father. He was a kind and generous man, and he made our family his life in Africa. It was rare to see mixed race couples in Kenya at the time, and, sadly, race was an issue that often impinged upon our daily lives. It was after losing Christian, when I was sixteen, that my life started to crash and burn.

The late Sarah Obama, my favorite aunt and Barack Obama Senior's oldest sister. Auntie Sarah led a hard life. She refused to accept the kind of abuse that Kenyan men at times visit on their wives, and ended up living with her children in the ghetto. Fiercely independent and stubborn, she was a plain talker. When I went to live with her in the ghetto, she did so much to help turn my life around.

In the gateway to my Huruma home, my late Auntie Sarah's place, with some of my ghetto buddies. In the ghetto they know me as their own "Obama president." On my right is Clyde Kagondu, a Kenyan tae kwon do champion. Clyde and I run tae kwon do classes for the ghetto kids in an effort to build their self-respect and -esteem. My Huruma home may look basic, but there are worse places to live in Nairobi—the neighboring slum of Mathare is more desperate and deprived. Some 4.5 million Kenyans live in such urban shantylands, but in spite of the privations there is a unique and powerful sense of community and brotherhood in the ghetto that I value hugely.

Rajab Obama, my cousin and the father figure who helped me pull my life together after the gangster and prison years. The example of Barack Obama Senior inspired Rajab to get a university education and an MA in Economics. For the first sixteen years of my life, my mother brought me up as a Christian, and it has been largely Rajab's influence in recent years that has helped steer me toward Islam, the faith of my father.

Shiyayo, the girl next door in the Huruma ghetto, and my sometimes sweetheart. Like so many in the ghetto, Shiyayo has a tragic life story. Orphaned as a child, she drifted into the Nairobi slums. A few years ago Shiyayo and I joined the One Love Youth Group, and then founded our own community group, the Huruma Centre Youth Group. It uses sports, crafts, tribal dancing, and even beauty contests in an effort to combat drug and alcohol abuse, and to give people back their self-respect.

Football team captain Kadenge Mathenge stands with me, giving a victory salute after we win a major game. I'm both the team coach and its main sponsor. Since my brother won the U.S. presidency, I have tried to help lift the ghetto youth out of crushing poverty and give them the break in life they dearly deserve.

Sitting in the center, with the ball, surrounded by my soccer team, Huruma Centre FC—"Obama's Champs." This photo was taken immediately after we beat our arch rivals, Sports Connect, 7–3, in a crucial match that helped us win the Nairobi Super League. I found sponsors to pay for the team's first ever uniform, and to buy them new boots—things that few ghetto dwellers could ever afford. Winning the Super League was an impossible dream for these players, and their sense of achievement and respect helps keep them out of crime, drink, and drugs. I was once a ghetto criminal myself, so I understand the guys and never judge them.

with Nicky, when the police swooped in. Normally the street kids would warn us of any threat, but this time the cops caught us off guard. The police Land Rover had been trawling the neighborhood, checking the regular hangouts for guys like us, and when the street kids raised the alarm, Nicky and I were too stoned to run.

In Kenya it is illegal to smoke hash, but a hell of a lot of people do so anyway. Whenever the cops turned up, we'd try to throw away whatever we had or even swallow it, so as to hide the evidence, but this time we were caught red-handed. We were thrown onto the metal floor in the rear of the police Land Rover, and the cops handcuffed us so savagely tight that the cuffs cut into our skin.

As the vehicle set off for the nearest police station, the cops in the rear settled onto the bench seats that ran down either side. One of the coppers was a fat guy, with a stomach bulging out of his white shirt and threatening to bust the buttons. I wasn't sure if he was the oldest or the most senior in rank, but for whatever reason he proceeded to lead the intimidation, and the negotiations.

He held up the tiny bag of grass, which was all that remained from our session. *Slap* went his wooden baton into a meaty palm.

"You know what happens to boys caught smoking hash? Eh? Let me tell you, you don't want to think about what happens." He turned to one of his colleagues. "Officer Kwaje, he doesn't even want to dream about what will happen, does he?"

Officer Kwaje laughed. "No, sir. It can be really, really bad, sir." He slapped his baton against his ankle-high boots. "No, sir, the cells aren't the place for young boys like these."

"So, what do you have for me, eh?" the fat policeman demanded, fixing me with his stare. "What do you have for me, for Officer Kwaje, and our other friends?"

"A little cash might keep you out of the cells," Officer Kwaje added. *Slap* went his baton. "So this is your chance."

"We're the nice guys," the fat officer added. "We don't want to see bad things happen to two young boys. So what do you have for us? Quick, before we reach the station and have to book you."

At that moment I would have paid any amount of money to get

released, for I knew the reputation of Nairobi's jails. We all knew people who'd been arrested and imprisoned, and their stories were like visions of the worst kind of nightmare. The trouble was that neither Nicky nor I had any money on us. We'd spent our last cash on the weed, plus a few plates of rice and lentils that we'd bought for us and our street kid friends.

"We don't have any cash," I muttered into the dirty floor of the vehicle. "We spent it."

The fat officer's baton went smashing into the metal inches from my face. "You're lying!" he snarled, his eyes bulging with fury. "We'll search you at Buruburu. If we find anything . . ."

"Just give us the cash you have and we'll let you go," Officer Kwaje snapped. "No cash and there's no way out." He tapped his baton impatiently against his boot. "Quick, tell us where your cash is hidden."

The police knew well enough how guys like us operated. Whenever we did have any cash on us, we'd keep it hidden. That way if we drank too much *changa'a*, or smoked too much hash, and were *KO*— knocked out—there was less likelihood of anyone stealing it off us. I stared at the floor, keeping my eyes down. I didn't want to provoke them.

"It's like I told you, we spent it all."

There was a hiss of rage from the fat officer. "*Idiots!* Stubborn little fools. Well, we're here now, so have it your way."

Moments later the Land Rover came to a halt and we were frogmarched into the police station. There was no talking or charming my way out of this one now. I was sixteen years old and I had never been arrested. Nicky was seventeen, and he too was a first-timer. As we were propelled into the reception area, I was dead scared, and I figured Nicky had to be shitting himself too. He'd gone quiet, which was unusual, for Nicky was a chatty kind of guy especially when stoned.

"Book these two idiots," the fat policeman announced, handing us over to a duty officer. "Caught red-handed in possession. Here's the evidence," he added, flinging the tiny bag of weed onto the desk.

"Name?" the duty officer announced, looking at me with a bored expression.

"Obama," I replied.

"First name?"

"George."

He took a few personal details and did the same with Nicky, after which we were made to sign.

"Take them to the cells," the duty officer announced.

The whole process had taken five minutes or less, and he was clearly glad to get rid of us. In Kenya, anyone who reaches the stage of being booked by the police is by definition a loser and a nobody. Only those with no money or access to money, or no power or access to those with power, would ever end up here. Anyone else would have paid the police their bribes and be long gone. Getting slammed into the cells meant you were an absolute zero.

There is no process of bail offered to absolute zeros, because the police presume you cannot afford to pay. There's no phone call offered, for who would an absolute zero possibly want to call? Certainly not a lawyer, for an absolute zero would never be able to afford the legal fees. The absolute zeros get slammed into a holding cell, where they remain until charged. In the interim, they are forgotten. Out of sight, out of mind. Left to rot in the cells.

As we were marched toward the far recesses of the police station, the only hope that I could grasp on to was that at least we had been arrested in Umoja. Some of our street kid friends must have witnessed the police taking us, and I just hoped and prayed that they would have the foresight to contact someone who might know my mother. While I dreaded her finding out what had happened, I was far more fearful of what awaited me if I was sucked into the Kenyan "justice" system. That was a black hole from which absolute zeros were known never to return.

The jailer clanked the keys on his belt, selected one, and inserted it into the lock on the cell door. Inside it was pitch-black, but from the murmuring of voices I could sense the number of people locked away in there. It was night by now and so the temperature had dropped, but the cell was hot, airless, and suffocating. The stench of stale sweat and unwashed bodies assaulted my nostrils even before we were shoved inside.

As the cell bars slid open, pinpricks of white showed in the darkness, eyes turning to inspect us.

"Two more to join the party," the jailer announced. Then to us, "Get inside!"

He shoved me in the back and I half stumbled into the cell, colliding with a wall of bodies. There was a chorus of angry voices.

"Hey! Watch it!"

"There's no room."

"Show some respect!"

"Get off or else."

The cell was about five yards by five, and I had no idea just how many men were packed into it, but it had to be dozens. There was barely room for Nicky and me to squeeze in before the cell door was slammed shut. The walls of the cell were painted a dull matte black and I couldn't see a thing in the darkness. It was as if we had been thrown into a room peopled by ghosts, except that the press of alien flesh was all too real.

For a moment there was a weird and ravenous silence. It was utterly terrifying. And then a voice rang out of the darkness, signifying a deep and predatory presence.

"Welcome. Welcome to the hotel from hell." A beat. "And what do you have for us this evening? Cigarettes? Drugs? Cash? Some nice clean clothes even?"

Thirty pairs of eyes peered at us, showing sickly white in the gloom. The silence lengthened as neither Nicky nor I could find the words to respond.

"Well, speak up." The predatory voice again, terrifying in its amoral authority, the rasping of a brute animal. "Speak up. *I can't hear you.* Surely you didn't come with *nothing*?"

"They took the weed off of us, and . . . ," I tried to reply.

"So it does speak. It speaks and sounds *so young*. What d'you reckon, lads? A couple of teenage kids is it they've given us this time?"

There were sniggers and jibes from out of the darkness, teeth showing white all around us like those of a pack of animals. I had no idea how long these men had been crammed together in this cell, but they seemed to know each other pretty well. They had bonded and formed a hierarchy, and we were the newcomers and the outsiders, the young ones at the very bottom of the pecking order.

I was terrified, and as Nicky had yet to speak a word, I guessed he was too.

"*Weed,*" the voice sneered. "A couple of teenage dopeheads. What are we going to do with them, lads?"

"Search them, for starters, boss," a faceless voice replied.

"Good idea. Search them," the commanding voice confirmed.

Rough hands grabbed me in an iron grip and slammed me against the bars. I could feel my face being squeezed into the cold metal, as hands frisked my pockets from behind. For a second I considered resisting, but there were two of us and dozens of them and no room in which to fight, even had I—the Mamba—fancied the odds, which I most certainly did not. In here it didn't matter a damn that I was the Mamba. Many of these guys would be hardened criminals, and we were as nothing to them.

"There's nothing," I tried saying.

"Shut up!" the man searching me snarled in my ear. "You speak when the boss wants to be spoken to, okay?"

"Okay."

"Pockets are empty, boss," the voice in my ear reported.

"Search them *properly*," the boss snapped. "They've got to have something on them."

I was horribly scared now. I knew the worst the police would ever do was give you a good beating. But these guys, they seemed capable of anything. Were they going to strip us, I wondered? Outnumbered, we were at their mercy. And one thing was for sure; the police weren't about to step in and protect us.

"Find anything?" the voice snapped, once the hands had finished.

"Not a thing, boss," the voice in my ear replied.

The voice of "the boss" sighed. "So, what now?"

That silence again—just the rasp of breathing in the crushing darkness—but this time laced with evil intent.

"What now?" the voice repeated. "Any suggestions, teenage dope-heads?"

"It's just *stoot* we're in for," I tried telling the darkness. "We were just caught smoking a joint. It's no big—"

"I'll be the judge of that," the voice cut in. "Tom, give them a space to crouch by the door. Crouching room only. And they can have one visit to the shower to drink. They've done nothing to earn any better. Just enough to keep them alive until morning. Once we can see the whites of their eyes, and their *fear*, we can judge what to do with them."

The same powerful hands manhandled me to a tiny patch of bare concrete by the cell door. I felt Nicky get shoved down onto the space next to me.

"Crouching room only, boys," the voice in my ear—Tom, I guessed—hissed. "And I wouldn't sleep if I was you. You never know what might happen in the night if you do."

I sat on my haunches, my back against the cell bars, arms hooked around my knees. I stayed awake, my fearful eyes patrolling the darkness. I had never felt so scared in my life, and I couldn't have slept even had I wanted to. While the rest of the inmates lay down side by side on the floor like sardines, Nicky and I squatted in silence, awaiting whatever the morning would bring. Fear and adrenaline kept me wired, and every now and then I was convinced that one or other of the humped figures was creeping up on us.

The heat in that airless hellhole was stifling, and sweat poured off me. Soon I was dying for a drink. I thought I could follow my ears to the noise of the dripping shower, which was the only source of water in the entire cell. But as I got to my feet and attempted to pick my way between the bodies, there was the hiss of a voice in the darkness.

"Hey! Where d'you think you're going?" It sounded like Tom, the boss's henchman.

I came to a halt. "The shower. I need a drink."

"You get one shower visit only," Tom's voice warned. "You heard what the boss said."

I thrust my head under the warm, rust-flavored dribble spattering out of the showerhead. As I held it there, I wondered how on earth my life had sunk to this—an absolute zero crammed into a cell sipping water from a dirty showerhead and facing a trial by mob justice come the morning. Once I had been a gifted pupil attending some of Kenya's best schools, with the promise of qualifying as an airline pilot before me. My previous life seemed an age ago, yet in reality it was only twelve months since I had first started to crash and burn.

At some time in the early hours I must have dozed off. I awoke with a start, my head leaning against the cold bars, my neck aching from sleeping in a sitting hunch. For a second I wondered what had woken me, and then I heard a voice calling my name. I tried to clear my mind, half fearing it was the cell boss beginning his morning inquisition. But then the call came again, and this time I recognized it for what it was.

"Obama! You have a visitor." It was the jailer, and he was unlocking the cell. He held the door wide. "You coming or not? If you'd prefer to stay . . ." He nodded at Nicky. "And bring your friend. You're getting out of here."

At the duty officer's desk I spotted a familiar figure. It was my mother. I was immensely thankful to see her, but my gratitude was mixed with shame. Now she knew just how far I had fallen. Yet in spite of my failings she loved me as only a mother could, and as she signed the forms to bail us out of jail, I felt deeply unworthy of her love.

Nicky and I had been arrested and booked on charges of possession, and possession of hash in Kenya carries a mandatory jail term, even for a first offense. But the reality was that once bail had been paid, the charges were dropped. The bail money would go into the pockets of the police, and it would be as if the arrest had never happened. Everyone understood the unwritten rules in Kenya—that with money came power and the ability to get away with just about anything.

I walked out of the police station a free man, but now I had to face my mother. She marched Nicky and me to the nearest *matatu* stop, her lips tight with fury. She placed Nicky on the first bus to Umoja and paid his fare. Like me, he was still living at home, and doubtless he would have to face the music with his own parents as soon as he got there.

My mother and I were left waiting to catch another *matatu*.

"You are a disgrace and a failure, you know that," she hissed, just as soon as Nicky was gone. "A complete disgrace and a failure. Look at yourself. Just take a look at what you've become."

Over the past few months I'd been attempting to grow dreadlocks, like my muse, Bob Marley, although the tufts of hair were still too short and unformed to look really cool. My clothes—black jeans and a Hilfiger T-shirt—were dirty and rumpled, a far cry from the smart uniform and polished shoes of my public school days. I didn't have an answer for my mother, so I chose to say nothing.

She couldn't bear to look at me. "I'm taking you to your Auntie Sarah's place," she snapped. "Maybe she can talk some sense into you."

I shrugged. I was shell-shocked from lack of sleep and the trauma of the jail cell. Plus I felt guilty and raw at having let my mother down.

"Have you got nothing to say for yourself?" my mother demanded. "The least you could do is apologize. If you continue like this, Lord only knows where it will all end."

"I'm sorry," I told her, and I tried a sheepish smile.

"Is that all?"

"And thanks for bailing me—"

"You put yourself in there and you only have yourself to blame," my mother cut in. "Don't expect me to come and save you next time. In fact, there better not be a next time."

En route to Auntie Sarah's, my mother took me to a barbershop to have my dreads shaved off so that I would look at least vaguely respectable. It was the least I could do, after all my mother had done for me. As the barber ran an electric razor over my scalp and the matted clumps of hair fell to the floor, a part of me hoped that I was shedding the worst of my bad life.

But in fact, the badness had only just begun.

CHAPTER 13

In the Ghetto

AFTER HAVING A private word with Auntie Sarah, my mother bade me a curt farewell and left. There was no one else at home, so it was just the two of us—Auntie Sarah and I.

She fixed me with her piercing gaze.

"So, I hear you really messed up. Your mother's told me everything, and it seems you've been a complete fool. D'you have anything to say for yourself?"

"Not much," I muttered. "No."

"I thought so." She snorted, derisively. "Think you can choose the life of a loser and get away with it, do you? Well, let me tell you something—not if I have anything to do with it. So, this is what we are going to do: you're staying here for as long as it takes for some of your late father's good grace to rub off on you. As long as it takes for you to see the error of your ways, and how you have to change things in your life."

"Fine." I smiled sheepishly. "I agree. And that way I'll have plenty of time on your stall to help you—"

She cut me off. "This is no laughing matter, George. Your father

149

would be appalled, you know that? Disgusted. He would be dismayed at how you've squandered your talents, and after all the privilege and opportunity that came your way."

"Auntie, it was only smoking some *stoot*—"

"It's not that which I'm referring to," she interjected angrily. "I don't want to know the details of your childish misbehavior. It's the squandering of your education, of your intellect, that is so unforgivable, plus the fact that you seem hell-bent on throwing your life away."

"Things just kind of started going wrong when Christian left," I muttered. "It kind of pushed me over an edge, into a crisis—"

"Then get a grip!" she snapped. "Pull yourself together. You've got no excuses, after all you've been given in life. You know what your father would say, if he was still alive? He'd tell you you're a fool to waste your abilities, and a fool to squander your chances. *A fool.* D'you know that? He'd say, How can a smart boy be such a complete fool at the same time?"

I stared at the ground. Auntie Sarah had a way of making me feel really, really small. I guess it was because of the blood ties, and that in her I came as close as I ever could to someone like my father.

"Your father would tell you that you're messing it up, George, and he'd tell you what an idiot you are to be throwing your life down the drain. He'd remind you that you are an Obama. *An Obama.* He'd say you are an Obama, George, and so act like one."

I stayed with Auntie Sarah for two weeks, and during that time she said all the right kinds of things to me, over and over again, and God knows I should have listened. She told me that I had to get back into the school system and restart my studies. She told me that my brains had come to me via my father, and that he would never have allowed me to waste my life. She told me that he would have kicked my ass had he still been alive, since nothing but achieving the very best academically had ever been good enough for his children.

I heard Auntie Sarah's voice, but I wasn't listening. She kept appealing to the memory of my birth father—the man who had been so highly educated, who had worked for the Kenyan government and faithfully served his country to the last, in spite of all its failings. She kept trying to make me see how my behavior would hurt my birth father, how it was an insult to his memory, and how I should place his example before me as my inspiration to change. By upholding his example, she tried to persuade me to turn my life around.

But I was closed to such persuasion. I had never really known my birth father, so his memory could only ever have so much sway over me. More importantly, if I were to do as Auntie Sarah suggested, I would make myself vulnerable again. I had placed all my belief and love in one father in my lifetime—Christian—only to have my trust thrown back in my face. I didn't want to risk the same again. And so I chose to reject Auntie Sarah's words, although I did so quietly and without her quite realizing how deep the wounds had cut me, or how fiercely the spirit of rebellion was burning in my heart.

By being a rebel, and keeping the rebel flame, I knew that no one could come close to me or hurt me. By holding on to my rebellion, I believed I could insulate myself from love and family affection—the things in life that had proven their capacity to cause me pain. I might fail on the one level—on the level of my education, my career, and my future—but I would succeed on another, that of emotional survival. I would nurture my anger and my rebellion and build the walls that surrounded me ever higher. That way no one could reach me, and I could never fall.

At one stage during those two weeks my half brother, Roy, and I got together. He was my father's firstborn, which made him the head of the family when my father died. In African and Luo culture he held a position of real influence and responsibility. We had spent precious little time together, but I looked up to him. Like me, he was happier being known by his African-Muslim name, Malik.

I guessed the entire Obama clan had to know about my problems by now. There were rifts and fault lines in the family, which meant that Auntie Sarah didn't talk to some of her sisters, but word still got around. Perhaps that was why Malik decided to take me to a mosque; perhaps it was in the hope that Islam might provide the stabilizing influence that was so clearly missing in my life. I didn't know where he was taking me at the time, although I did know that Malik was trying to live as a good Muslim.

"Let's go," was all he said to me. "Come on, Hussein, I've got something I want to show you."

"Where to?" I asked him.

"Just come. There's something you need to see."

In the center of downtown Nairobi sits the Jamia Mosque. Its richly decorated entranceway is flanked by two sentinel towers, each topped by a small white dome that seems to hover in the air, piercing the cloudless blue of the sky. At least that's how the façade looked to me as Malik led me toward it along tree-lined streets and through swirling crowds. I knew what he was intending to do even before he announced it.

It was a Friday, the Muslim holy day, and he'd brought me here to pray. But after the experiences of the past year, nothing could have been further from my mind than faith—faith of any sort. I didn't believe I belonged in any house of God anymore. I belonged on the streets, with my brethren—the dispossessed street kids and my fellow gang members, along with any other assorted rebels and absolute zeros who fell in with us.

I put one hand on Malik's arm and halted him in his stride. "I'm not sure I want to do this, Malik," I told him. "I'm not sure I'm up for this. Not today."

Malik let out his characteristic booming laugh. "There's no time like the present, Hussein. Come on. Come inside."

"But—"

"But nothing, Hussein. It's good to know who you are, George. It's the faith of our father, the old man's religion. Think about it, Hussein, before you decide to turn away."

Because he was Malik and the head of the family, I went with him without further question. Inside, I was struck by the silence and the stillness. Light streamed in through the high-arched windows. I had never imagined that in the heart of this heaving, roaring, pulsating city such calm and peace could exist. I glanced around me at the crowds of people bowed beneath the graceful arch of the domed roof. I felt shamefully underdressed in my battered jeans and T-shirt. The men wore spotless white and gray robes that fell to their ankles, with richly embroidered skullcaps to match.

What the hell am I doing here? I wondered, self-consciously. *I should never have allowed Malik to entice me in.* But he led me across to the washing area and showed me how to cleanse myself by performing *wudu*, the ritual washing of hands, face, and feet that a Muslim must do before prayer. And then he took me over to the prayer area, where mats were spread on the cool floor. Malik stood for a moment facing the east—the direction of Islam's holiest shrines, in Mecca—his hands cupped before him in silent contemplation.

He glanced at me out of the corner of his eye, a faint smile playing on his lips. "You know how to do this? To pray?"

"Some," I whispered back at him. "Yeah, I guess I'll be okay."

Malik nodded. "Great. You get lost, just follow what I do."

I racked my brains, trying to remember just what I had done and said at Dagoretti, when breaking fast and praying with the other Muslim boys. We had always started with the Shahadah, the Islamic creed that is a declaration of belief in the oneness of God. I mouthed the words, as Malik did likewise, our murmurings joining those of the countless other figures in the crowd.

Laa ilaha illa Allah,
wa Muhammad ur-rasul Allah.

There is no God but God,
and Muhammad is the Messenger of God.

As I mouthed the prayers, following Malik whenever I got lost, I suddenly felt as though I were back at the Busara Forest View Academy, in a line of young boys dressed in our smart school best, murmuring the catechism in the chapel on Sunday morning. Now I was a sixteen-year-old street hustler brought to the heart of Islam by my dead father's eldest son. I was a teenage rebel and dropout, forever restless and angry, a lawbreaking gangster who had only narrowly escaped jail. God knows I couldn't fall much farther.

For a moment I wondered how and where my fall would end, and if I would ever find rest and be at peace. If only there was a way for God to show himself, to prove himself, and to guarantee to abide by me and take away my hurt, then I might be able to trust again and to stop falling. I would accept him as my father—a father to replace the first that I had never known, and the second who had disappeared from my life.

For an instant I waited for something close to a miracle. I opened myself and dropped all my barriers, and in so doing I felt hot tears pricking at my eyes. But when I felt nothing—absolutely nothing at all—I withdrew into my shell once more. For an instant I had let out a cry for help, but I had received not even the whisper of an answer. The mask of the unreachable teenage rebel gangster fell across my face once more and the moment was gone.

Malik and I were preparing to leave when my eye fell on a poster displayed near the door. "Ayah of the Week" was its title.

> *If you avoid the heinous sins which you have been forbidden, We will do away with your small sins and cause you to enter a place of great honour (paradise).*
>
> HOLY QUR'AN, AL NISAA 4:31

I read it over a couple of times. *The heinous sins which you have been forbidden.* After my year of living dangerously, I guess I was steeped in those "heinous sins." It wasn't my small sins that needed forgiving, it was the really, really big ones. And now as I stepped out into the harsh city daylight, I could feel the hot rebellion and fierce anonymity of those sins pulling me back toward that life again.

Malik turned to me and placed one hand on my shoulder. He had a serious look in his normally laughing eyes. He repeated the phrase that he'd used earlier.

"You see, Hussein, it is good to know who you are."

I nodded. "Yeah. Thanks."

"This is your religion, Hussein, the religion of your birth. You have to get to know your God."

The trouble was, I didn't know who my God was anymore. I couldn't speak to him or touch him or reach out for his help, for I didn't know how to trust. And anyway, I felt better on my own, rebellious and isolated and entombed within my anger.

At the end of those two weeks with Auntie Sarah I returned home to Umoja, but I drifted back into the old ways. The pull of that life, with its familiar, angry rebellion that made me an untouchable was too strong. And, I craved the wasteland of forgetfulness that I found in the dope and the *changa'a*.

Our Umoja home felt even more like a body that had been stripped of all its living flesh when Christian had disappeared. I hated being there, for each time I set foot in the dead hush of the skeleton house, it reminded me of all that had been lost. I hung out more and more with the street kids, and I felt more at home among their cardboard and plastic shacks than in our neat and cloistered bungalow.

I was reunited with my gang. We were the disaffected sons of the Umoja class of Kenyans. But in the street kids' shanty land we could gather in relative safety to chat and to plan our day, and to smoke our weed and drink *changa'a*. It had become our base of operations, and was the first place we all went to whenever we'd pulled off another mugging or street robbery.

But for me it was becoming more than that—it was my home. Most people in Nairobi treated the street kids as if they were absolute scum. Mostly, they'd pretend the *chokora*—"street urchins" in Swahili—didn't exist. If those raggedy kids were thrust into their faces, they would abuse them horribly. The very idea that the son of an Umoja family might actually want to *live* among the street kids, to become an honorary member of their tribe—that was anathema. It was as inconceivable to most Kenyans as walking to the moon.

But I found something among their number that touched me, and reached me in a way that nothing else seemed able to—not my

mother's distress, nor Auntie Sarah's wisdom, nor my dead father's memory, nor Malik's Islam. The street kids had welcomed me in. They had no pretensions and no false pride. Life with them was about pure survival, for there was nowhere left for them to fall. And strangely enough for outsiders like me, their life was about brotherhood and community and a boundless generosity.

I experienced more acts of unsolicited kindness with those kids than perhaps I ever had before—the kindness of those who had nothing. They had nothing in terms of material possessions, but whatever they did get their hands on, they seemed happy to share. They looked after their own with a fierce, burning intensity. And no one judged anyone. Not ever.

From the very first our gang had treated those kids as if they were our younger brothers. That kindness and respect was never lost on them. At first they didn't understand it. All they ever expected from outsiders was abuse and cruelty. But they came to cherish our brotherly kindness, as much as we valued their scraggy wasteland home as our own. And I decided that if I was to live among them, then I would live as they lived, and that meant eating the same food as they did whenever we couldn't afford to buy a few plates of rice and lentils.

The street kid I was closest to was known as "Scram." I guess he was a year or two younger than my brother, Marvin, but of course Scram didn't know his real age. If he ever had known his birthday, it was long forgotten, for who was there to share it with these days? Scram had no parents or family to buy him any presents or to bake him a cake, or to light the candles and to sing him happy birthday. All Scram had was the fellowship of the other street kids and the daily fight for survival.

I'd been drawn to him by his eager good spirits and his laughter. His dusty, wiry hair stood out in crazed angles, as if he'd just been electrocuted, and his one pair of shorts and T-shirt were full of burn marks and holes. He had a big gap between his two front teeth, and that gave him an extremely cheeky look. He seemed to have a permanently running nose, which he was forever wiping on his sleeve, and his bare feet were dirty and scabbed, with cracked and broken toe-

nails. But somehow all that just seemed to add to his indefinable charm.

On the day that Scram fed me my first street meal, he'd spent his time scavenging on the rubbish dumps around Umoja. I found him crouched over a choking cooking fire, one made of a few sticks and some burning rubbish, and stirring a cooking pot made out of an old vegetable oil tin. As he stirred the indescribable mess with a stick, he chatted away with the other kids, spinning a tale of nonsense and craziness, spreading warmth and laughter and light.

"You know what I'm going to do when I'm as old as the Mamba?" Scram announced to no one in particular. "I'm going to have a jumbo jet and fill it with dancing girls and a casino for gambling and a huge swimming pool and the girls will have come from all over—Nairobi and Russia and China and London and Planet Mars and America; yeah, loads of Miss USA on my jumbo—and all of you lot will be real welcome because you're my *brothers* and you'll be *there* and I'll give each of you loads of *maganji* to gamble in Scram's casino and I'll throw the biggest party Nairobi's ever seen and we'll fly around and around the city dropping empty champagne bottles and cigarette butts and girl's bras and stuff so that everyone will know what a damn fine party we're having up there and they'll all be so jealous and want to come, and the music, the reggae and the soul and the beat, will be blasting out *so loud* that no one in the city will be able to *sleep a wink*, and behind that jumbo I'll be flying a huge banner with a massive sign saying, Scram's Jumbo Party—By Invitation Only!"

"Yeah, well, you don't even know your own age, Scrambo," Cheesy, one of Scram's street buddies, countered. "So how will you know when you're as old as the Mamba?"

"Plus where's all the dough gonna come from, Scrambo?" Jeff, Scram and Cheesy's buddy, added. "You need a lot of *maganji* to hire a jumbo."

"Easy," Scram scoffed. "I'm not *hiring* a jumbo, I'm *buying* one, like that Arab guy we saw on TV." He glanced up at me and grinned his gap-toothed smile. "And the Mamba—he's gonna tell me when I'm as old as he is."

I cracked up laughing. "Yeah, no problem. I'll let you know when you're as old as me and it's time to party."

Whenever Scram and his street buddies weren't foraging on the rubbish dumps or touting for the *matatu* drivers, they'd hang out in downtown Nairobi staring into shop windows, eyeballing all the stuff that they would never in their lives be able to buy. Their favorite hangouts were the electronics shops with the TVs playing in the windows. Via an odd mixture of MTV, CNN, and children's programs like *Scooby Doo!* and *Tom and Jerry*, they were given a window onto the world, and that was the source of Scram's weird mishmash of cultural references.

Of course, they could never watch for long before the shop owner or the security guards or the police chased them away. It wasn't good for business having scraggy street kids like Scram and his buddies clustered outside your window.

Scram cocked his head to one side and fixed me with a curious look. "You eating with us?" He gestured at the cooking pot. "Scram's finest rubbish dump stew. It ain't quite *nyama choma*, barbecued meat, but it might keep you alive until morning."

"That's unless you're gonna buy us some rice 'n' lentils?" Cheesy added, hopefully. "It sure beats *that*."

I shrugged. "I'm all out of cash."

"What the hell are you guys on about?" Scram demanded. "Cheesy, the Mamba, are you saying Scram's rubbish dump stew ain't good enough for you? 'Cause if you are . . ."

There was nothing like a set of eating utensils in Scram and Cheesy's world. Once the tin was hoofed off the cooking fire and had been left to cool a little, we sat around it and scooped out the contents with our hands. I had no idea what Scram's stew consisted of, though some of the contents were just about recognizable. There were some beans in there, and what looked like chunks of potato. But I figured that if Scram and the others could survive on it, then so could I. I forced myself to suppress the gag reflex and shoveled in a few handfuls, and in no time it was all gone.

After sharing that first meal with Scram and his buddies, it was as if I'd crossed some invisible line. I had become one of them. I guess they had never had an outsider come into their world and share it without blame or regret, and without looking down on them. None of the kids ever talked about their lives before the streets, and I understood why: the memories were too painful. They hadn't chosen a life on the streets. It had been thrust upon them, so who had any right to look down on them?

This life was their only means of survival. The oldest were thirteen or fourteen at the most, for by that age either they had found some way to make a more permanent living, and had left the streets, or the street life had killed them. Many were orphans. One or both of their parents had died, mostly from AIDS. And subconsciously I felt myself half orphaned twice over—once by my dead father, and once by my adoptive father who had deserted me. Perhaps that was another reason why I felt so at home with the street kids.

Because we all had lives that were dark and painful, we shared an unspoken understanding that the past was taboo. On the few occasions when one of the street kids made mention of a long-lost parent or sibling, just the very memory made them angry and hurt. And so they did their best to bury the memories so deep that nothing could bring them to the surface.

The favored route to such oblivion was drugs, and the cheapest drug that the kids could get their hands on was glue. All over Nairobi you'd find rickety old stalls—on the streets and in the parks and outside churches and near the *matatu* stops—and among the tradesmen selling their wares were the cobblers. The shoe menders did a roaring trade with city dwellers who couldn't afford to throw an old pair of shoes away, as most do in the West. A pair of shoes was a real asset, and they would be resoled and resoled countless times over. The cobblers used a powerful glue, which the kids were into sniffing.

The cobblers knew the street kids were sniffing glue, but they sold it to them anyway. The kids would take a small plastic medicine bottle that they'd scavenged from the rubbish dumps and dribble a little of the glue into it. They'd thrust the neck of that bottle up one nostril and inhale deeply. The glue was volatile, and in the enclosed space of the bottle the fumes were thick and heady and rushed into the kid's brain. I had never sniffed glue, but I'd seen the shattering effect that it had on those who did. Its draw was total oblivion; its horror was the way it destroyed people's minds.

The first time I caught Scram sniffing, I found him slumped in his shelter, resting on a strip of old cardboard, his hand gripping the tell-tale plastic bottle. I squatted next to him, but his eyes were glazed and half turned up into his head, the whites showing horribly, as if he had died.

I reached out and prized the bottle from his sticky grasp. He was so out of it, his fingers barely resisted. I held the bottle up in front of his unseeing eyes.

"Damn, Scrambo. No more of this, you hear me? You know what this does to your mind? It fucks your brain, Scrambo. No more of this, you hear?"

I hurled the bottle as far as I could into the waste ground, where I hoped none of the kids could retrieve it.

"Gioivve mey oworet . . ." Scram tried to say something, to object, I guess.

My intervention must have registered somewhere in his messed-up mind. But his words were an incoherent mess, and a frothy dribble formed on his lips as he tried to speak. In this state Scram was utterly vulnerable, and there were those on the streets of Nairobi who would prey on defenseless street kids. And if the kids had bought glue in bulk from one of the cobblers, and if they all had been sniffing, they'd not be able to raise the alarm or defend themselves.

I stayed there all that night, bedded down beside a comatose Scram on a thin strip of cardboard. In the morning I found him shivering, but it wasn't from the cold. His face was sickly yellow, his eyes puffy and inflamed, the lids horribly gummed together. When Scram was finally able to open his eyes, I could tell that he felt like something worse than death. He knew that I knew what he'd been up to, and there was a sullen, guilty resentment in his gaze that was unlike Scram. He felt around for the glue bottle, before realizing it was gone. I guess he couldn't face the day, or his memories, and he craved another hit, another sweet rainbow journey into the sunlit fields of oblivion.

"Where is it?" Scram demanded.

"I threw it," I replied. "It's gone."

He eyeballed me for a second, lips tight with anger, and then he rolled away from me and hunched into a ball.

"You have to stop doing that stuff." I spoke to his back. "It'll fuck you up, Scram. I'll come back one day and find you dead. Is that what you want? Is it?"

Scram didn't answer.

"You want to die, glue's the way to do it," I added. "I catch you sniffing, Scrambo, I'm taking it off you. Every time."

"You saying this is a life worth living?" Scram muttered.

"Whatever, you don't die that way, Scram, not with glue. You sniff, it messes with your head, and anyone can come and mess you up, Scram. You sniff, you're like a zombie, like the walking dead. And I won't always be here to watch over you."

"You do *stoot*," Scram countered, his voice laced with resentment. "What's the difference?"

"There's a big difference. It doesn't make me like that, Scram. It doesn't fuck with my head. It's not a chemical."

There was a moment's silence between us.

"You remember your jumbo jet party, Scram?" I ventured. "All that gambling and partying and the girls? You really want to die before all of that?"

"It's just a stupid dream," Scram muttered. "A stupid kid's dream. That's all."

I didn't know what to say.

Later that day Scram was back to his happy, crazy self, and it was almost as if nothing had happened. There was another reason I and my gang buddies snatched those glue bottles off the kids. They had precious little money, and to spend it on glue as opposed to food was just senseless. I could tell they were ravenous, and they were forever rubbing their bellies and telling me how hungry they were.

Most of the kids were aged around eight or nine. They were mainly boys, but there was a handful of girls. They earned what little they could by scavenging glass, cardboard, plastic, and metal from the garbage heaps. They'd pile their findings onto a makeshift handcart—an old, discarded pram maybe—and wheel it off to a dealer's place. The dealer would pay them the going rate for whatever they had and resell it to one of the big recycling operations. From a day's scavenging the kids would be lucky to earn a dollar each, so they could little afford to squander it on glue.

Everyone in our gang had done glue at one time or another, all apart from Ramjo and I, but none of us was doing it anymore. I knew from the others what it did to you. It put you completely out of your head. And for the street kids who were trying to survive a life barely worth living, that proved irresistible. When they sniffed, they chose forgetfulness no matter what the cost. More than anything, that testified to what Scram, Cheesy, and the others had been through in their young lives.

The street kids also did pills, which was another big taboo for me. You could buy just about anything you wanted from the chemists around Nairobi. No prescription was required. The most popular pills with the street kids were some big yellow ones. I had no idea what they were for, but I would snatch them away.

"You're not sick," I'd admonish them. "You only need to swallow pills if you're ill. You're fine, so stop doing them. You don't need pills to get high."

I went back to the Umoja house only occasionally now, and it was usually when I needed something—a wash, or a change of clothes. I'd sneak in when I knew my mother would be out at work and leave long before she came back again. And each time I returned to my home with the street kids, I tried to bring something with me that might lighten their lives. The first time I picked out some old toys—the indestructible metal Tonka cars that I had cherished in my youth.

Scram and the rest were at the age I'd been when I'd loved those toys, and I hoped they'd be overjoyed with them.

But the reaction I got when I presented the kids with my gifts was totally unexpected. Scram, Cheesy, and Jeff inspected the toys as if they were just another lucky find on the rubbish dumps. They didn't view them as toys or for one moment want to *play* with them. Instead, the talk was all about where they might sell them, how much they could get for them, and what they might do with the money. I realized then that for these kids, there was no childhood anymore. Play wasn't in it.

As it was for many an adult, life for them was a daily battle to find money and survive.

CHAPTER 14

The Hood

THE NEXT TIME I returned to the Umoja house, I was determined to do better at finding Scram and his buddies something useful. I went through the cupboards in my bedroom and pulled out some old clothes. They were far too small for me, but they would fit Scram and his fellows well enough. I stuffed them into a plastic garbage bag and carried them back to the waste ground, whereupon I emptied out the contents in front of the gang of urchins.

I'd never seen kids so overjoyed at receiving a bunch of old, secondhand clothes. This was like manna from heaven. Scram chose a set for himself and disappeared into his hut. He emerged a few moments later dressed in a pair of smart jeans and one of my old T-shirts.

That T-shirt had *Hakuna Matata*—Swahili for "no worries"— emblazoned across the front of it. I had a vague memory of my mother or Christian having gotten it for me when I was around Scram's age. Scram struck a pose and strutted across the waste ground as if he were a model on the catwalk or some performer on one of the MTV videos he'd seen in a downtown Nairobi store window.

He froze in midstride and fixed me with a look, his head held high, eyes shining bright.

"How do I look?" he announced.

"Damn, Scram, you're the man!" I replied. "You look like you're dressed for a damn fine jumbo jet party."

"Yah!" Scram grinned a wide, gappy smile. "I'm the man! And next time, can you bring me some shoes?"

A few days later I fetched Scram a pair of sneakers from home. It was a worn-out white pair stained brown with overuse, but for all I knew they were the first shoes he'd ever owned. He was totally lit up. As he pulled them on, he declared that life on the streets with us around was so sweet. It was so, so good, he avowed. My gang buddies and I had done more for him and his friends than anyone else before us.

Scram went on to tell me a story about the time he'd been taken into a children's home. Occasionally, Kenyan-based "charities" tried to do roundups of the street kids, promising them security, food, and a dry bed in a place where they could learn a trade, like carpentry or metalwork. A trade would mean work and an income and a route out of their hopelessness. A year ago Scram had been taken into one of those homes, but it wasn't long before he realized what was going on there.

He was shown how to bang a nail with a hammer and use a screwdriver, and then he was set to making furniture. Every day he was given the same task; he was learning absolutely nothing. Those who ran the home were selling the furniture, but none of the money came back to the kids. He was a child laborer with no pay, his only reward a roof over his head and some half-edible food. In Scram's eyes he was better off on the streets, and at the first opportunity he ran away.

This was the kind of story that my gang buddy Nito treasured. It was a perfect excuse for him to do some real intellectualizing. Nito's big thing was that in Kenya, the rich and the powerful lived on the backs of the poor and the powerless, setting a terrible precedent. The corruption and the abuse filtered through the system, and at the very bottom were the street kids. Scram's story was proof that some people were willing to live off the backs of even the poorest and most disempowered.

"In this country, money and power has the right," Nito remarked. "You can do whatever you want and get away with it. Ministers cream off millions at the top, and they do so with no danger of ever getting caught. The corruption and graft are all for the rich and the powerful. So what we are doing—stealing from those who have, to feed those who have nothing—is it really so bad?"

"It's just small stuff," I concurred. "Just a bit of cash here and there and no one gets hurt. It's the big men who are the real criminals."

Scram was listening to what we were saying, and I could see him nodding his spiky-haired head in agreement. We were passing a joint around, and it fueled our imagination and our philosophizing.

"At least with us there's a kind of karma to what we're about," Nito continued. "We do something bad, we do something good to offset it." He waved a hand expansively at Scram and the others, the joint glowing red as he swished it through the air. "We steal someone's wallet, we buy these kids a meal. We mug a rich guy in Umoja, we do something good for the poorest, and that makes it kind of all right. You know where I'm coming from here?"

I nodded. "You remember that guy we took with all that cash?"

Nito grinned. "How could I forget it? The one with—"

"Yeah, the one with sixty-four thousand shillings in his trouser pocket," I confirmed.

I could see the eyes of Scram and the others going wide with amazement. Sixty-four thousand Kenyan shillings was over a thousand dollars. It was four o'clock in the morning the night of the mugging, and we'd caught the guy drunk and stumbling home from a nightclub. The most you could ever spend on a good night out in Nairobi was two thousand shillings, so the only reason we could imagine anyone would have all that cash would be to impress the girls. Whenever he pulled out that fat wad of thousand-shilling notes to buy them a drink, he was showing what a "big man" he was.

But he was drunk as a skunk by the time we got to him. He

wouldn't feel like such a big man in the morning, when he woke up with the hangover from hell and his money all gone.

"Sixty-four thousand shillings—that's a fortune!" Scram exclaimed.

"It was a good night's work." I grinned, taking the joint from Nito. I inhaled deeply, holding the smoke in, letting the burning hit take me back to the memory of that mugging. "There were four of us," I continued, speaking through a cloud of smoke as I exhaled. "So when we divided the cash, it was sixteen thousand each. Sixteen thousand. Almost enough to buy Scram that jumbo jet he's after," I joked.

Scram rolled his eyes in delight. "You guys! Damn! I'm gonna be just like you guys when I'm grown."

"Yeah, but the point is this," I interjected, passing him the butt end. "We used some of that money to do some good. There was this kid we knew—a street kid like you, but he lived in a park downtown. The kid had helped us a lot. A couple of times we were running from the cops and he and his mates had covered for us. Hidden us. Anyway, the kid was real sick. He had cholera or something. So we paid for him to go to the clinic and get well."

"You ever hear of any of the big men in Kenya doing that?" Nito added. "You ever see them coming to help the people at the bottom of the heap? You don't. They throw some cash around to their families and their friends; they act like the big man and look after their own." Nito paused, but I knew there was more. Once he was on a roll he was hard to stop. "And you know what else they do? They silence anyone who tries to investigate just how much they've stolen. You all heard about that Robert Ouko affair?"

"Ouko was a guy who served as a big minister in the government," I explained. I gave the kids a quick rundown of the Goldenberg scandal. "Ouko was called in to investigate, but instead of nailing the bad guys, Ouko was found murdered."

"That's right," Nito continued. "Ouko had gotten too close to uncovering those who had stolen the money, so they had him killed. It's like I said, those at the top have absolute power, and they use it to corrupt absolutely."

"You know, the Kenyan government had to call in the British to investigate," I added. "Imagine that. In order to try to get to the bottom of who did away with Ouko, they called in Scotland Yard. *That's the British police.* And even when people were arrested, the Kenyan cops released them for 'lack of evidence.' We had to call in the British police because no one in Kenya had the courage or commitment to investigate such a crime, and even then we failed to do anything about it. How messed up is that?"

The smoke was finished and Scram tossed the butt into the bush. He mimed rolling a joint between his fingers, suggesting that I make another. When we had grass, we'd smoke it until it was all gone.

"So what happened about Ouko's murder?" Scram asked.

Nito snorted derisively. "It's never been solved. No one's ever been punished. Those who ordered it are free to do whatever they like and continue to abuse their power. There's talk of another inquiry, but it'll never get anywhere. In Kenya, when you have that much money, you can bribe your way out of anything."

I mixed together some of the grass with tobacco in the palm of my hand, to prepare the next smoke.

"That's why the gap between the rich and the poor is so huge," I continued. "That's why there's street kids like you, and street gangsters like us, and then there's guys living in palaces in places like Westlands and Lavington—with gardeners and maids and nurses and nannies and cars and jeeps and swimming pools and private helicopters. You name it, they got it. And they just keep getting richer."

"So how do we get what they've got?" Scram asked.

It seemed a reasonable question. Any number of superrich in Kenya could well afford to lay on Scram's jumbo jet party in the skies above Nairobi, *by invitation only.* But I didn't have any easy answers as to how you went about acquiring that kind of wealth.

"I don't know," I replied. "I guess you've got to grab some of the cake, like the others are doing. And do it before they've stolen everything and the country goes completely broke."

"If the way we're going is any indication, it won't be long now before we are broke," Nito remarked. "You know, at independence

Kenya was on an economic par with Malaysia or Singapore. We were at the same level in terms of development. Look where we are now, and where they are. They're practically developed and industrialized, while Kenya's still a basket case. So what does that tell us?"

"You should listen to Nito," I told Scram and the others, as I sparked up the new smoke. "That's the most crucial part. The British granted those countries independence about the same time as us, so what's the difference? What's our excuse for failure? We don't have one. We've only got ourselves to blame, or at least those at the top of our messed-up society."

"Well, I want what those guys have," Scram announced. "Those big guys in the big palaces with all the money."

"Me too," agreed Cheesy.

"Gotta be," added Jeff.

I chuckled. "Well, good luck, guys. I hope you get some. Go grab your slice of the pie." I knew where they were coming from, and I couldn't say I blamed them. I took a pull on the joint, then held it up to the others. "So, who's next for a good blast of *stoot*?"

Our partnership with the street kids went from strength to strength, and not just with Scram, Cheesy, Jeff, and the gang in Umoja. The kids in downtown Nairobi were getting more and more familiar with our steal-from-the-rich-and-give-to-the-poor philosophy. Whenever we got into a chase downtown, we'd head for one of the dark alleyways or patches of waste ground where we knew the street kids had their hangouts. As soon as they saw us coming, they'd point us to a hiding place and swarm around whoever was after us.

"Mister! Mister! Something to eat, mister!"

"Buy me a meal, mister!"

"Please, mister, please!"

"Shilling, mister! Shilling!"

"Mister! I'm starving . . ."

By the time our pursuers fought their way through the begging, clamoring kids, we were long gone. More often than not the victim of a street robbery would conclude that the perpetrators were the street urchins, but it was rarely those kids. It was street gangsters like us. The street kids were only our cover.

When all the fuss of the chase had died down, we'd take the kids for a good meal. Invariably the best we could afford was rice and lentils or rice and beans, but to the street kids a meal like that was a luxury. There was a kind of brotherhood among us—street kids and street gangsters—that cut across everything. It was the haves versus the have-nots, and now I had definitely fallen on the side of those who had nothing.

Sometimes after one of those street robberies, I'd catch myself in a moment of stillness and reflection. I'd wonder if the person we had deprived of money or possessions had deserved it. Mostly they were small people like us, not the big guys at the top. You'd rarely get a chance to get to any of those fat cats, with their chauffer-driven Mercedes and their bodyguards, their walled and gated compounds ringed with electric fencing and razor wire, and their 24/7 security details.

The person we had mugged was probably going to use the money to buy his family some food or maybe pay a relative's hospital bill or even cover his kid's school fees. Losing that money was surely a real blow to him. I had to console myself with the thought that we had to live too, and that at least we shared some of our ill-gotten gains with the real have-nots. And then I'd think about the good times ahead, and all the remorse and the regret would be forgotten.

I had a new girlfriend now, one who lived in Umoja. I knew her from around the neighborhood, and I'd discovered she was a great girl to party with. Sarah was a pretty slip of a thing from the Kamba tribe, with dark hair cut almost boyishly short and an ebony black complexion. I managed to keep hidden from her the worst stuff that I was up to, for she was mostly at school when I was out doing my street crime, studying for her final-year exams. I was seventeen when we got together, and she was sweet sixteen, and for the next two years she would be my girl.

Sarah was a dancer to die for, especially when she was dressed in miniskirts or tight jeans. Her favorite nightclub was New York, in downtown Nairobi. I was still big into reggae, but Sarah was a die-hard hip-hop and soul girl. I had to take her to the kind of place where she could really dance, and New York was it. She used to tell me to my face what a crap mover I was, whenever I tried to keep up with her moves. She had a great sense of humor and was always teasing me, which was a foil to my badass gangster attitude. She knew how to take me down a peg or two, which was no bad thing.

None of us in the gang had quite been kicked out of home yet, so we could go back to our Umoja houses to freshen up a little before a night out on the town. We'd usually sleep off a night's partying with the street kids. Home had become a pit stop between wild nights out or days spent doing street crime. Marvin was too young to understand much of what I was up to, and I felt a yawning gulf had opened between us. For me at least, home most certainly wasn't where the heart was anymore.

My mother must have realized that if she threw me out, all contact would be broken. I think she knew it would drive me into doing worse stuff, and God knows, there was far worse out there. The parents of us street gangsters feared that if they drove us away completely, one or more of us would end up dead. I wasn't really talking to my mother much those days, but at least she saw me now and then and knew that I was alive.

As time went on, my past life faded into a hard-to-reach and hazy place of childhood hope and innocence. As the months rolled by, this life became the only way that I seemed to know. I was becoming what I had wished to be—a badass gangster—and losing a grip on my past. But as they say, you should beware of what you wish for.

I was seventeen and a half when my mother announced that she was leaving Kenya. She was going to work in South Korea and leaving my little brother, Marvin, in the care of one of her sisters. Auntie Janet lived in Satellite, a Nairobi suburb a little like Umoja, and Marvin would stay with her and go to a central Nairobi school. She was letting the Umoja house go, and no provision had been made for me. I didn't expect or want any.

I presumed that we couldn't afford to keep the Umoja house, not with Christian gone, but I didn't give a damn. Home was dead to me. I was glad it was over. It was the final page in that chapter of my life, and I was pleased that it was slamming shut on me. Mum seemed to want me to ask more about why she was leaving, but I just wasn't going there. She seemed hurt, but I wasn't about to open myself up to that pain.

"Don't you want to know what's going to happen to this place?" she asked. "All your things . . ."

I shook my head and shrugged. The message was, *Do I care?*

"Everything is being sent to Grandma Dorcas's place. She's promised to look after it for us."

"That's a relief," I muttered sarcastically.

There was nothing in the house that I wanted, least of all the memories. Anything I'd had of any value I'd already given to Scram and the other street kids. I was going to be just like them now: I was homeless, and all I owned were the clothes that I stood up in.

"Don't you want to know why I'm going?" she asked. "Where I'll be? When I'll be coming—"

"I'm fine," I cut in. I tried to soften my tone a little. "Mum, I can look after myself."

"I'm not leaving you, George. I'm just making a life for myself. For all of us. I'll call. I'll send you money."

I shrugged. "I can look after myself."

"I know you can, but I just wanted you to know . . ."

I nodded. We didn't say much. What more was to be said? I wasn't angry at my mother, I was angry at the world. At times I was enraged, but mum wasn't the focus of it. I had forced myself to bury the memory of Christian in the deepest recess of my mind. If he had tried to see me, I think I would have attacked him physically, so great was my sense of betrayal and rebellion. I was closed and had to remain closed, for that was the only way to keep ahead and to survive.

A small, hidden part of me wanted to reach out to my mother, to tell her that I loved her and to ask for a second chance—a chance to start my life all over. She was still trying to pull me back into school whenever I was around and would listen. But the part of me that wanted to grab that second chance was small and feeble, and while I heard her pleading, I didn't listen.

In spite of everything, my mother was still trying to support me financially and trying to give me the little she could to stop me doing all the bad stuff that I was involved in. I guessed that her leaving for Korea was driven by her need to earn money, and in part it was to support Marvin and me. My mother could have dumped me. She could have told me that I was a disaster and an embarrassment and disowned me. I knew that. Instead, she tried to take the path of understanding. She wasn't stubborn like me, but she was strong. She might bow with the wind, but she wouldn't break. She loved me, and that's why she hadn't deserted me completely now that I had turned bad. I wasn't angry with her. It just wasn't possible for her to control me anymore. It was hardly her fault. I needed a father to stamp his foot and to yell at me to do my homework, to get my hair cut, and to study for my future, and to be proud of me when I did, but that man was gone.

And now my mother was leaving. So be it. I was on my own now. This was who I was.

CHAPTER 15

Gangland

THE UMOJA HOUSE was shut down and my mother and Marvin were gone. I returned to Scram and the other street kids, my fellow homeless orphans. Umoja was still the turf of our gang, and that's what kept me anchored there—that and the brotherhood of the streets.

If I needed a pit stop, I'd go with Ramjo to his parents' place, but it was far from ideal. It was at this point that Auntie Sarah reached out to me, knowing the state that I was in. She and my mother had been close, and she decided to extend to me the basics of life now that my mother no longer could: a roof over my head, somewhere to sleep and to wash, and a hot meal whenever I was around. This was the way of the extended family, something that is common all over Africa. Recently, she'd built a couple of new shacks clustered around the wall of her Huruma compound. One was situated just inside the main gate, and she told me that I could stay there whenever I was in need of sanctuary.

That shack was very basic, but it was nowhere near as bad as the makeshift shelters that I'd shared with Scram, Cheesy, and the others. With galvanized tin walls, its one room was smaller than my old bedroom in Umoja. There was a bed, a couple of chairs, and a table. The door had a padlock and Auntie Sarah gave me a key to the padlock on the door, and told me I could come whenever I needed to.

It went without saying that Auntie Sarah didn't expect me to pay any rent, but if I had money, giving her a little to help with household expenses would be no bad thing. In spite of my descent into darkness, Auntie Sarah still saw it as her responsibility to help me if she could.

"I know what you're about, Hussein," Auntie Sarah remarked, as she finished showing me the tin shack. "Your mother told me and I can read it in your eyes. But that doesn't mean we disown you. That's not your mother's way, and it's not my way either. That's not the way of the clan. You're still an Obama, Hussein. No matter what you do, you're still an Obama. No one will disown you here. This home is your home."

"I'm not up to anything much, Auntie," I tried telling her. "It's nothing to worry about. I'll grow out of it, you know, and then—"

"And what then, Hussein?" Auntie Sarah fixed me with one of her looks. "I want to tell you something, and I want you to listen good, okay?"

"Okay." I shrugged.

"You may know this or you may not know this," she continued, "but either way I want you to put this into that stubborn, boneheaded skull of yours. Your mother has had a very hard life, and she's done everything she has and struggled like she has for you and little Marvin. Don't you ever forget that. Don't you ever, ever turn away from that."

"Fine," I muttered. "I'm not."

"When your father died, do you know what your mother asked for from his estate?" Auntie continued. "If you don't know, it's high time you heard. All she ever asked for was money enough to put you through school, for you were the youngest and the one who most needed help. At that terrible, tough moment of her life, when you were not yet one year old and her husband had died, she thought first and foremost of you. That's your mother for you, George. And I really think you needed to hear that."

"So what happened?" I asked. "Did they—"

"You know, in Luo tradition things can often be very hard on a woman," Auntie remarked. "After your father's death your uncles came and removed from your mother's house all of his possessions. That is how it often works with the Luo, but that doesn't make it *right*. Your mother got a rough deal, Hussein, but she dealt with it. She moved on and built a life for herself and a life for you guys. And in case you hadn't realized, that's what she's still doing today. She's a strong woman, Hussein, and she is a mother full of love."

A mother full of love. I guess I should have told Auntie Sarah that I knew that, that I appreciated my mother for who she was. But I was too closed and stubborn to admit that to anyone. Instead, I let her wander off to do the cooking, while I stretched out on the bed in the tin shack that was my new semi-home. It felt good to be around Auntie Sarah, that was for sure, but I missed my brothers—the street kids and my street gang. I guessed this would be my pit stop now, but my base would remain on Scram's wasteland.

The more time I spent in Huruma, the more I saw of the dark and menacing underbelly of the place. At this time it was wild. It wasn't quite Mathare—the valley ghettoland that I had driven past in Christian's Danger-mobile—but it was only one step removed. Auntie Sarah's compound was crammed fence-to-fence with those of other families, and between those dwellings ran the dark and shoulder-narrow dirt alleyways—the arteries of the ghetto.

Open and broken sewer gutters ran down those dirt alleys, a loose wooden plank providing a bridge to give access to someone's home. Passersby had to dodge the gray, putrid sludge that leaked from those open trenches. On every corner there were heaps of rotting garbage, wherein choking fires spluttered and coughed their rancid smoke. Even lifelong inhabitants of the ghetto never got used to the stench. Dodging garbage and sewage in the half-light of the smog, that was the "dance" of the ghetto, and for many it was a twice-daily routine.

Many of the ghetto dwellers did have some kind of menial job. They worked in the city as hotel cleaners, hairdressers, or laborers on building sites. The journey to work would begin before six each morning, as the workers picked their way along those grim alleyways in the half darkness of dawn. If you were of the ghetto, you were pretty much safe there, but still people were getting mugged and robbed on a daily basis.

A young woman could walk down a darkened alley and thieves would suddenly spring out of the shadows. She'd be surrounded, and they'd order her to remove all her jewelry and hand over her purse. They might even force her to remove her clothes, especially if she was dressed smartly, for those too could be sold for good money. The victim would be left marooned in the ghetto dressed only in her underclothes.

Huruma was a crazed and dangerous place. I was no longer the posh little rich kid who had gotten down from Christian's gleaming car with his polished shoes and smart clothes and gazed out over the expanse of the slum in fascinated horror. The ghetto didn't feel anywhere near as alien to me as it had those four years ago, and I had a good sense of how to get by here. But I was still an outsider, and the only way to feel truly safe was to get *inside* the ghetto. And I had a good idea how I might do that. Indeed, I wanted to prove that I could survive and *thrive* in the ghetto. I thrilled to the idea, to the pure, crazed, adrenaline-fueled danger and promise of it all.

I set about drawing my Umoja gang into Huruma and joining forces with some of the ghetto's main players. The only way to make ourselves "worthy" of the ghetto was to up our game. A spate of pick-pocketing, a little casual mugging—neither was going to be enough anymore. As we had in Umoja, we would have to prove ourselves on our new turf, and we would have to do so in battle. I drew Ramjo into Huruma with me, but most of the others balked at where my life was taking me.

I left Nito, Scram, Cheesy, and the others, and with Ramjo I was sucked into the undertow of the place. Over the next few months I descended into a world of darkness and violence and chaos. My lost years began. My mother had been sending me money from Korea, and checking up on me by phone whenever she could, but as I submerged myself in the carnage and darkness, I stopped picking up the cash she sent me or taking her calls. In time I was lost to my mother, and lost to my brother, Marvin, and finally I was lost even to myself.

I got myself "tooled up." I started using a gun. No one could be a gangster in the ghetto without carrying a weapon. I traded gunfire with rival gangsters, although no one ever managed to put a bullet in me. And that was part of the draw and the high—the electric buzz of sheer survival, of getting away with it and staying alive. My new gang brethren were doing all sorts of drugs, swallowing whatever pills and chemicals they could get their hands on, but that was where I drew the line. I smoked dope and I drank *changa'a* like there was no tomorrow, but no way was I ever going to do the chemical stuff, because those chemicals wrecked your body.

I lost my girl, Sarah. The love just died a gradual, lingering death. She was training to be a nurse while I was a ghetto gangster, and our lives were worlds apart. I couldn't hide from her who and what I was becoming, although amazingly she still wanted to be with me, in spite of everything. But as the ghetto sucked me in and chewed me up, I reached the stage where I didn't want to see her anymore. I had money, and the ghetto girls were chasing after me, and they came to feel more like my own kind.

I carried a pistol and I went about my "work." Guns. Guns. Guns. One day we'd start early, at four or five in the morning, when it was still dark. We'd head for the city center and rob people on their way to their places of work. Another day we'd sleep until late afternoon and go out robbing at night. The people we were stealing from could be any race, color, or creed, and once we'd done our "work," we'd go clubbing until the sun rose and sent us back to our beds. Often there was no bed. I'd sleep on a patch of waste ground or on someone's bare dirt floor or wherever I could get my head down.

Most of the time I couldn't go back to Auntie Sarah's place: I was in too bad a state. I was so out of my head on weed and *changa'a* that each day melded into the next in a blur of drug- and alcohol-induced oblivion. I have few if any clear memories of this time, and little sense of a connected sequence of events. Mostly I have a series of stark images burned into my mind, but little idea of how they relate or what they might mean.

I say this with no pride. I say it with shame. These were bad times, the very worst of days. But the absolute worst was the "work" that Ramjo and I and the rest of the gang were doing.

We were a big group now, some twenty to thirty gang members at any one time. We had no formal name or structure, but we were the Huruma gangsters, and that's what defined and united us. During the day we'd split up into groups of three or four, and go about our business. By sundown we'd get back together, two or three dozen of us with money in our pockets and the hunger to drink and to smoke and to party.

My speciality was carjacking. Usually, I held up *matatus*. It was a stand-and-deliver operation, and I was like a modern-day highwayman robbing a coach and horses. The economics of a *matatu*-jacking were simple. In a full minivan with sixteen people each person would have a mobile phone and a wallet. It was sixteen times what I could make from street robberies. There was rarely any resistance, for I had the gun and looked like the mad, crazed thing I had become. I had truly become the Mamba now. I was living the Mamba. I was the Mamba squared.

That first *matatu* job I went out with Ramjo and our two closest gang buddies, Stevo and Mandeka. We had one weapon among us— an old and well-worn pistol. The hard, cold steel was thrust inside my jacket, its weight dragging at my shoulders. We chose a busy downtown *matatu* stop, on a route leading to an upmarket suburb of Nairobi, and waited. No one paid us any mind, for the place was crowded with people returning home from work.

A *matatu* slowed. It had STREET KILLER emblazoned along one side of its battered, dirty white paintwork, in lurid spray-painted letters. We'd received good advice from one of the older, more experienced gang members on how we should go about doing this. The secret was to divide forces; one went in the front, to force the vehicle to a stop; three dispersed around the back to swiftly relieve the passengers of their phones and cash. And we were to choose a spot to strike where a patch of waste ground or bush was in easy distance, so we could make good our getaway.

As the vehicle pulled to a halt, I yanked open the passenger door and slid in beside the driver. The four of us acted as if we didn't know each other, and Ramjo and the others disappeared into the back of the vehicle, sliding in alongside the unsuspecting passengers. Just as soon as we were onboard, the driver gunned the engine and lurched into the main stream of the traffic, blaring his horn to clear a path. Nairobi *matatu* drivers are notorious, and few vehicles choose to get in their way.

I waited, tense and coiled and primed to pull the weapon, as the vehicle plowed onward toward the suburbs. Deafening reggae music blared out from the four speakers set into the roof. Conversation was all but impossible, which was a good thing. I didn't want to have to make small talk with the guy that I was about to rob.

I glanced at the driver out of the corner of one eye. He looked to be in his late forties, and he had the thin, gray look of a man who'd spent a life battling his minivan through chaotic and pollution-filled streets. A gold band encircled one of the fingers that gripped the steering wheel. For an instant I wondered about that man's wife and kids back home. For sure, they'd done nothing to deserve what was coming. But then I told myself to harden up: I wasn't about to hurt him. I was just going to relieve him and his passengers of some of their hard-earned cash.

Ahead of us a darkened stretch marked where the tarmac was worn away, the road left rutted and cratered by deep holes. Dust hung heavy in the headlamps of passing cars and trucks. Vehicles had to slow to a crawl to pass here, and a stretch of parkland was just across the far side of the road. This was the spot where we planned to make our hit.

As the brakes bit and the *matatu* slowed, then slumped into the first crater in the road, I slipped my fingers around the cold pistol grip. We slowed still further, the vehicle bucking and groaning on the uneven surface, and I steeled myself to strike.

We reached the roughest, darkest stretch where the streetlamps weren't working properly. The driver proceeded at a slow and painful crawl. I whipped out the gun, leaning back into the open passenger window, and leveled it at the driver. He swung his head toward me, eyes going wide with fear as he spotted the weapon.

"Stop the fucking vehicle," I snarled at him. "Pull over! Now!"

The driver did exactly as I'd said. I held the gun on him as he stared unblinkingly ahead, the engine idling away but the vehicle going nowhere. He raised his hands from the steering wheel and put them above his head, in a gesture of impotent terror. I felt my pulse racing with a mixture of excitement and fear. Fear of the gun; fear of being forced to really hurt someone; fear of my own brute power.

"It's a holdup!" I yelled behind me. "Your phones and cash—now! I've got the gun, so do it! *Now!*"

From behind I could hear Ramjo, Mandeka, and Stevo yelling at the passengers to empty out their pockets and hand over their cash. A woman began wailing hysterically, as Stevo grabbed her handbag and threw its contents onto the scuffed and dirty *matatu* floor. He scrabbled about for her phone, then chucked the empty bag back into her lap.

"You! And you!" Ramjo yelled at the passengers beside her. "Phones! Cash! Pass it over—now!"

The driver stole a glance behind him, and I gestured with the muzzle of the weapon for him to keep his eyes to the front. The fewer witnesses the better.

"We're done!" Ramjo yelled. "We're out of here!"

I heard the metallic screech of the side door sliding open. My three gang buddies bailed out, their pockets bulging with phones and cash. I kept the gun on the driver for a few moments more.

"Don't move. Don't drive," I ordered, coldly. "You stay here a full minute before you go anywhere. I see you move, I'll open fire. I'll shoot you. You got it?"

The guy nodded.

"I can't hear you," I snarled. "Tell me you understand what I said."

"I understand," he whimpered. "I'm not going . . ."

The last words were lost in the slam of the passenger door, and with that I was gone, feet pounding across the road. I thrust the weapon inside my jacket and vaulted the gate that led into the parkland. I made for the prearranged rendezvous, where the four of us would divide the cash. The phones we'd sell to unscrupulous traders, and the money would go for maybe a little food—and definitely booze, drugs, and partying.

The risks in what we were doing were legion. Average Kenyans were sick to death with the crime rate in the city. It hadn't been dubbed "Nairobbery" for nothing. More often than not if they caught a thief, they'd take the law into their own hands. An angry mob would beat and burn the culprit half to death. The police would not intervene, for in their eyes the bad guy was getting what he deserved. And to the public and police alike, *matatu*-jacking was an especially hateful crime.

The police had instituted a shoot-to-kill policy. Even if the robber had surrendered, more often than not he was gunned down. One of our gang had been caught smoking pot in Huruma. The cops hadn't bothered arresting him, they just put a bullet in him. That very night the cops had shot three people dead in the slums. Another night it was five. If you came from the ghetto, you didn't have the money or the status or the power to fight back or resist.

The life expectancy of a gangster was never very high, but then again no one was guaranteed a long life in the ghetto. Over half of Kenyans lived below the poverty line, and more and more of those dispossessed were ending up in the ghetto. Four million people were crammed into the vast Kenyan slumlands, where every day was spent teetering on the very brink.

Auntie Sarah's tin-walled shack was a palace for the majority of the ghetto dwellers. Most families—grandparents, parents, kids, and babies—lived crammed into a one-room shack the size of my own. And in those families the children would be starving because their folks couldn't afford to buy them enough of the cheapest food to survive.

The ghetto dwellers consumed the detritus that the rest of the city rejected: chicken heads, boiled up in big vats to make chicken-head stew; the hooves and heads of goats, pigs, and cows, whenever they were lucky enough to find them; animal intestines fried in a little oil—a luxury most could ill afford. You could survive on that stuff, if you could afford to buy enough of it. Many families lived on one meal a day, and that was only when they could afford it.

In Huruma people were truly desperate in ways that most people in the outside world could never imagine. Outsiders had not the slightest understanding of what that desperation was like—of the slow, suffocating death of hope of the ghetto dweller. There was no social welfare safety net, no education without money, no way to gain qualifications and a future, no security or status. And for many, life was horribly short. Death was often the only way out of the ghetto. It was hardly surprising that so many resorted to crime, for what other options were open to them?

The competition for legitimate work was fierce, and if you could find any—as a domestic servant, a gardener, a watchman—rarely would it earn you more than five dollars a day. That was five dollars with which to feed, clothe, and house an entire family, plus paying for school fees and medical care, for nothing comes free in Kenya. Those who couldn't find such better jobs would hustle—collecting garbage in handcarts or scavenging off the rubbish dumps. And that would earn you a good deal less than five dollars a day.

Doing my "work" as a gangster, I could earn one hundred times that amount. I could net five hundred dollars from one good *matatu* jacking. The economics were glaringly simple, so people turned to crime as the only way to survive. You'd find a single mother living in a one-room shack with seven kids. Her husband might have died from typhoid or malaria, diseases that are rife in the ghetto. She couldn't afford to feed her children, let alone pay their school fees, so by the time they reached their teens, they'd have no education and no prospects.

If you were the oldest child, you'd turn to crime and use the money to help your mother feed the family and maybe put your younger siblings through school so they might have a better life. Boys would turn to robbery at the age of twelve or thirteen, and girls would turn to prostitution. I'd see the girls leaving the ghetto in the evenings, dressed in their one set of smart, "sexy" clothes, heading for the city. They'd likely have enough money to buy themselves just one drink, then they'd sit all evening waiting for customers.

With drugs so readily available, some of those girls would have pills on them. If they got a chance, they'd slip a sedative into a man's drink and rob him of all his possessions. It was soul-destroying work, but it was a ticket to survival.

Beneath all the drugs and the drink and the criminality, a part of our Umoja gang philosophy still endured. The karma side of it survived, no matter what I was doing. When I was a school kid, I'd seen a cartoon of Robin Hood, the figure from English medieval folklore who stole from the rich to give to the poor. He was a good guy using criminality to fight for those who had nothing. It had struck a chord with me, for it seemed to me modern Kenya needed a Robin Hood, as England had done in those days.

That was never more glaringly obvious than it was in Huruma. Kids died of hunger or of simple, curable diseases, while the big men in the exclusive suburbs lived a life of luxury, funded by corruption. Society was rotten from the highest level, just as it had been under England's evil and Machiavellian King John, the wicked ruler who had driven Robin Hood to become a bandit in Sherwood Forest. In Kenya the rot had set in from the top down, and that in part was why the crime rate was so high.

Ramjo, myself, and the other Huruma gangsters were part of that crime wave. We weren't political in any sense; we didn't read the newspapers or watch the TV news. We felt we were outside normal society, and we didn't believe that politics or current affairs affected us anymore. Many in the ghetto felt likewise, for we were the unnoticed, powerless nonpeople, the excluded and voiceless underclass.

But deep down the ghetto dwellers were complaining, if not with their voices then in their hearts. They knew that Kenya was rotten to the core, but this was a wound of the heart, not one of the conscious mind. Things had been like this for so long that people felt there was no sense in complaining anymore. The all-consuming need was to survive, and that universal need united the ghetto dwellers in an uncommon brotherhood.

The ghetto dwellers looked after their own, and we gangsters were no different. None of our bad stuff was perpetrated in Huruma. We did our "work" in the glittering world of downtown Nairobi, where the ghetto dwellers moved only as the unseen slaves of those with money. And when we had money, we would give something back to the brotherhood.

One day a girl came and found me. I was playing soccer with some of the slum kids using a rag-and-string ball. The girl waited patiently for a break in the game. Her name was Rachel. She was a pretty thing around twelve years old. It struck me with a mute anger that a couple of years more and she'd likely be a *shangingi*—the Swahili word for a working girl. She told me she had a nine-year-old brother who was desperately ill.

Her kid brother was at death's door, her mother was long dead, and her father was a *changa'a* addict. This left her more or less the head of the family, and there was no one to whom she could turn for help. Her few relatives lived in a village upcountry. There was no money to pay for her kid brother's treatment, but a friend of hers had told her that I—or one of the others in the Huruma gang—might be willing to help.

I didn't need to see the kid brother to know it was the truth. Even in the ghetto, people didn't lie about such things. In fact, beneath the carnage and the need there was a truth and an honesty that was breathtaking. I knew she wasn't lying. I gave her around a thousand shillings, the equivalent of fifteen dollars. It was nothing to me, but for Rachel that was the equivalent of two weeks spent scavenging glass bottles, cans, and plastic. She left me with an embarrassed murmuring, and with tears of hope in her beautiful eyes.

I never expected to see her again or to hear from her. I never expected the favor to be returned. But in terms of karma, had giving that money to save her brother made up for my stealing a businessman's wallet? I didn't think much about it back then. I didn't really care. We fed the ghetto kids, clothed their sisters, paid a gifted slum kid's school fees. Small things. It didn't make us the good guys and it didn't absolve our sins, but maybe it afforded us some limited redemption.

A few days later Rachel came and found me again. She told me her kid brother had been stricken with typhoid, a fever all too common in the ghetto. She'd gotten him to the hospital just in time. The doctors had wanted to keep him in for a week or more, but Rachel wouldn't allow it. From the thousand shillings that I'd given her, she had to buy the rest of the family some maize flour and other basic foodstuffs. "Keep my brother alive," she'd told the doctors. "That's all I can afford. Until the next time."

On the spur of the moment Rachel gave me a little peck on the cheek, a girly, childish thank-you. It struck me then what a waste of a life it would be if that angel of a girl ended up selling her body on the streets. She was certainly beautiful enough to make it as a *shangingi*. She had huge, smoky eyes speckled with flecks of gold, like diamond-studded chocolate, and a grace and a poise that belied the weight she carried on her tiny, delicate shoulders.

Rachel's father had wanted to come and thank me himself, but the draw of the *changa'a* monster raging in his soul had been too strong. Instead he'd taken fifty shillings from the money I'd given Rachel and gone on a drinking binge. I didn't blame him. God only knew what his life had been like, what trials and tribulations he'd lived through.

I had no idea how Rachel's mother had died, and I didn't ask. We were so used to death that we never normally inquired of someone how a relative or friend might have perished. A few months previously I'd witnessed a shooting of a woman. It could have been Rachel's mother, for all I knew. The police had come charging into the slum, their guns drawn and their bullets flying, chasing a thief who'd fled into Huruma to lose them in the dark, labyrinthine alleyways.

My attention was drawn by the gunshots, and I thought that it might be a rival gang come into "our ghetto" to cause trouble. But then I caught sight of the thief—wide-eyed with terror as he vaulted across open sewers with the police not far behind him. Shots rang out as the cops tried to gun him down. At the very moment that he darted around an alley corner, a woman stepped out of the shadows to cross the path. One of the policemen's bullets struck her in the stomach, and I watched as she clutched at her wound and crumpled to the ground.

An instant later blood was spurting from between her fingers, and her agonized screams echoed around the fearful streets. Rage sparked like a wildfire. A crowd gathered, myself at the forefront, and we chanted for revenge against that policeman who'd gunned down an innocent mother of the ghetto. The cops realized the ghetto was rising and that they were the target of its fury. There were cries of "Kill the cops," as our rage fueled our hunger for mob justice.

A policeman raised his pistol and fired over the crowd, the bullets snarling through the air above our heads. Men, women, and children dove for cover, as those bravest, or most foolhardy, tried to press forward and get to the fallen woman. An instant later the cops had fled up a darkened alleyway. We picked up the wounded woman, leaving behind a pool of blood congealing on the dirt path. We hoisted her high above our heads and rushed her to the nearest clinic, a white-walled place on the fringes of the ghetto.

The woman needed treatment, and fast. But nothing comes free in Kenya, not even emergency, lifesaving medical aid. No one knew who the woman was or where her family might be to pay for that treatment. We barged into the clinic, and threw a handful of bloody banknotes onto the desk in front of the white-coated doctor. A couple of the others chucked in a few hundred shillings, and soon we had enough to pay for her treatment—if she could be saved. I don't know if she survived.

The intense rage that I felt at the woman's shooting fueled the anger within me, and that rage drove me to execute more robberies and carjackings. It was a vicious circle. The gang life is a one-way street that leads to an early grave. Although I did my best to hide it, Auntie Sarah saw the state that I was in. She sensed that I was breaking the law and doing too much *changa'a* and weed. She knew I was living on the very edge, and she kept trying to talk to me and reach me, to bring me back from a place of no return.

She continued to tell me about my Obama birthright, the moral and intellectual legacy of my father. Time and time again she put the example of my Obama father before me, in the hope that it might shame me, and spirit me out of my bad ways. But it was going to take more than talk—much, much more—for me to change.

CHAPTER 16

Imprisoned

In December 2002 a spirit of hope swept through the ghettolands. A presidential election was scheduled, and all predictions were that Daniel Arap Moi, Kenya's president of twenty-four years, would lose. Moi had been implicated in the multimillion-dollar Goldenberg scandal and subsequent cover-ups, among many other allegations of corruption. People eagerly anticipated the end of the "Moi era," and with it a reduction in venality, unemployment, and crime.

I was twenty years old and eligible to vote, but I didn't bother to register, for I doubted anything would change. More importantly, it didn't seem to make the slightest difference who the ghetto dwellers voted for. Aspiring politicians—those hoping to win a place in parliament—would turn up in the slums the month before the election, handing out fifty-shilling notes to secure votes, and then they wouldn't be seen again in the ghetto until the next election. With a five-year term ahead of them, each vote cost them ten shillings a year that they were in power, or less than twenty U.S. cents. I wasn't about to become a part of that.

In the run-up to the elections everyone was talking politics, including our ghetto gang. Some agreed with me and opted to stay out of politics altogether. Others decided to cast their vote. A couple of the guys tried to persuade me to do likewise, but no way was I voting for more of the same, and I was convinced that that was all we were going to get.

"Hell no, I'm not into politics," I told them. "Here in Kenya it's fucked us up big-time. No way am I voting. Politics is a dirty, dirty game."

"You don't vote, you can't change anything," Stevo told me. "You don't vote, *then* you're voting for more of the same."

"Listen, you know what politics is in Africa?" I responded. "Politics is money and wealth, that's all it is. They give out money to buy your votes. They have middlemen going around buying votes for nothing. For fifty shillings. *For nothing.* I'm not even applying for a voting card."

"So what's new? Politics is like that everywhere," Ramjo remarked. "It's all money and corruption. Wherever you are, that's all it ever is."

"Well, maybe it's not," I countered. "Maybe it's not like that *everywhere.*"

"So where is it any different?" Ramjo demanded.

"Europe maybe. Maybe America," I suggested. "It's not squeaky clean anywhere, but it sure as hell isn't anything like as dirty as it is here."

"You're always trying to back up the whites," Ramjo declared, mockingly. "What is it with you, Hussein? You want to bring colonialism back to Africa or something?"

"Race doesn't come into it," I replied. "But let me tell you something. Look at South Africa. They were under the whites until the 1990s, and look where they are now. They're practically a developed nation. The corruption there is nothing like what it is here. So who is better off? Us, who kicked out the British, or the South Africans? Maybe if we'd let the whites stay a bit longer, we'd be where South Africa is today."

"Whoa . . . It's just like I said!" Ramjo exclaimed. "Hussein wants to bring the British back to rule us."

"You know what, Ramjo?" I continued. "Had we been alive during colonial times, we'd have been some of those 'freedom fighters.' You and me, Stevo—all of us Mau Mau warriors killing the white man. The British did a hell of a lot of bad stuff in Kenya and I guess we would have risen up against them. But if we had, you know what we'd have been fighting for? We'd have fought for the right of our leaders to be corrupt, that's all. So, go think about that when you cast your ballot and vote for more of the same."

I was forever being accused of "backing up the whites." I wasn't. I was simply a pragmatist, and I didn't believe the myths people told about our country and the cause of its ills. I didn't believe someone should be considered fair game simply because of the color of his skin or because of history. As my muse, Bob Marley, had put it, "Who the cap fit, let him wear it," not "Who the cap fit, let him wear it, as long as he's a black man."

In the end Moi stepped down just before the December elections, and a new president, Mwai Kibaki, and his Rainbow Coalition government came to power. Celebrations swept the nation, but I didn't share the spirit of hope. Corruption was a disease that had eaten into the Kenyan soul, and who knew what would ever bring it to an end?

In fact, corruption was eating up much of Africa. Even the foreign aid programs were subject to corruption, and in many cases it was poor Africans who would have to pay for the aid money in the long term, especially if it was given in loans. The rule of law had to come first in Africa; without law and accountability, nothing would ever change.

A few months after the elections, Ramjo, Stevo, Mandeka, and I paid a visit to Umoja. Recently we'd found a damn fine *changa'a* den there, and it was good to spend some time hanging out in the old territory. Scram, Cheesy, and the others seemed to have moved on, and a different bunch of street kids were in possession of the wasteland, but it was still good to go there and hang out once in a while. We had money, and so we spent the day chilling out and drinking.

Toward evening there was the squeal of tires and a couple of police Land Rovers pulled up outside. The cops came in and rounded up the four of us, plus the lady serving the *changa'a*. At first we presumed we'd been picked up for being in an illegal drinking den, which wasn't exactly a serious crime. It was the kind of thing that we'd bribe our way out of easily enough, so no one was particularly worried. But once we got to the police station—Buruburu again—we realized things were a little more serious.

We were booked under a charge of robbery, for an incident that was supposed to have happened that very day. In fact we'd spent the entire day drinking *changa'a*. I tried pointing out that we couldn't have done it, for we couldn't have been in two places at the same time. All the police had to do was ask the *changa'a* lady, and she'd confirm what I was saying. But the police had already let her go, and they made it clear they weren't interested in any alibis.

The cops knew that we were bad guys, and they were intent on nailing us, invented though the charges might be. It was a sting operation, but at least the four of us hadn't been shot dead, which could easily have happened. For a second time I found myself thrown into the Buruburu cells. They hadn't changed a great deal since my last visit. But I had changed. After three years as a ghetto gangster, being locked away here was nowhere near as terrifying as it had been the first time. There were four of us, we knew how to handle ourselves, and we weren't about to be intimidated.

We spent a week in the cells, during which time it became obvious that none of our parents were about to come and bail us out. No one but the *changa'a* lady had seen the police take us, and even if someone else had, who was there to alert? I'd lost contact with my mother, and Ramjo, Stevo, and Mandeka had little contact with their families. We were pretty much on our own.

On the morning of the eighth day we were bundled into the police Land Rover for the short drive to the Makadara Law Courts. At this stage we still weren't particularly worried. We knew the charges were a frame-up. We intended to plead not guilty and hope that justice might prevail. Having never yet been before the courts, we had little idea what we were up against.

In Kenya lawyers are only provided by the state to those charged with a capital offense such as murder and who are facing the death penalty. For everyone else a lawyer is only available if you can afford to hire one, and nearly everyone who has that kind of money would never end up in the cells in the first place.

On arrival at the Law Courts we were offered the last chance to buy our way out. The courts have an imposing, colonial-era stone façade, with arched windows and fountains complete with water-spouting cherubs. Yet the grand exterior hides a shadowy reality. Along with dozens of other first-timers, we awaited processing into an overcrowded holding cell. The air here stank of corruption. Those who went before the magistrate would then be in the system, and once they were sent on to prison, there was no way out.

We joined the line of suspects. Names were called and matched up to cases to be heard, but no one seemed able to pass without getting a crack from one of the three policeman's batons. One old man failed to answer to his name. A policeman stepped forward and smashed him in the head. The old man collapsed to the ground, his glasses falling from his face and splintering. For a moment he scrabbled around on the floor, fingers groping blindly in the broken glass, as the three policemen pointed and jeered.

It turned out that the police had actually recorded the old man's name incorrectly, which was why he hadn't answered the call. But there was no hint of an apology; the police seemed to get a kick out of visiting mindless violence on the defenseless. I wondered if they would like to see their elderly fathers or mothers beaten in that way. Would they beat a minister or a big businessman with equal relish? And I wondered how they'd fare in a one-on-one fight against myself—the Mamba—or Ramjo or the others. We'd make mincemeat out of them, of that I was certain.

When my name was called, I eyeballed the cop who had smashed the old man's spectacles. I felt Ramjo and the others bunched up behind me. I gave the cop my crazed and dangerous look, the same one that put the fear of God into my opponents in our gang fights. The policeman went to raise his baton, but I stared him down, almost willing him to strike. Instead, he gave an antagonistic grunt and shoved me in the back, pushing me forward into the dark holding cell.

A dozen prisoners at a time were taken into the courtroom. There were two reasons we weren't buying our freedom: we knew we didn't have the money to put up a bribe of suitable size to get ourselves off such charges, and we balked at paying for a crime we didn't commit.

We emerged from the dark cell into the wood-paneled court. Bright sun was streaming through high-arched windows. I stood with the others awaiting my turn and eyeing the proceedings. The judge was a jowly, middle-aged man dressed in a formal business suit and wearing chunky-framed glasses. The gray of his pinstripes matched the tired gray of his features, but I detected something honest about his face, in spite of its jaundiced weariness.

Most of the prisoners were pleading "guilty" for petty charges. Few seemed to have the will to deny them. Two men in their early twenties stepped forward. We would be next.

"Simon Mwenje and Peter Ndodo," the judge announced, looking up from his charge sheet. "You are charged with touting. How do you plead?"

"Guilty, Your Honor," the prosecutor responded, speaking on their behalf.

"Three days' community service," the judge announced. "Case dismissed."

Next the four of us were propelled forward by the court guards, as the judge read out our names. Back in the Buruburu cells, Ramjo, Stevo, and Mandeka had appointed me as the spokesperson of our group. I knew that if we stood any chance of getting out of this, the judge was the key, and making a personal connection with him would be crucial. I'd watched the previous cases closely and hoped that I had mastered the correct way to address the man. I intended to speak to him directly, as opposed to letting the prosecutor speak for us.

For a moment I cast my mind back to the time when I'd appeared before the headmaster at Dagoretti High. It was five years and a whole world ago, yet I still remembered how I had spoken to him with respect but with determination to see justice done. Being forced to do the prefect's dirty laundry hadn't been fair punishment, and I'd won that argument. Conviction for a violent robbery carried a sentence of up to fourteen years. Fourteen years—and in Kenya there was no such thing as early release for good behavior. Spending that long in a Nairobi prison would be little short of a death sentence. I tried to cast my mind back to the spirited and smart, yet polite schoolboy I had been at Dagoretti High. But it had been so long since I had been on the right side of society or the law, I wondered if I could drop my badass gangster attitude now that I needed to. I had to try, for myself and the others.

The judge glanced up at the four of us briefly, then down to the charge sheet.

"You are charged with robbery," he declared, raising his voice at the gravity of the charges. "How do you plead?"

"The four accused pl—" the prosecutor began, but I cut him off.

"We would like to speak for ourselves," I told him. I glanced at the judge and held his gaze. "Your Honor, I plead not guilty to the charges."

The judge scrutinized me over the top of his glasses. "You deny the charges against you?"

"I do, Your Honor. We didn't commit this robbery, and so I am pleading not guilty, as I believe are my co-accused."

The judge eyeballed Ramjo. "And your plea?"

"Not guilty," Ramjo confirmed.

He repeated the process with Stevo and Mandeka, who pleaded likewise.

"Very well, the four accused in *The Republic versus Obama and Others* plead not guilty," the judge confirmed. "You will be held on remand until the full hearing." He checked something on his desk for a moment, then glanced back at us. "Your full hearing will be listed for three months hence, and I will be scheduled as the presiding judge at that hearing. Two weeks from today you will return for your mention, at which you will be given another opportunity to consider your plea. Is that clear?"

"It is, Your Honor," I confirmed. "And thank you, Your Honor."

"Very well then."

I didn't understand all that he had said, but I felt it hadn't gone too badly. He had accepted our not-guilty plea and we had a hearing date. That had to be a good start. We were led out of the courtroom and handed over into the custody of the prison guards. Around the back of the court a truck was waiting. It was already packed with guys like us making their first journey to prison, along with inmates who'd been at court to attend their hearings. We were shoved into the back, and with a grinding of gears and a lurch the truck set off for Nairobi's Industrial Area Prison.

As the first prison gates clanged shut behind us, I tried peering out of the mesh side of the truck to get a first glimpse of our new home, but a crush of other faces were doing likewise. It was only after we were unloaded and marched through the second gate that I saw the defenses ranged against us. Any hope of escape was instantly dashed. The Industrial Area Prison, built in 1911, consisted of a maze of chain-link fences, rolls of razor wire, and guard towers, set within concentric circles. The prison buildings were enclosed within two walls four meters high or more. And over everything were the watchtowers, each with a contingent of guards carrying unmistakable G3 assault rifles. The G3 is a heavy weapon, but it is highly accurate at long range, and it would be perfect for picking off prisoners attempting to climb the walls or scale the wire. It was abundantly clear that there would be only one way out of here, and that would be via the ruling of that middle-aged judge seated in the Law Courts.

We were herded into the processing facility. A prison warden started compiling a list of the new prisoners' details—name, age, date of birth, and next of kin. As we waited in line, I considered what I was going to say. No way was I willing to give out all my details, for the last thing I wanted was Auntie Sarah or my mother or my little brother, Marvin, finding out that I was here and how I had been charged.

I had no faith that any of them would *believe* in my innocence, for they knew the kind of life I was leading. They would do their best to defend me, of that I was certain, yet all the while they would judge me guilty as charged. I didn't need to deal with that on top of coping with whatever prison life was going to throw at me. I needed a clear mind so I could prepare to win my own freedom and that of Ramjo and the others at trial, and I knew that having my family's guilt and shame on my shoulders wouldn't help.

I gave my real name, but when the warden came to ask for my address, the only one that I could think of was Auntie Sarah's. I didn't want anyone tracing me to her place, so I made up an address that I could remember. Likewise, I gave a name for my next of kin that was memorable but fictitious. Next the warden asked for details of my tribal chief. I thought back to the infant years that I'd spent with Grandma Dorcas, but I couldn't even remember the name of the village chief. Instead, I gave the first convincing Luo name that came into my head.

That was my smokescreen, and I figured that once I got inside the final set of prison gates, no one would be able to find me. Before moving forward we had to remove our watches, belts, and phones, all of which we had to sign for. The belts of the new arrivals were tied together in one big bunch and dated. We'd collect them in two weeks' time when we returned to court, for our mention. I wasn't sure what a "mention" was exactly, but there had to be those in prison who could explain it to us.

In Kenya prisoners on remand keep their civilian clothing, and so we were marched those final few yards dressed in the clothes in which we'd been arrested. We were searched one last time, and then the final, massive set of gates swung shut behind us. I felt an odd mixture of emotions as I stared up at the white painted exterior of the prison. On the one hand I was daunted by what might lie before me. On the other, I counted my blessings that I'd been taken along with Ramjo, Stevo, and Mandeka.

If I had to be here, then I was in the very finest of company. We were four tough sons of bitches, and I thought that if anyone should be able to look after himself in prison, we should. And we were four Huruma brothers, so I knew for sure we would stick together no matter what. I'd managed to avoid prison during five years as a street gangster, and I thought I'd learned all the tricks. Yet here I was in jail. So be it. We were where we were.

We entered the prison via gate four, and were corralled into compound number one. The first thing that hit me was the smoke from the kitchen fires mixed with the smell of rancid food and the reek of raw sewage. The prison assaulted the senses just as Huruma did, but here there was no laughter, vibrancy, or light. A sullen, leaden atmosphere hung over the place, like a dark storm waiting to break.

The Industrial Area Prison buildings still had a grand Victorian-era feel to them. But now, some ninety years later, four-thousand-odd prisoners were crammed into an area designed to hold a fraction of that number. There were sick and insane prisoners, debtors, murderers, and child criminals, all in theory segregated from one another. But in practice imprisoned street kids, lunatics, and the very worst of the worst were all mixed in together.

It was four o'clock in the afternoon and we were ordered to queue for food. In the kitchens the cooks strained over massive, soot-blackened pots, stirring their contents over open fires. The staff were dressed in identical off-white uniforms, and it didn't take a genius to work out that they had to be the convicted criminals. In fact cooking was a cushy job for a con to get, and we were soon to find out just how sought-after that kitchen work was.

I reached the front of the queue and grabbed myself a prison-issue metal bowl. As I did so, I couldn't help but remember a different queue and a different mealtime—the line for breakfast on my first day at Busara Forest View Academy. Mount Kenya had been cloaked in the heavy mist of a freezing dawn. I'd turned my nose up at the ladle-ful of porridge, the hunk of bread and butter, and mug of sweet milky tea back then, but now, as I watched the server slop a gray, watery mess into my bowl, I wished for all the world that I were sitting down to a meal at the Academy.

During the truck journey from the courtroom, the other inmates had warned us about prison food. Apparently, the authorities fed each of their inmates on less than thirty Kenyan shillings—under fifty U.S. cents—a day. Some of the prisoners had been on remand for five years, and remand time was dead time, for it was never taken away from your sentence. Those long-term prisoners were bone thin, like walking skeletons. They had the sunken, desperate look in the eyes that denoted the gnawing pain of long-term hunger. In this prison people died from the starvation diet, or diseases brought on by the hunger. That was one of the ways the prison authorities tried to keep the numbers down. I knew that the food was supposedly inedible, but still I couldn't believe the foulness of that first meal. It was a half-cooked, rancid, stomach-churning mess, and I'd have preferred one of Scram's rubbish dump stews any day.

We squatted in the open with the other prisoners. I pushed my bowl away from me across the rough cement floor. A dozen eyes glanced up hungrily at the noise of metal scraping on concrete. The nearest prisoners paused from shoveling the gruel into their mouths with their bare hands. Eyes stared at my bowl, then flicked to my face and back to the bowl again, before one of the prisoners spoke.

"Not eating?"

"Nope. Take it." I kicked the bowl across to him.

Without a word he snatched it up and tipped the contents into his own bowl.

"You got to eat, Hussein," Ramjo remarked quietly. I could see he was trying to force some of the gruel down his own throat. "You don't eat, you don't live."

"I'm not eating that shit," I muttered. "You wouldn't feed it to animals."

"You got to eat," Ramjo repeated. He glanced around at some of the other inmates. "Don't you go dying on us, Hussein. I got a feeling we're going to be needing the Mamba around here pretty soon."

There was no telling who our cellmates might be, but some at least were bound to be evil bastards. We were determined to prevent being split up. We Huruma brothers had safety in numbers, and if it came to it, we would come out fighting.

The guards were dressed in green fatigues with matching berets and black boots. None of them carried guns in here, but each had a long wooden baton. Under their watchful gaze, we went into a huddle.

"This is so fucked up," I remarked. "One moment we're drinking *changa'a*, the next we're in this place. You know how long we could be facing? *Fourteen years.* That's fourteen years of food like this and staring at these four walls, and we don't even know what other bad stuff. I'm twenty years old. I'd be thirty-four when I got out. *Thirty-four.* And all for a charge that we know is a setup. Fuck that. *Fuck that.*"

"So what're you suggesting?" Ramjo asked. "You got an alternative, Hussein? You got an escape plan or something? What you gonna do, Hussein, call up your buddy with a helicopter and get him to fly us out of here? 'Cause anything less—"

"No one's escaping." I cut Ramjo off. "You saw the walls and the fences and the guards with guns. What we've got to do is keep our heads and our shit together and get ready for that trial date. You heard the judge: three months. Three months and we get the chance to argue our case and get out of here. I can do three months. That I can survive. Three months and we're out of here: that's what we got to aim for."

"Fair enough," Stevo agreed. "You're our voice, Hussein. You got to do the talking."

"You got the charm, Hussein," Mandeka added. "Anyone can charm us out of this place, you can."

"You spend all the time you need thinking about that trial," Ramjo remarked firmly. "You work out just how you're gonna charm that judge, Hussein. In the meantime, we're watching your back. All for one and one for all. No one fucks with the Huruma brothers and gets away with it. All for one and one for all, you got that?"

Ramjo raised his fist and held it out to the three of us. As one we raised our own fists and cracked knuckles against knuckles. It was our Huruma salute, and it signified our togetherness. Over the coming months we would need that brotherhood more than ever before.

Mealtime over, we were ordered to our feet to be shown our cells. One overriding thought was running through my mind: thank God for Ramjo, Stevo, and Mandeka. Thank God for the four of us.

Thank God I'm not here alone.

CHAPTER 17

Absolute Zero

THE FOUR OF us were led to a cell block at the far end of the prison.
It was one of two massive edifices kept for prisoners on remand. In
each three-story brick building, the cells ran off a central metal stairwell. On the ground floor was the eating area.

We were marched to the top floor of the wing that faced the sick
bay and the block that housed the insane, and propelled down the
echoing landing. A door was flung open and the first things that
struck me were the heat and the bodies. The room was more like a
dormitory than a cell. Ranks of fluorescent strip lights marched across
the ceiling, revealing a sea of comatose forms. The remorseless African sun had been beating down on that room all day. There was no
ventilation. There had to be one hundred prisoners in there, and all
seemed to be stripped to their underclothes, baking in the scorching,
suffocating heat.

Without a word the guards shoved the four of us forward and
slammed the door shut. There were disgruntled mutterings as we
tried to claim a patch of standing room on the bare cement floor. I
glanced around me. The walls may have been black once, but great,

dirty gray gashes showed where the paint had peeled and the plaster was crumbling onto the floor. Wary, hostile faces gazed out at me: blank expressions, predatory ones, the vacant stare of hopelessness.

Everyone was stretched out in the stultifying heat. Not a bare patch of floor was visible. For a few moments the four of us stood rooted to the spot like idiots, announcing our arrival as the new kids on the block. We were saved by the appearance of a guard.

"Roll call!" he yelled out, banging his baton on the bars of the door. "Roll call!"

There was a fetid shifting among the prostrate forms, as prisoners coalesced into some ill-defined, halfhearted action, but I didn't know what we were supposed to do. At Mosocho and Dagoretti the nearest to roll call had been the daily register, where a matron or teacher called out the names to check that all were present. Was it the same here? I wondered.

"You're new," a voice on the floor muttered. "Come on, you can make a five with me. Here."

The speaker was an older-looking guy, with hair going gray around the temples. He had a wide-eyed, permanently surprised expression, as if he couldn't understand how life had dealt him this hand. He was painfully thin, and I guessed he had been here for some time.

"Make a five with me," he repeated, shifting to make a little space. "Squat. They count us like that—in fives."

Sure enough a pair of wardens started to make their rounds, marking off each group of five prisoners. We huddled down with the old man. He muttered something to us.

"There's one hundred and twenty. Makes one hundred and twenty-five what with you four and the other new guy. That's less space for the rest of us, and less air to breathe, not that you can breathe in here. So no one will be too pleased."

"Is it always this hot?" I asked.

The old man shrugged. "Pretty much. They leave the lights on all night long. It's supposed to help stop, you know, *trouble*. But there's nothing will stop that, so better get used to it."

I nodded. "Get a lot of trouble, do you?"

"Some. More than enough. Not so much for an old one like me. You young guys need to watch yourselves." The man nodded in the direction of the door. There were four bulky-looking prisoners grouped around a fifth man, who had an indefinable air of authority about him. "See that guy? That's Charge. He's the top dog. He runs things in here. You getting too much trouble, you might want to have a word with Charge. He runs all the rackets in here—cigarettes, food, weed, the usual. You need something, Charge can sort it."

"Thanks, it's appreciated."

"You got any cash on you?" the old man queried.

"Some. Maybe. Why?"

"You might want to buy yourself a space by the wall. It's up to you, but . . . Your first night in prison, is it?"

I nodded.

"Take the advice of an old man who's been here awhile: buy yourself a space by the wall. Charge can sort it. That's what I did when I first got here, before the money ran dry."

The old man glanced at me with that wide-eyed expression of his. "What you here for?"

"Robbery."

I thought for a second of adding that we didn't do it, that we'd been framed, but I figured that had to be bad form in here. In here you wouldn't deny your crimes. I figured the more extreme they were, the more respect you'd garner.

"What about you?" I asked the old man.

"Squatting on police property," he replied.

"What?"

"I rented a house off a landlord," he explained tiredly. "The house was owned by a cop. The cop and the landlord had a falling out, and so the cop got me arrested and charged with squatting on police property."

"So how long have you been here?"

The old man shrugged. "I lost track of the time. A year maybe. Day by day, month by month, nothing ever happens. There's no way to count the days."

That evening we used a little of the money we had hidden on our persons to purchase a sleeping place by the wall. For a few shillings more, Charge found Ramjo and me a thin, stained mattress, and another for Mandeka and Stevo. As Ramjo and I slumped down on our jail bedding, a smell rose from the mattress of sweat, stale urine, and worse. Even so, I counted our blessings.

Those sleeping away from the walls were packed like sardines in a tin, bodies pressed onto the hard, bare floor. As one moved, all would have to move, for otherwise there was not even the space to roll over. Being in here was like putting a dog in a cage, I reflected, and throwing away the key. In fact it was worse than that, for when was a dog ever locked into a cage along with 120 other dogs?

In the heat and the harsh light I began to sweat. I felt rivulets running down my face and my shoulders, and I began to itch as well. It was then that I realized the mattress was alive. It was crawling with lice, and they were feasting on the newly arrived occupants of their home—*us*. That was another reason the prisoners stayed in their underclothes—to keep their one set of clothes lice-free, so that they might have something vaguely respectable to wear at their next court hearing.

I thought back over my life. What had happened to the dreamy kid who'd listened to stories of far-off times on Grandma Dorcas's knee? Once I'd had a world of opportunity before me, yet I had burned it up for this. In a rare moment of clarity I knew that I was the author of my own destiny, as are we all. As much as I might blame my absent or dead fathers for my fate, I knew I had only myself to blame. I had put myself here through my own aimless rebellion and misguided arrogance, and the quest for notoriety.

My train of thought was broken by a blow to the small of my back that sent a jolt of agony up my spine. Ramjo had taken the space on the mattress next to the wall, I the outside.

"Get the fuck out of my space!" a voice at my back snarled.

I spun around to face him. "What did you say?"

The guy got to his feet. "I said, get the fuck out of my space. I need the bathroom, so get the fuck out of my way."

He went to tread on my side of the mattress—on me—but by now I was on my feet. I could feel Ramjo at my shoulder, tensed and ready. The prisoner had his back toward me and he was heading for the toilet block, at the far end of the cell. He was a tall, bulky guy, doubtless one of the "big men" in our cell—the kind of guy who liked causing trouble, the kind of guy the old man had warned me about.

"Hey, hold up," I called after him.

He spun around. "What the hell does a new fuck—"

He didn't get to finish the sentence. Without warning I punched him twice in the face. As the guy went down among a crush of bodies, all hell broke loose. My specialty had always been the "start and stop" fight, which was pretty much how this had gone.

It took Charge and his band of strongmen to break up the melee and pull me off of the prisoner, whereupon we both were marched to Charge's end of the cell. Charge got the two of us facing him, with his bruisers on hand to stop any further trouble. Charge wasn't an overly big guy, but I sensed a keen intelligence and a ruthlessness behind his eyes.

"You're a new guy," Charge announced. "What's your name?"

"Hussein," I answered.

"Well, Hussein, you may have heard, I'm the Charge and I run things around here. And I don't take kindly to fighting. Take a look around yourself, Hussein. You see how packed it is in here. I don't like fighting 'cause there's no room for it, you see that?"

"I see it," I confirmed.

"So, you better have a good story for me, Hussein." He nodded in the direction of the other prisoner. "You pretty much KO'd Charley there. Put him down. Messed up a load of the brothers' sleep. So what's the reason, Hussein? And don't tell me it's 'cause you like fighting, 'cause then you're the kind of punk I don't want in here. Then you're the kind of guy we put in the sick bay or the wing for the insane, and you really don't want to go there, Hussein, you really do not. So why the fighting?"

"My buddy Ramjo got a mattress from you and a place by the wall," I replied. "I'm lying there and this guy punches me in the back, and starts bad-mouthing me. I ask him what the trouble is and he tells me to get the fuck out of his way. He walks all over our mattress, the one Ramjo just paid you good money for, and bad-mouths me some more. I don't take that kind of shit from no one. It's unnecessary. So I hit him."

Charge turned his gaze on the prisoner beside me. "Charley, there any truth to what the new guy's saying?"

"Yeah, but he's a new guy, Charge. You just don't expect that kind of attitude from a new guy. You expect a bit of cooperation, a bit of respect. I been here a year or more, and hell, Charge, all I wanted was him out of my way so I could get to—"

"I don't like what I'm hearing, Charley," the Charge cut in. "The new guy paid good money for that mattress. You disrespect the mattress, you disrespecting me."

"Ramjo bought the wall space, and Ramjo saw the whole thing," I added, before Charley could say anymore. "Ask Ramjo. He'll confirm what I'm saying. I'll respect a fellow prisoner, Charge, but I won't take shit off anyone for no reason."

"Charley, you want respect, you got to earn it, even from the new guys," the Charge announced. "But most of all you never disrespect my business, you got it?"

"Sure, Charge, I got it," Charley muttered.

"You got punishment duty, Charley. You're on toilet duty for a week. That's the end of the matter, Charley. It ends here and now with what I say, okay?"

"Okay, Charge," Charley muttered. "No problem."

"Okay, you go use the bathroom."

The Charge turned to me. "I run a tight ship, Hussein. You seem like a smart guy. Stay out of trouble. And you need anything—weed, tobacco, all that shit—you come to me, okay? You tell Ramjo and your brothers, they need anything, I'm the man."

A strange kind of democracy had developed in that cell, which made the unbearable slightly less hellish than it might have been. The Charge ran things with the threat of muscle behind him. He ran all the rackets with the cooperation of the bent prison guards, who took a cut of the profits. But actually Charge had been elected by his cellmates. If Charge were convicted or released, a new man would be elected in his place. Without that kind of iron system in place, the cell would descend into anarchy. God knows it was bad enough as it was.

The following morning there was roll call at six sharp. I'd slept fitfully, tortured by the lice, my body a mass of crawling and biting. I could feel them in my clothes and my groin and my hair, and I was covered in their red and itchy bite marks. The urge to scratch and scratch my skin until it was raw was all but irresistible. I couldn't imagine how I was going to endure their incessant chomping. Three months of that alone would be enough to send me to the wing for the insane.

The first to be called for breakfast were those scheduled to appear in court that day. Then the rest of us followed, a human mass surging down the zigzag stairwells in an effort to be first in line. Breakfast turned out to be a pint of watery porridge. But this wasn't the porridge of the Academy—oats cooked in water and milk with sugar and salt to taste. This was a thin gruel of boiled maize flour. It was gritty and tasteless, but my hunger drove me to eat. I managed half of it before my stomach started to revolt.

After eating we were marched back to our cell. There were none of the luxuries here of a prison in the West: no exercise time, no gymnasium or TV room, no movies, no prison bands or theater groups, no library or career development or study opportunities or computer rooms. Apart from the mindlessness of the lockdown, there was purely and simply nothing. You were locked into that cramped and baking cell all day long and left to grapple with the stultifying boredom and the complete pointlessness of what your life had become.

If prison was about punishment, then this was the ultimate.

During the day it wasn't the guards who locked you in, it was fellow prisoners. These were the equivalent of the school snitches, and here their way to feel the thrill of a little power was to act as guard on their fellow prisoners. The rest of the inmates called them the "Loud Mouths," for they were invariably the guys who loved the sound of their own voices but were soft as shit if it came to a showdown with a fellow inmate.

That first day I tried to observe things, to work out how the cell ran itself. Pretty quickly it was obvious that the lockdown was selective. The Loud Mouths let certain individuals come and go as they pleased. Of course Charge was exempt from the lockdown, for he had to be free to do his deals with the guards. I figured we'd have to secure for ourselves the same kind of freedoms if we were to have any chance of remaining sane.

We had one big advantage in getting what we wanted: we were a gang of four. Apart from Charge and his bruisers, there were few other recognizable groups as far as I could tell. Prisoners arrived mostly in ones and twos. The four of us had bonded over our years in Huruma, and I reckoned few would be willing to take us on. The least we should be able to do was muscle our way past the Loud Mouths.

I was sharing some of my observations with Ramjo and the others when I felt the first griping pains in my stomach. Whatever they had put in that porridge, I was cramping up real bad. I made a dash for the echoing space of the toilet block and washroom, and jammed myself into one of the cubicles, crouching over the squat-down toilet. The smell in there made me gag, but no more so than the stench of what I was voiding from my bowels.

I hadn't had time to shut the cubicle door, but it looked to be unusable anyway. It was half smashed up and hanging from its hinges. I'd been there barely a minute when two figures arrived at the far end of the line of cubicles. I heard them before I saw them.

"New boy in here with a cute little ass," a voice growled. "Where the hell's that new guy hiding?"

"Bend and pick up the soap, new guy," a second voice rumbled. "Bend and take the soap."

I heard the pad of bare footsteps across the cement floor. What the hell was I going to do? All I could think of was unleashing unlimited violence on whoever had pursued me in here, in the hope that the shock and surprise would buy me the chance to escape. I grabbed at my trousers and prepared to spring, when I heard a familiar voice echoing across the bare expanse of the toilet block.

"You looking for someone, brothers?" It was Ramjo. "You got a friend in here or something?"

"Who's asking?" the voice that had told me to grab the soap answered. "I ain't seen you around before."

"Our friends is our own business," the other figure added menacingly. "New guys got to learn some respect. And fast."

I emerged from the cubicle to see Ramjo, Mandeka, and Stevo facing off against two bulky prisoners.

Ramjo glanced past them to me. "Hussein, brother, you know these jerks or something? They friends of yours?"

"I never saw them around, brother."

Ramjo fixed the two guys with an iron stare. "Hussein says he doesn't know you, and the Mamba never lies. And we don't want to know you. So get the hell out of here."

The guys were bigger than Ramjo, but I'd never seen him back down in front of anyone. He was slower to anger than me, but his skill as a boxer meant he was a street fighter par excellence, and he seemed to know no fear. He had an aura about him of calm invincibility and it had the two prisoners spooked.

The bigger of the two licked his lips. "You hear that? New guy's ordering us out of our own bathroom. Trouble is we like it in here. This is where we bring us friends, like Huss—"

He didn't get to finish speaking my name before Ramjo's fist made contact with his jaw. The guy went down hard, the back of his head smashing into a cubicle door.

"I guess you didn't hear right, asshole," Ramjo snarled. "Hussein said he doesn't know you."

The guy on the ground was barely conscious and he didn't seem in any hurry to get up again. Now it was one of them against the four of us, and the guy who had ordered me to pick up the soap clearly didn't like his chances. We left him in the bathroom to clear up the mess Ramjo had made of his brother, and returned to our space by the wall.

Ramjo and I had been inseparable before prison; we had been like brothers. Prison brought us closer still. We would share that one mattress by the wall of the cell, and we would fight back to back for as long as it took to get us out of here. That was the brotherhood.

In the coming days we went about trying to establish some kind of regime that would keep us sane. Word had gotten around pretty quickly that the four of us would look after our own, and few seemed keen to take us on. That was fine by us. We didn't want trouble. All we wanted was to be left to our own devices for the three months it would take our case to come to trial, at which point we intended to get the hell out of here.

The four of us kept pretty much to ourselves. We ate together, shared any cigarettes we might have, and if we had none, we didn't beg or scrounge from the others. We kept our self-respect. We knew if we started borrowing from other prisoners, that would give them an opening to invade our space. We were civil to others, but we kept our own counsel. We four were different, and we wanted to be left alone. Respect that, and we'd behave. Cross us, and we'd take no prisoners.

The Charge seemed to notice this difference, and he respected it. The Loud Mouths soon understood that we expected free passage during the day. Outside the cell block we could sit in the shade of the prison wall and the relative cool of the "fresh" air, and while away the hours. We'd take our two mattresses outside and try to get the air and the sun into them, to blow away some of the stench and rid them of the worst of the lice.

We made a game of ludo, crafting a die from a chunk of cow bone that one of us had found in our stew, and using a flattened cardboard box as the board. We drew a cross on the board, the aim of the game being to roll the dice and race your board pieces toward the center of the cross. In time our ludo matches took on epic proportions, with many of the prisoners betting cigarettes, money, and food on the outcome. They'd gamble recklessly on combined poker and ludo matches and lose everything.

By contrast, Ramjo ensured that play on our side was strictly disciplined. We played to win, and we had a system of watchers and signalers put in place among the four of us to ensure that we rarely lost. We'd scrutinize another poker player's hand and signal the details to his opponent on our side. We were cheating, but we were doing so to look after our own. We reckoned all was fair in the dog-eat-dog world of the jail.

With the help of corrupt guards, people smuggled anything and everything into that jail. There were bottles of Kenyan gin and whisky, bags of weed, pills by the bucketload, and even bundles of fresh *mira*—qat, a local plant that is chewed as a speedlike drug. People gambled it all on the poker and the ludo games. They even gambled their clothes, and that was how we acquired extra boxer shorts and vests, so we could keep our main clothing relatively clean and lice-free for our pending court hearing.

We stopped using any alcohol or drugs. We went dry in that jail. Anything we earned from our gambling was used to barter for sleeping space on a wall-side mattress or better food from the kitchens. Those things would keep us sane over the next three months. And rest and sustenance might provide me with the energy and space to work out just how I was going to argue our defense at trial.

The only thing we had to make sure of when we spent time outside was to be back in the cell for the seven o'clock roll call. If the numbers didn't add up, there would be trouble. Guards turned a blind eye to select prisoners being out of their cells, but only for so long. After I'd witnessed a few prisoner beatings by the wardens, I realized I really did not want to be on the receiving end of the same.

One lunchtime the queue was moving forward in its usual sullen silence when the guy at the front complained that he hadn't gotten his full ration. The con serving had ladled it out but half had missed his bowl. Lunch was invariably *sukuma-wikki*, a boiled spinachlike green, but unless you had a man on the inside of the kitchens, all you'd get was a bowl of boiled water left over from the greens. The prisoner seemed determined to argue for his full ration.

"Give me my fair share," he demanded of the server.

"Move on," the server countered. "I have all these behind you."

"Not a half ladle!" the prisoner insisted. "A full share!"

I noticed a group of three guards moving in from the sides.

"I'm not moving till I get my full share!" the prisoner yelled.

The voice sounded familiar. I shifted slightly so I could see. It was the old guy with gray hair who'd given us the advice on our first night in the cells.

"Just move on," the server repeated, refusing to give him any more.

"I haven't had my—" The prisoner's last words were lost in the crash of a baton smashing against his metal bowl.

It went flying out of his hands, the contents spilling across the floor.

"Trying to get a double helping!" the guard yelled.

The baton came swinging down again, this time connecting with the prisoner's head. It made a horrible, hollow, wounding crack, as the bewildered older man collapsed to his knees. His hands went up to shield his face, as the three guards set upon him. Each savage blow of the batons was punctuated by a screamed insult.

"We'll teach you, old man—"

Smash.

"Crafty bastard needs a good lesson—"

Smash.

"A lesson—"

Smash.

"You'll never—"

Smash.

"Ever—"

Smash.

"Forget!"

Smash.

As the three guards beat the prisoner to a semiconscious heap, a fourth guard came forward and started taking photos on his mobile phone.

"Nice work," he remarked to the others. "He was an ugly old dog. Reshape his face a little . . . Hold it." A beat. "Click. There, something to remember him by."

It was sickening, but I knew that if any of us tried to intervene, we'd get savagely beaten. And I knew the guards could do worse to prisoners. This was nothing—just a little spontaneous violence to keep the lunch queue in line. If they took you off for a private, bespoke beating, they'd use bamboo poles and plastic strips to flay you alive.

Food was the trigger for everything. Unless you had an inside track in the kitchens, the meals you were given couldn't keep a grown man alive. Lunch was boiled vegetable water; the fat and the oil and the solid greens would never make it onto your plate. Every Thursday there was a meat ration, but without a guy in the kitchen, you'd get a single chunk about the size of a cigarette butt. I can remember the first few times sucking and sucking on that meaty morsel, making it last as long as I could.

Luckily, I've always been a small eater, but still I found myself dreaming about food.

"If you had cash and freedom, what would you buy to eat?" I'd ask Ramjo and the others. "Anything. You can go anywhere and afford anything. What'd it be?"

"Pilau," Ramjo would answer. "Every time, no contest, it has to be pilau."

Pilau was a kind of fried rice flavored with spices and with chunks of meat or chicken thrown in. It was one of our favorite meals when we had money and were out on the town.

"Nah, *matoke*," I'd counter. "Has to be *matoke*. Nothing fills your belly like *matoke*."

Matoke was a traditional, thick Kenyan stew made of cooked plantains, potatoes, and meat.

"Stop going on about *food*!" Stevo would complain.

"*Matoke* and pilau," Mandeka would moan. "You're just remind-ing me how hungry I am!"

I'd never appreciated the power of hunger before, and what it could do to a man. During those first few weeks I was always hungry, and the pain gnawed away at my insides. Hunger broke a number of the prisoners, destroying their sense of self-respect. Some of the younger inmates sold their bodies for extra food and were sodomized by the "big men," who used their money or their muscle to work some extra rations out of the kitchens.

The big men called those prisoners their "wives." Openly, like it was no secret what was going on and what they were doing to them. And some of those "wives" adopted feminine ways—the high-pitched voices, the lady-boy walk—as if they were embracing the role the big men had assigned to them. They went into the prison pretty much as normal young men; they came out completely broken, with their self-respect and their confidence smashed beyond repair. Or they'd try to kill themselves, or they'd end up in the insane wing, which was pretty much a death sentence in itself.

Two weeks into this brutal regime, I reckoned we could survive. We'd last the three months and it wouldn't break us. It hadn't taken long for me to stop thinking about home—Huruma, Umoja, wher-ever. Instead, for better or worse this place had become home. If you learned to forget life on the outside, you could survive here. If you kept lamenting all you had lost in the world, then this place would break you apart.

At the end of those two weeks our names were called at dawn roll call to be first down to breakfast. This was the day of our mention, and we would be going back to the courts. We donned our best clothes—the ones that we kept tied up in a plastic bag. Our plan was to see who turned up from the prosecution's side, and what they might have to say against us. None of us was changing his plea, but it might be an opportunity to help build our case for trial.

Dozens of us were crammed into the rear of the prison truck, and the shorter guys were half suffocating. But the tall guys like me could see out. As we pulled out of the prison gates, I slipped my fingers through the wire mesh at the top and gazed out at the teeming city. I raised my face to the wind of the truck's slipstream and inhaled deeply. I could smell the freedom out there and see the riot of life going on all around me, the people on the streets experiencing all that I was craving. It was torture.

The journey from the prison to the Law Courts followed a similar route to that used by the *matatus* serving Umoja. I knew most of the drivers, from my time spent touting for them. As the prison truck snorted and gasped its way through the chaotic Nairobi traffic, I saw faces I recognized. But not a person among them knew that I was here, in this truck, in that prison, or what my life had become. The city that had for so long been my own was now lost to me. This was as I wanted; I didn't want anyone knowing. But that didn't make it any less unsettling.

At the Law Courts the procedure was a repeat of our first appearance, as we were processed to go before the judge. I don't know what exactly I had been expecting from this mention—perhaps a mini trial. In fact, it was nothing of the sort. There were no prosecution witnesses, no statements from the police, no case presented against us at all. With little or no preamble, the four of us were shoved before the judge.

"*The Republic versus Obama and Others,*" he announced, tiredly. "At your last appearance you pleaded not guilty. Have you changed your plea?"

I shook my head. A part of me was tempted to ask him, *Why would we have changed our plea? We've been stuck in that hellhole for two weeks. How would that ever have made us change our minds?*

Instead, I answered respectfully. "No, Your Honor."

"You still plead not guilty?" he queried.

"Yes, Your Honor."

The judge repeated the process with Ramjo, Stevo, and Mandeka, and all confirmed their not-guilty pleas.

"Very well," he announced. "The defendants in *The Republic versus Obama and Others* plead not guilty."

And that was it. We were bundled into the prison truck and

driven back to jail. Every two weeks we had to appear for another mention, which was the exact repeat of the one before. Each drive through the teeming city was psychological torture, a reminder of all that we had lost. I witnessed inmates change their plea to one of "guilty" out of sheer desperation, at which moment they were given their sentence, which got them out of the Industrial Area Prison and into a place where they could serve their time.

In our prison, people had been on remand for years; imagine the sheer willpower needed to plead not guilty every two weeks for five years, when each time you knew it would send you back into the remand prison—a place close to hell. If I could have opted not to go to those mentions, I would have done so, for they were a pointless exercise. Worse, they were designed to break you and destroy any sense of hope you might have, thus forcing you to change your plea to guilty.

We could have changed our plea and banked on the fact that since we were first-time offenders the judge would show clemency and grant us a light sentence. A few years and we would be out. It was tempting, but I told myself I had to keep some faith in the justice system and those who presided over it.

Surely, the system had to balance the prosecutor's case with that of the defense, and in our case, we would be defending ourselves. The judge would know that he had the four of us with no legal training facing a state prosecutor, and surely he would balance that in the scales of justice and try to find where the truth lay. We had to live in hope, and the hope was that the judge would hear us. He seemed a reasonable enough guy, and who else were we to pin our hopes on?

For without faith in something, all hope dies.

CHAPTER 18

Survivor

ONE DAY MERGED into another, and the greatest enemy to the soul, apart from the hunger, was the boredom. Ramjo, Mandeka, and Stevo started to get some visitors after word got out to their families that they were here. When one of them was called by name and marched to the visitor facility, it was the highlight of their days. But for me there was none of that. I didn't want my family knowing that I was in here.

I was too stubborn to accept any help. I'd lost contact with my mother not long after she'd left for South Korea, and with Marvin, who I guessed was still in Nairobi living with our aunt. I couldn't face Auntie Sarah knowing that I had fallen this low, and have her throw the Obama family example in my face again. Before my arrest it wasn't unusual for her not to see me for days on end, but I had been absent for weeks now. I guess she had to know that I was in serious trouble, and possibly she even thought that I was dead. I had to hope that when she spoke to my mother by phone, she wasn't saying anything too disturbing. I couldn't allow the worry to consume me, for I had to concentrate on getting us out of there.

If my family had learned that I was in jail, I knew they would have found some way to hire me a lawyer. I didn't want that help, for it would come with the guilt and shame they would unload on me. In any case, I was convinced that we could win our own case at trial; I had an arrogant confidence in my abilities. I'd retained a certain erudition, and I knew how to charm and cajole. That was what the defense lawyers and the prosecutors seemed to do in court, and I aimed to do likewise.

As I saw it, our defense rested upon some fairly simple absolutes. First, we couldn't have committed the robbery, for none of us was present at the time and place of the crime. Our alibi was simple: we were in the drinking den enjoying some *changa'a*. Each of us could provide an alibi for the other. Second, the *changa'a* lady was an eyewitness who could corroborate our story. I intended to call her in our defense, plus her teenage daughter who'd also been present that day. Via Ramjo's relatives we had people working on the outside to secure their support.

Third, none of us had been in an identity lineup, so how was it that the robbery victim had identified us as the perpetrators? We'd never even met or seen the robbery victim. I intended to call the police as witnesses and cross-examine them. We hadn't been picked up at the scene of the crime, red-handed; we'd been arrested in an Umoja drinking den. So what was the chain of evidence that had led them to us? The more I thought about it, the more I hoped that I could demolish the prosecution's case, but I hadn't seen the evidence that they might introduce.

We had been arrested in February, and it would be May by the time we got back before the judge for our hearing. As the date approached, our hopes soared. I got all four of us preparing for the trial in great detail. Apart from my copious notes, I had each of us draw up a set of questions for the robbery victim. On the morning of the trial, we did our best to dress as respectfully as we could in our somewhat less lice-ridden clothes.

During the drive to the court I could smell freedom through the wire mesh of the truck. I was convinced that I would soon taste it for real. Curiously, I wasn't nervous. In fact, I was looking forward to arguing our case at trial. We were back before the same judge, and after six appearances for our mentions, the scene was getting to be somewhat familiar.

"*The Republic versus Obama and Others,*" the judge announced.

I was getting used to hearing that phrase. Hopefully today would be the last time.

"Prosecutor," the judge continued, "I presume you have your case ready to present to the court?"

"Er, well, as of yet, Your Honor, the complainant hasn't turned up, but I am confident that he will at any moment."

"Harrumph," the judge grumbled. He fixed the prosecutor with a stern eye. "Please ensure he gets here. I'll hear another case while we're waiting."

He consulted his list. "I'll hear *The Republic versus . . .*"

We waited all morning until the judge was about to break for lunch. There was still no sign of the complainant, and the judge was clearly getting irritated by the prosecutor's failure to deliver. I wondered what the outcome of all this might be. Did a no-show mean no case to answer? Did it mean that we would win by default? It ought to, for if the complainant couldn't be bothered to get to court, it was clear he didn't take seriously the charges against us.

Finally the prosecutor seemed to accept that the complainant wasn't going to show. Or perhaps there was no complainant, and that's why the prosecutor couldn't produce him. That would fit with the whole case being a setup. Finally the judge brought proceedings to a close, but he did so by delivering to us a shattering blow.

"I am adjourning the trial for three months," the judge announced. "At that time I expect to hear all the evidence in this case, including that of the complainant."

And that was it. We had barely gotten to speak a word. We were bundled into the truck and driven back to the prison. On the journey I stared out at the streets of Nairobi in a sullen silence, as did my three buddies.

Back in our cell one or two of the inmates asked us how things had gone. None of us felt inclined to say very much. There were those in the prison who liked to brag about what they were in there for. We weren't among their number. When people asked me what charges I was facing, I'd taken to not answering. It was my business, and I'd keep it to myself, just as I would now the outcome of the hearing.

If anything, the long adjournment of the case strengthened the bonds among the four of us. We now knew we were in this prison for the long haul; we'd have to rely on our fellowship to see us through. But some things would have to change. For a start we were running short of cash, and without money we couldn't keep our precious, lice-ridden mattresses and our places by the wall. We could gain a little cash in the poker and ludo matches, but what we really needed was an injection of funds from the outside.

There was only one way to get it: we would have to fall back on the support of our Huruma gang brothers. We sent out the word via our visitors, and the members of the gang responded. They came to the prison visiting room with rolls of cash hidden in places where the wardens would never find it and watched for an opportunity to get it to us.

At first, they passed cash to us in the form of a tightly rolled thousand-shilling note stuffed inside a section of drinking straw. The straw could be pushed through the wire mesh separating prisoner from visitor, when no one was looking. But the guards finally caught on to what was happening, and our visitors had to turn to more ingenious methods.

The starvation diet was taking its toll. Through Charge we had located a prisoner in the kitchen who could look out for us. In exchange for a little cash he agreed to pass us extra food, the best he could get his hands on. We knew that without extra sustenance, the months ahead would be horrible, and so the money the gang smuggled in went to a fine cause—to pay off our inside man in the kitchens.

In Kenya, *ugali*—maize mash—is usually served in all-you-can-eat portions the size of a brick, but in prison you got a ration a finger-tip deep in the bottom of your bowl. It wasn't enough for a child to live on. Over time the hunger gnawed away at your body and your mind until you just couldn't take it anymore. That's what usually broke people.

Some of the starving prisoners lost their minds, and ended up on the wing for the insane, from which few ever returned. Others ended up selling themselves as "wives." Others succumbed to one of the diseases common in the jail—tuberculosis, typhoid, or malaria—and were carted off to the sick bay, which was a place of death, not recovery.

If a young guy cracked and offered himself as a "wife," so be it. That was his decision. No one was going to intervene or to help. I remembered a saying from the Bible, one I had learned as a kid: *man was made to suffer*. In here, it had taken on a different meaning. In here, if you were a man and you couldn't endure suffering, then you had real problems.

In my mind the only family that I had now were Ramjo, Mandeka, and Stevo. We were family, and we knew we had to accept our lot and endure. *We are where we are,* we used to tell each other. *We'll deal with it. We'll survive.* By paying off that guy in the kitchen, we could make our days a little easier. We weren't putting on the weight we'd lost during our first three months, but we weren't losing any either. We could stay alive like this.

We established a routine. Compared to the claustrophobia of the cell, the toilet block and washroom was a huge, echoing space. Over time even the smell became bearable. We started a daily exercise routine. The four of us would take over an entire bathroom and shut it down to others. That became our makeshift gym. We'd do push-ups and sit-ups on the bare floor, and pull-ups on the doorframe. Each week we'd dream up a new exercise to keep body and soul together.

In this way we managed to survive until our second hearing. This time I went to court well prepared but with more pragmatic aspirations. I hoped we might have our day before the judge, but we all knew that this hearing might not be the end of these darkest days.

The hearing started out as a repeat performance of our first. The judge called the case, but the prosecutor admitted that the complainant had yet to arrive at court. Again, it became a waiting game, as the prosecutor kept insisting that the complainant would be there. With lunch fast approaching, I knew that the court was about to recess and that the judge would more than likely set us another trial date three months hence. We would be nine months in, having achieved absolutely nothing.

I raised my hand as I had seen others do, seeking the judge's permission to speak. It was a while before he noticed me, and each minute took us closer to another adjournment and a further three months in hell. Soon it would be a year, and still we would be trapped in this stultifying limbo. Finally the judge paused and peered at me over his glasses. He checked the listing on his desk.

"Obama, is it? You wish to make a point?"

"I do, Your Honor," I replied. "Am I permitted to speak in English? I find it a more suitable language to express what can be complex arguments."

In Kenya, English is the language of the ruling classes. Only those with a fine education can speak it fluently, and no one in that court had been speaking anything other than Swahili. My question was a ruse to unsettle the prosecutor, and perhaps even the judge. Of course, the judge had to accede to my request, for the language of the elite had to be his language too.

"Permission to speak is granted," the judge replied. He switched to English. "And please, of course you may argue your case in English, if you so wish."

"I'm grateful, Your Honor."

I paused for a second to marshal my thoughts. And then I began to outline my argument. "Your Honor, while I fully respect the process of the courts," I began, "I feel I must point out that this case has been going on for six months now. And with respect, Your Honor, that is six months in which little or nothing has been achieved. This is our second hearing, and again the complainant has failed to appear at court. How serious can this person's case be, when two times running he has failed to make an appearance?"

The judge was scribbling some notes on a pad in front of him. He glanced up. "Go on."

"Moreover, I fail to see any of the police present in the court, witnesses whom I had presumed would be central to the prosecutor's case. The police have apparently made no effort to appear. The complainant has apparently made no effort to appear. And this has happened not once, but twice. It begs the question, what serious effort is the prosecutor making to progress—"

"Objection!" the prosecutor announced, jumping to his feet and fixing me with a glare. "Accused has no right—"

"Overruled!" the judge growled. "Sit down, prosecutor. I trust you are following Mr. Obama's arguments? A fine thing to see such a command of English, don't you agree?"

He turned back to me. "Continue, Mr. Obama."

"Your Honor, on the evidence to date, I question the prosecutor's ability to progress this case. And the point is this, Your Honor: it is we who are suffering—myself and my three co-accused. We are the ones who are being hurt here; we the ones who are deprived of our liberty; we the ones who are being denied the right to argue for our innocence at trial. How much longer can this go on? Another six months, another year?"

"And so your argument is?" the judge queried.

"Your Honor, I'm not a lawyer," I replied. "But I presume it is within your power and that of the courts to give us some relief. I presume you have the power to dismiss this case, because the prosecutor has done nothing whatsoever to progress it—"

The prosecutor shot to his feet. "Object—"

"Overruled!" The judge glared. "In your seat, Mr. Prosecutor. In your seat."

He nodded to me. "Continue, Mr. Obama."

"I'm more or less done, Your Honor, but it seems to me there is no justification in keeping the four of us locked up when there is nothing happening on our case and apparently nothing is being done to progress it. We are, as you know, mounting our own defense. Your Honor, we cannot afford lawyers. But I am ready to argue my case today, this very minute, as I was at the last hearing. It is the prosecutor who has twice failed to deliver the complainant, witnesses, arresting officers, or a single shred of evidence."

The prosecutor shot to his feet again, but one look from the judge silenced him.

"Is it fair to keep us locked up under such circumstances?" I continued. "Your Honor, I believe it is not. Your Honor, we too have rights, and the prison we are being kept in is a torture chamber. If you saw it, Your Honor, well, you would, I feel sure, release us right here and now."

The judge finished scribbling his notes. He glanced at me. "And you speak for your three . . . colleagues, do you?"

I turned to Ramjo and the others, switching to Swahili. "You guys happy with what I said?"

"Sure," they confirmed, though they'd probably understood only half of it.

"Your Honor, I speak for us all."

"Thank you, Mr. Obama." The judge glanced at Ramjo and the others. "Is there anything you wish to add to what your co-accused has just outlined, and very eruditely if I might say so?"

Ramjo, Stevo, and Mandeka added a few words in Swahili, backing up what I had said. As they did so, I was aware that just about everyone in the courtroom was staring at me. My three gang buddies were equally bemused. I hadn't told them that I intended to argue the case in English. In fact, it was something that had come to me on the spur of the moment. But it was the prosecutor who was eyeballing me the most. I could feel his resentment and anger, and I have to admit that I was enjoying it.

"Mr. Prosecutor, I've noted a number of attempts to raise an objection," the judge remarked. "Do you have anything to say for the prosecution's part?"

"Thank you, Your Honor," the prosecutor replied. "You know, the complainant is sick and he is out of town. That is the only reason he is not here today. He wished to be here with all his being, to present the damning evidence against these four ruffians, but alas he is prevented—"

"Sick or out of town, which is it?" the judge snapped. "And which was it at the previous hearing, sick or out of town?"

"Your Honor, I will need to speak to the complainant to ascertain exactly which is the foremost problem—"

The judge silenced him with a wave of his hand. I'd noted that the prosecutor was struggling to conduct his argument in English. It was an effort not to crack up laughing. I raised my hand to speak.

The judge pointed in my direction. "Mr. Obama. But make it quick, for lunch will soon be upon us."

"Your Honor, what about the police officers who arrested us?" I asked. "Are they also sick and out of town? I note the prosecutor carries a walkie-talkie, via which he can communicate directly to the police, I believe. Why doesn't he call them and ask them to attend? Buruburu Police Station is but a fifteen-minute drive away. It should be a simple matter to get them here so they can give evidence and I can cross-examine them."

"Mr. Prosecutor?" the judge asked. "How do you respond to the defendant's query? It seems a very valid one to me."

"Er . . . I have no way to answer that at present, Your Honor."

The judge scribbled a few notes, then glanced at his watch. He cleared his throat.

"I am aware that time is against us," he declared. "So, in *The Republic versus Obama and Others*, my ruling is that I will adjourn the case for a further three months. However, let me make one thing absolutely clear." He fixed the prosecutor with a glare. "There will be no further adjournments. If the complainant and key witnesses fail to turn up for a third time, I will rule in the defendants' favor. Court clerk, please ensure that is clearly noted in the record."

On the drive back to the prison we were in an ebullient mood. We hadn't won this thing yet, but we were a big step closer to doing so. Three more months. *Three more months.* We had to presume that the complainant would fail to show for a third time because there was no complainant, and then it would all be over.

Ramjo, Mandeka, and Stevo were flabbergasted by my performance. None of them had known that I was fluent in English, for all I had ever spoken with them was Swahili or Sheng. They'd managed to get the drift of what I was saying, but more importantly they'd seen the effect my arguing in English had had on the judge and the court. It was clear what everyone had been thinking: *How can this guy have emerged from the Industrial Area Prison and be here on robbery charges, and yet he speaks English as well as any judge? How on earth can he do that? Who is that guy?*

Of course, once we were back in the prison, we were pretty much back to our old life, but at least we had something to sustain us now. In three months we'd be going back to court, and either we'd win our freedom or face whatever case the prosecutor might have cooked up. We were almost certain that there was no complainant, but even if we were tried and found guilty, we wouldn't be returning to prison without a verdict. It was the not knowing that was so unendurable.

I knew now what it was like to have my freedom taken away, as did all of us. The last six months had taught me the value of freedom, how truly precious it is. And in the private, quiet hours it was that which I dreamed of most—*freedom, sweet freedom*. It would have been better to be starving and free than be fed and in that prison. I'd rather have been sleeping on the streets and free than locked up in a cell. I dreamed of breathing clean air, of seeing the wide and open sky, of walking down a street and being free to cross a road. Simple things. Things that are only appreciated when they are taken from you.

I had changed in other ways too—ways that forced me to contemplate whether the brutal regime of the prison actually worked. We were not guilty of the crime for which we were accused, but for sure we were guilty of countless other crimes. It was only luck and our street skills that had kept us out of prison before. And there was a part of me that felt as if we were getting what we deserved. I felt a sense of contrition, a sense that my doing time here was justified by all the wrong that I had perpetrated in the past. Of one thing I was certain: I did not ever want to end up here again.

Shortly after we'd returned from that second hearing, I caught Ramjo in a moment of peace and quiet, something rare in that hell-hole.

"Damn, Ramjo, I've got to change my life," I declared quietly. "No way do I want any of this again."

"Brother, there isn't a day goes by when I'm not thinking the same," he replied. "It's the end of the road, brother. No more fucking around."

"So what d'you plan to do? When we get out of this shithole, I mean."

"I got to find a legal way to make a living. Enough is enough, Hussein. You seen what this place does to people. End up here again and you're a dead man."

"You know what I've realized, Ramjo? It's the system has the power. It's the system has the power to do anything it wants to us. And we're like nothing."

"I tell you something, brother. Without you we'd have been lost. If you hadn't argued that case like you did, who knows how long we'd be rotting in this place. Who knows . . ."

"What about the others?" I asked. "What're they planning?"

"Same as us, I guess," Ramjo replied. "Once we're out of here, it's the end of the fellowship, brother. Whether we like it or not, we're all going our separate ways."

"You got any idea what you'll do?"

"I dunno. I'm not sure. Teacher maybe. Something working with kids, and keeps me out of trouble. That was always you and me, Hussein; we were always good with the kids. You remember? No matter how bad we got, we were always trying to help the kids."

For a moment I thought about Scram, Cheesy, and Jeff, and the other street urchins for whom we'd tried to do a little good. Ramjo was right. If there was one thing that I had always loved, one thing that I'd always had time for, it was the kids. I remembered Ramjo and me kicking a scraggy ball of plastic and string around the wasteland in Umoja, the wild cries of the kids ringing in our ears. Under our tuition, Scram and his team had gotten pretty good. Maybe working with kids wasn't such a bad thing to aim for.

But there was one crucial difference between me and Ramjo and the others. We had never discussed it, but Ramjo, Stevo, and Mandeka were a couple of years older than me, and they had all had the good sense to complete their high school studies before getting into the gangster life. They had passed their exams and so they had prospects, whereas I had not one qualification to my name.

For our third trial date, word got out that we expected a result. When we arrived at court, the four of us were led into a packed courtroom. The Huruma gang had taken over the public gallery. The judge called the case, and it was hardly a surprise when the prosecutor announced that the complainant hadn't quite made it yet but was expected to arrive at any moment. I raised my hand, and this time I didn't ask if I could speak in English.

"Mr. Obama." The judge smiled. "Permission to speak is granted."

"Thank you, Your Honor. I'd like to respectfully remind the court of what the ruling was last time we were here. This is our third hearing, and it is supposed to be the very last adjournment on this case. Once again, we have no complainant, and I presume no evidence, and so there is a gaping black hole where the prosecutor's case should be—"

"Objection!" the prosecutor declared.

The judge fixed him with a withering gaze. "You object, do you, Mr. Prosecutor? *Interesting.* I'd be most interested to hear upon what basis you think you can object. So, let's hear it."

"Your Honor, I can assure you the complainant will be here by two o'clock sharp," said the prosecutor. "Two o'clock and not a moment later, and then we will have a complainant here to give evidence."

"And do you think the court should wait for the man to deign to put in an appearance?" the judge demanded icily.

"Your Honor, I would crave the court's indulgence—"

"Would you indeed?" the judge cut him off. "And when exactly do you think the court runs out of patience? This repeated failure to present a case makes a mockery of the court process, not to mention the justice system."

The judge turned to me. "Mr. Obama, I see you have your hand raised. What would you have to say on the matter of the complainant's punctuality?"

"Your Honor, if I'm not mistaken, it is more than the complainant alone who is absent from the court," I replied. "Once again I see no police, no other witnesses, and I conclude that the prosecutor has again failed to persuade them of the importance of attending your court. Your Honor, this is unacceptable, for it pertains to our liberty, and to justice being done. Those are important concepts, Your Honor, and they should be valued and respected."

"I have to say I am inclined to agree with you, Mr. Obama," the judge mused. "You and your fellows have been deprived of your liberty for, what is it, nine months now? And still I have yet to see a single scrap of evidence or to hear from a single witness to suggest that that is either fair or just. Mr. Obama?"

"Your Honor, it astounds me. I'm at a loss for words. As you say, the prosecutor's failure to present any case at all makes a mockery of the court process."

The prosecutor jumped to his feet. He was red in the face with rage. "Your Honor, I must object—"

"You will do nothing of the sort!" the judge thundered. "Back in your seat. Any objections you may have are overruled." The judge grabbed his gavel and banged it down hard on the desk in front of him. "By the authority vested in me by this court, the case of *The Republic versus Obama and Others* is dismissed," he declared. "You four men are being released under section two-one-zero of the Kenyan Penal Code . . ."

The judge's last words were lost in our cries of delight and the roar that went up from the gallery as the Huruma gang broke into round after round of cheers. For a second the judge looked dumbfounded, and then he let a slow smile of satisfaction creep across his normally gray features. For a moment I caught his eye. He returned my gaze with an odd look, as if for a second he was trying to fathom who on earth I was.

And then the moment was lost, and we were being manhandled out of the courtroom by the guards. My last sight of the court was the prosecutor bolting out of the door ahead of me, his face like thunder. We were propelled into the processing cell for the last time, where our few possessions were returned to us.

And then I took my first step into freedom and onto the teeming streets of the city. The four of us, along with the rest of the Huruma gang, headed directly for the nearest cafe. Ramjo ordered pilau and I ordered *matoke*.

That was our first, delicious taste of freedom, precious freedom.

CHAPTER 19

The Awakening

I WAS RELEASED from prison on September 11, 2003. Jail was the worst time in my life, the lowest, darkest days, and it changed me forever. Prison was a place of utter hopelessness and despair, but if I hadn't gone there, God only knows what might have befallen me. I might have been shot dead, either by the police or by rival gangsters, and my family might never have known what had happened to me. I would have become one of the ghetto's countless disappeared.

I had learned a vital lesson in prison: the true value of freedom.

The day after my release I managed to get a phone call through to my mother. Apart from sporadic reports on my fortunes, I had been lost to her and my brother Marvin for three years now. And for the last nine months I had disappeared completely. I was horribly nervous about speaking to her, for I didn't know how she would react.

It was wonderful to hear her voice again, but I then realized what I had put her through over the last year. She had been worried sick at my disappearance, the silence had been so deep and sustained. She had feared the very worst. Now, with this phone call, it was as if I had come back from the dead. She was both furious and hurt that I hadn't told anyone what had happened to me.

"Why didn't you get a message to me?" she demanded. "I'd have found a way to help. We'd have bailed you out. Hired a lawyer. Saved you those nine months in jail. You put us through torture, George. Why didn't you let anyone know?"

"I'm sorry, Mum," I told her. "But, you know, you wouldn't have believed that I was innocent. You'd have helped, but decided I was guilty at the same time. That's what I didn't want. I didn't need that, Mum. I couldn't have dealt with it."

My mother accepted what I told her. She loved me still and had never stopped doing so, in spite of everything. When others in the family had reached the conclusion that I had to be dead, my mother had never once put me out of her mind or given up on me. She was the best mother in the world.

During the time that I had been rotting in jail, my mother had met and married an African American man and moved to the United States of America. His name was Hosea Dixon. When I had called my mother I had done so via a number in Atlanta, Georgia. She told me that I had a little sister now, named Chrissie. She was two years old and quite beautiful, and everyone was proud of her. She put little Chrissie on the phone so we could share a few cooing words.

Before finishing the call, I promised my mother that the wild days were over. I had been too wild even to remember my own mother, but I would be a lost son no more.

I spent the following year driving a *matatu* around Nairobi. It was the first legal work that I had ever had, and it was the best that I could manage with no qualifications. I earned around ten dollars a day, which was a decent enough wage by Nairobi standards. It allowed me the time and space in which to think and to reflect upon all that had happened. Mostly I was just happy and content to be free.

Among the noisy, street-roaming touts that helped me fill up my *matatu* were Scram, Cheesy, and Jeff—my street kid friends from the Umoja wasteland. They'd never forgotten me, and it was good to be around them again. I kept in touch with Ramjo, Mandeka, and Stevo, but the fellowship was well and truly over. Each had chosen his own path on the straight and narrow. Sure enough, Ramjo was training to be a teacher, and I was glad that he had found his way and was happy.

Most of the rest of the Huruma gang had followed our example and stopped surviving from crime and doing the worst drugs. They'd seen what prison had done to us, and none of them wanted any of that. They'd found legal work of one kind or another and had stopped drinking and doing drugs. In a way, those nine months in jail had done us all a big favor. We'd meet once in a while, but it was mainly for a quick catch-up and then back to whatever work we were doing.

The gang wasn't my family anymore; the streets weren't my home. I was standing on my own feet now and trying to rebuild the bridges that I had burned—especially those with my family. I was twenty-two years old, life was simple, and the worst of the stress had gone. I was more sorted out than I'd been since the age of fifteen, when my life had imploded so spectacularly. I was trying to learn whatever lessons the past seven years might teach me and trying to find a new way, a new path.

I started easing myself back into normal society, having the kind of informed conversations that Kenyan citizens are wont to have. During my time locked away, war had broken out in Iraq, one spearheaded by "Coalition forces," chiefly from the United States and Britain. But as I read about the ongoing struggle in the Kenyan newspapers, the reasons given to justify the war made no sense to me. If it was all about destroying missiles and weapons of mass destruction, why hadn't the Coalition invaded North Korea, or Iran for that matter?

Alternatively, if it was all about removing a dictator from power and ushering in democracy—the other reason given to justify the invasion—why hadn't the Coalition invaded Kenya's southern neighbor, Zimbabwe? If there was a crazed and autocratic dictator who needed removing from power, Robert Mugabe was it. If there was one people who truly needed "liberating," it was the Zimbabweans, but no one in America or Britain was talking about an Operation

Zimbabwe Freedom. Mugabe was a far worse despot than Saddam, but no one was threatening Mugabe with "regime change."

The only difference I could see between Iraq and North Korea or Zimbabwe was that Iraq had oil. Depending on which way you looked at it, Iraq was cursed or blessed with oil. I didn't care about the religious aspects of the conflict, for I didn't feel I shared a religion with anyone just then. But the humanitarian side of it was all wrong. The idea that all people in the world were equal, the sense that regardless of where you were from, you had the same rights—that had been badly damaged by the war in Iraq. One casualty of the Iraq War was our universal equality.

A few months after my release from prison, Christian reopened contact with me. He had called one of my aunties and told her that he wanted to meet. He was still living in Kenya, working for a French-Kenyan cultural exchange organization. I was of two minds about seeing him. On the one hand, I still resented his leaving. On the other, I was on a new path and thought perhaps the time was right to do this. I agreed to meet him at his downtown office.

It had been seven years since I'd last seen Christian. He was meeting a very different person from the fifteen-year-old kid whose life he had last known, but he himself was pretty much the same. Seven years hadn't aged him greatly, and in many ways his life was as it had been when he was the father figure in our household. We tried to make some small talk for a while, playing catch-up on the missing years, yet I didn't have much to say.

What was I to tell him—that after his leaving, I'd flunked school, become a gangster, done nearly a year in jail, and that now I drove a *matatu* for a living? I related the basics of what had happened, but it sounded like a catalogue of such utter failure, and it seemed to rub salt into the wounds of his leaving. Perhaps sensing this, Christian tried to apologize for disappearing from our home, and he apologized for the lack of contact over the intervening years.

We parted promising to stay in touch and to try to rebuild the closeness that we had lost. But even as we said those words, I think we both knew that it was a pipe dream. I had heard Christian's apologies, but I guess I didn't really feel them in my heart. Too much time had gone by. We'd grown apart, and I felt it was time to let it go. His influence in my life was gone, and it was time to move on. The contact petered out on both sides, and I think we knew that it was best that way.

But as I closed the door on the relationship with my white father, another seemed to open. Auntie Sarah was older now, and her once tireless energy was fading. As time went by she became weaker, and it was clear that she was ailing. I felt at home in her compound, where I had spent most of my time since leaving prison. Recently, one of her sons, Rajab, had come to live with us in Nairobi, so that he could help care for his sick mother.

Rajab was her fourth child, and he struck me as a kind and caring guy. He sported round, wire-rimmed spectacles and he had a gentle, studious manner, but there were hidden strengths beneath his quiet exterior. He was in his late thirties, and he had a wife and three children upcountry, in Eldoret. He'd requested a transfer with his work so that he could spend weekdays in Nairobi, looking after Auntie Sarah, and travel to Eldoret to spend the weekends with his family.

Pretty quickly Rajab and I became close. What drew me to him was the aspect of his nature that he shared with Auntie Sarah—his plain-talking, no-nonsense ways. He started chatting to me about my life and the wider Obama clan, and telling me stories about my father. His intention was to straighten me out and give me some grounding in life.

My father had died when Rajab was twelve, but Rajab remembered him well. Via his recollections, we set about trying to rediscover my father and build a clearer picture of who the man was. Rajab spoke to me of my father's kindness and his big heart and how he'd helped people whenever he could. In a way he had been generous to a fault, even helping those who had refused to help him when he was in need—people my father would have had every right to treat as his enemies.

He was a man of principle, perhaps naively so in a country as venal and corrupt as Kenya. He was a man of strong beliefs who'd tried to stand against the rot that was setting in, and to live the dream of a post-independence Kenya run by its own citizens for the good of the country. Had he still been alive, he would have kept me on the straight and narrow, Rajab explained.

Under my father's tough love I would have stuck with my studies, Rajab assured me, and gotten to where I had wanted to go. He told me that there was a lot of my father in me. Beneath the angry young man and the rebel without a cause there were common traits that united us—not least of which were my intellect, my stubborn willfulness, and my natural affinity for the underdog.

It was hard for me to know how much truth there was in all this, but Rajab struck me as being scrupulously honest and caring. I felt I could trust him. Auntie Sarah had told him all about my lost years, so there was little I felt I needed to hide. Everyone on my father's side knew that I had been no angel.

Rajab was a good listener, as well as frank in his opinions, and I felt he was like an older brother to me. I talked to him about the lost years and the reasons why my life had fallen apart, as I had never done with anyone else.

"What's past is past," Rajab told me, once I had finished saying all that I had to say. "What's done is done. It's time to sort your life out. You have the one chance to do so, which is now, and you have to grasp it with both hands. You've taken the first step; you've stopped doing the bad stuff. Take the next one; start building a future."

"But how?" I asked him. "I left school with nothing. No qualifications. You can't do anything in this country without an education."

"The best time to plant a tree is twenty years ago," Rajab replied, "but the second best time is now. It's never too late, Hussein. Go back to school. Study hard. Get some qualifications behind you and start your own business. You can still make something of your life in Kenya. Trust me, with a brain like yours you can."

"You really think so?"

"I do." Rajab gave me one of his looks. "But listen, Hussein, let's not pretend you haven't walked on the dark side. You have. You flunked high school. You did the gangster stuff. You did prison. There are people who'll never let you forget that. They'll keep punishing you for all you did wrong."

"To hell with them," I muttered. "Why should I care?"

"You shouldn't," Rajab confirmed. "But you need to be aware of it. There's even some in the family who may judge you. Some of your half brothers and sisters—they may try to deny you as one of the family. It's better to know that and to be prepared."

"Why? What's been said?"

Rajab shrugged. "There's just been some bad, stupid talking I've heard around Nairobi, that's all. People saying your mother wasn't really your father's last wife, and so you aren't his son. It's just an attempt to deny you, Hussein. But if you know about it, you can be ready for it. Forewarned is forearmed."

"And you, Rajab? What do you think?"

A smile lit up Rajab's face. "Hussein, you're the image of your father. *You are him*—just a young, angry version who's had nowhere to channel that anger. And there's lots of people that won't judge you, Hussein. They'll accept you for who you are. Those are the people you need to be around—the kind of people who will support you."

I smiled. "Guys like you, you mean?"

Rajab shrugged, good-naturedly. "Who am I to judge anyone? My life took a different path, that's all. It doesn't make me any better than you."

That was the most important thing for me. Rajab accepted me for who I was and without judging.

Rajab had a fine job as an economist with the Ministry for Livestock, but he was also studying for an MA. He told me that it was my father's example as the first truly educated Obama that had inspired him. My father had studied in Hawaii and at Harvard, Rajab explained, and he had been an economist, just as Rajab was today.

"It's a pity you never got to know him," Rajab remarked. "He was a generous man and an inspiration. But you can still make him proud, Hussein. Start doing something with your life, before it's too late. The ancestors are always watching." Rajab was a Muslim, but he believed in a relaxed and mellow kind of way. And beneath the surface of his faith were scattered enduring facets of Luo traditional belief—like the influence and presence of the ancestors.

I started accompanying Rajab to the mosque in Huruma. There was no flash of light or lightning conversion; I just felt happier exploring Islam. I felt more grounded in the faith of my fathers. I felt at home somehow, or at least as if I was coming home. But in a sense this was more about identity and family than belief per se. I prayed to Allah to protect those whom I was close to, and to help me find my path. In that sense praying in the mosque didn't feel particularly different from praying in a church.

Although I was drawn to Islam, I believed that there was only the one God and that he was the same for all faiths, for otherwise there had to be a whole pantheon crammed full of gods, one for each religion in the world, and that struck me as being impossible. I had chosen to call the prime being Allah; a Christian would call him God, but in the end we were all praying to the same entity. Stressing religious differences struck me as destructive and futile.

Invariably, it seemed, religion was dictated by place of birth, family, or tribe. If you were born in Pakistan, you were more than likely a Muslim; in Tibet, more than likely a Buddhist; in Rome, more than likely a Christian. That was even more reason to believe that there could only ever be the one God, and that any worship in any religion that was conducive to the greater good had to be to him. That was my innate sense of things, and it was the place that I had reached on my spiritual journey where I was happy.

Rajab and I might share a beer or two in Huruma, and we'd often take Idi with us, Auntie Sarah's youngest son. In our eyes alcohol wasn't strictly forbidden—or *haram*—in Islam. How could it be? In the Koran, Issa—Jesus, in the Bible—is one of the holy prophets. He not only drinks wine but at one point he turns water into wine. It seemed to me that if wine was good enough for a holy prophet, it should be okay for us. It wasn't what went into your body so much that mattered, it was what you did in the world.

A year or so after I'd gotten out of prison, I decided I was ready to learn again. I enrolled in the Unity College of Professional Studies.

I was starting a five-year course, at the end of which I'd get a diploma in mechanical engineering. I still drove the *matatu*, so I could earn money to live, and my mother was sending me funds to help with my studies. At the end of the course I would do as Rajab had advised and start a business. It wasn't quite being an airline pilot, but it was realistic, and at least it was something.

In this moment I realized the difference between myself and 99.9 percent of the slum dwellers: I had the family contacts—some of whom lived in the affluent, developed world—from whom I could secure help. The vast majority of the ghetto dwellers did not. Even the meager money required to pay school fees—a few hundred dollars per year, per child—was beyond most of them. I had asked for—and had been given—a second chance. Most in the ghetto had never been given any chance at all.

It was hardly surprising that the ghetto was the source of the prostitutes who plied Nairobi's streets and nightspots and the angry young gang members who robbed and carjacked indiscriminately. Having been one of their number, I understood the anger and desperation that breed such behavior. And having grown up in relative privilege, I knew the other side as well—the sweetness of having all the things of which those who live in the ghetto can only dream.

I felt an intense loyalty to the Huruma community. The people of the ghetto had shown me what true friendship was, for they had stuck with me during my darkest days. They had demonstrated an openness and a unity that you rarely find in the world outside. In the streets of upmarket Nairobi, the neighbors don't even know each other. But in the ghetto everyone knew everyone, and of course your neighbors were your friends and you'd help them if you could.

One of our Huruma neighbors might ask us for a little firewood for their cooking stove; for some sugar, detergent, or maize flour. These were small but important things, and if we had the ability to help, we would give. Everyone needs a little help once in a while, and in the ghetto we knew the favor would be returned.

The ghetto dwellers would keep an eye out for strangers and watch each other's properties. With houses so closely packed together and so flimsy, fire was a big risk, and if one person's house burned, the fire could sweep through the ghetto like an inferno. Mostly, fires were caused when a cooking stove was left unattended or someone left a candle alight. We knew the fire brigade wasn't going to make it to the ghetto, so we had no one to rely on but ourselves.

On one occasion thick black smoke billowed out of the house next door to Auntie Sarah's place. We knew that the neighbor was away at work, so the house was deserted. We smashed down the door and formed a human chain passing buckets of water to douse the flames. A crowd gathered in the smoke and the sweltering heat, and people thundered about with buckets in all directions.

Rajab was at work in downtown Nairobi, so I stood at the front of that human chain with a niece of Rajab's, called Mwanaisha, who had recently come to live with us in Huruma. The heat was unbearable, and by the time the owner had returned we were completely exhausted, our clothes and faces blackened with soot and smoke. The homeowner found his door kicked in, and the inside of his home a scorched and stinking mess, but the fire had been reduced to sodden smoldering and at least the structure of the house had been saved.

The Kenyan elite try to pretend the slums don't exist. They are ashamed of how some of their fellow Kenyans live. But it wasn't like that for me. I valued life in the ghetto. I valued people's vibrancy and the sheer belief in life that kept them going. And then there was the camaraderie. People cared for each other in ways the outside world has no concept of. In the generosity of those who had nothing, I realized that the ghetto had a lot to teach the wider world, if only it would listen.

Huruma is a Swahili word that means "mercy." The Huruma ghetto had taken me in when I was at my lowest ebb—showing me its mercy—and I wanted to give something back. I talked it through with Rajab, and he told me that I should get involved with the community. It would help me build my self-esteem, and it would give me a sense of purpose in life. My first step was to join the Pendo Moja— "One Love"—Youth Group. There were maybe a dozen youth groups

in Huruma, and One Love covered my area, so it was the natural one
to sign up with.

But there was another reason that I chose One Love, and that
was a girl. Shiyayo was a fellow ghetto dweller in her early twenties,
and for as long as I could remember she'd been Auntie Sarah's next-
door neighbor. To most outsiders her house would look pretty much
like mine. It was made of galvanized iron and wood tacked together
on a patch of waste ground. Inside it was cramped beyond belief, five
or six sharing a bed and a sofa and sleeping on the floor.

Shiyayo was petite and dark and striking, and she was something
of a sweetheart. For ages we seemed to have admired each other from
a distance, never quite becoming "an item." She was the archetypal
girl next door, and I was forever getting Auntie Sarah to send me over
to her place on some errand.

"Auntie, send me across to get some sugar from Shiyayo's uncle's
place," I'd tell her.

She'd give me one of her looks. "But we're fine for sugar, Hussein.
We don't need any."

I'd give her one of my winning smiles. "I know, but just send me
anyway."

"Why, you're sweet on one of those girls, aren't you?" she'd snort
derisively. "Like father, like son. He was one for the women too. Well,
if you have to. Here, go get this sugar bowl filled."

Shiyayo was also a member of the Pendo Moja Youth Group.
That alone was enough to make me want to join.

CHAPTER 20

From the Streets

PENDO MOJA HAD a pretty simple set of goals, most of which were designed to counter the kind of gangster influences to which I had fallen prey. It worked with the ghetto youth to combat the ills that plagued the ghettoland—most specifically crime, prostitution, drugs, and alcohol abuse. And it aimed to provide alternative, legal sources of income to the young unemployed of the slums.

I was twenty-three years old when I joined Pendo Moja, and I was excited to be helping the ghetto kids. But I also wanted to help myself. I hadn't stopped drinking, and I still smoked a little weed. It was nothing like I had done during my lost years, when I had regularly drunk and smoked myself into a comatose wreck, but still I reckoned the support of the youth group might help keep me on the straight and narrow. I didn't want to backslide. I couldn't afford to. I might never pull myself back up again.

My first project with Pendo Moja was environmental cleanups. Huruma was plagued by makeshift garbage dumps that doubled as informal toilets. There was one on a patch of waste ground between Auntie Sarah's place and Shiyayo's, and when the wind blew in the wrong direction it made life less than bearable. Pendo Moja received some small funding from aid organizations. With that it had managed to buy a handcart, some rubber gloves, and rubber boots—the bare necessities for setting up a garbage patrol.

I started taking the kids on house-to-house garbage collections, for which each household was supposed to pay fifty shillings—less than a dollar—a month. The garbage we collected was sorted into recyclables—glass, tin, copper, plastic, paper—which could be sold to dealers, with the remainder taken by cart to a collection point, from where the garbage trucks would haul it away. At the end of the month the fees paid by the households were pooled together and split among those doing the cleanup operations.

The money was a rare source of legal income for the slum children. I really gelled with those kids. Doing this work reminded me of the time I'd spent with Scram, Cheesy, and the others in Umoja, only now I had something really useful to offer. I could talk to the kids on their level and relate to their lives. I never tired of entertaining them and keeping their spirits up during the monotonous and sometimes downright revolting work of the garbage rounds.

There were many decades' worth of rotting garbage and ordure to remove. I took to carrying a rag football with us. Whenever things got really bad we'd take a break and have a kick around. There was nothing like a wild game of soccer to lift the kids' spirits. The cleanups offered them a tiny sliver of hope—the promise of doing some good, of helping sort out their own communities, and of earning a little regular income.

But I didn't kid myself that this was any kind of cure-all. Sometimes, children would turn up for the garbage patrol almost too weak to stand. I'd find out they hadn't eaten for two days, because their father or mother was ill and had no money to buy food. I'd get them a plate of rice and lentils from a roadside stall and maybe a Coke, and tell them to join the patrol when they had the energy to do so. Kids turned up for work battered and bruised, and unwilling to tell me what had happened. No one wanted to miss a garbage patrol and the few shillings they would earn.

Perhaps it was the closeness we forged with the kids, but for whatever reason Shiyayo and I seemed to shine together whenever we were out cleaning up the garbage. It was hardly the most romantic of settings—she and I bonding over the rubbish heaps—but it was about as good as it got in the ghetto. There was precious little chance of finding romance here anyway, for there was never the space or the privacy to do so. But over time we grew close, and over time we shared with each other some of our life stories.

From her earliest memories Shiyayo's life had been one of struggle. In many ways hers was a typical story of the ghetto, but what struck me most powerfully was how it contrasted so baldly with my own. Had Shiyayo lived my life, I knew for sure she would have made great things of it by now.

Shiyayo was from the Luhya tribe and hailed from a town in the west of Kenya. She was the last of five children, the only daughter, and her father's favorite. He worked for Kenya Power and Lighting, and he brought in a half-decent wage, but he died when she was four years old. She had few memories of him, and her recollections of childhood were mostly of growing up in a one-room shack in Kisumu as her mother struggled to raise her and her four brothers.

After her father's death the in-laws had taken all of his possessions away. As with the Luo, that was the tradition of the Luhya tribe. Renting a one-room hut was all that her mother could then afford. She scraped together a living by knitting cushion and seat covers, and by braiding women's hair. From the little she earned, she had to pay the rent on the house, buy food and clothes, and pay school fees. Eventually Shiyayo's brothers were sent to live with their grandparents in the rural area. There was never any money to visit, and so Shiyayo grew up not knowing her siblings.

Shiyayo was sent to Lake Primary, a state-run school in Kisumu. Her favorite subjects were English, Swahili, and history, and she regularly ranked among the top five students in the class. In her history lessons, she, like me, had been taught that all Kenya's problems were owing to the British colonial legacy. The British had come to Kenya and stolen all the wealth and the fertile land and turned tribe against tribe. At the time Shiyayo hadn't known any better, and so she had believed what she was taught.

She used to dream about becoming a flight attendant, just as I had dreamed about becoming a pilot. She had first got the idea during a school trip to the airport, when she'd seen the young women in their smart uniforms looking so pretty, with their fine jobs that took them all over the world. It struck me that in another life and another reality we might have met on an airliner as opposed to a garbage heap in the ghetto.

She told her mother about her dream to be a stewardess. Her mother backed her wholeheartedly, for she was determined Shiyayo would have a better life than her own. If Shiyayo was out playing and she hurt herself, her mother would scold her to be more careful: *if you want to be an air stewardess, how can you do so, with scars all over your body?* But as Shiyayo grew older, she realized that she'd not been blessed with her father's long limbs. She took after her mother, who was rather short. She knew that flight attendants had to be tall, so she had to find another dream to sustain her.

Many of her fellow pupils wanted to be nurses or teachers or lawyers. Shiyayo decided she would happily settle for something like that—a good job where you didn't have to be tall! But when she was eleven years old, her mother died. Ill with diabetes for some time, she was one of the many victims of the lack of free medical care in Kenya. Shiyayo went to stay with her mother's youngest sister, who lived nearby and was married with two children. She took Shiyayo in and cared for her as if she were her own.

Shiyayo's aunt became like her mother, her cousins like her family. Shiyayo called her aunt "mamma," and her aunt called Shiyayo "mammy"—a nickname originally given to Shiyayo by her grandmother. Shiyayo studied hard for her KCPE exams and was overjoyed when she came in second in her class. But the teachers were forever bending the rules for the wealthy children, and Shiyayo's aunt was asked to pay a bribe to secure her a scholarship for secondary school.

Then relatives on her father's side complained that Shiyayo should be living with their side of the family, for in Luhya tradition, as with the Luo, the father's side "owned" the children. Shiyayo was sent to live with an uncle in Nairobi, and that's how she first came to spend any time in Huruma. That uncle was a kind man, and Shiyayo warmed to him immediately, but he was married to a tough and cruel woman, who started to beat Shiyayo.

One awful day she tried to strangle Shiyayo. The neighbors heard the screaming and rescued Shiyayo. They hid her in a church, until money could be found to send her away from Nairobi. They put her on a *matatu* and the driver was given strict instructions not to let her off until she reached the marketplace near her auntie's home. From there she knew the way home.

Her auntie had cried and cried when Shiyayo had been taken away, and now she was welcomed home again. But there was still the problem of paying the bribes to get Shiyayo into a high school, which her auntie couldn't afford. Shiyayo had missed more than a year of her studies, while being bounced around among relatives who didn't want her. Then another uncle—one who claimed to be impressed with Shiyayo's KCPE results—offered to fund her through high school.

Shiyayo went to live with him and his family, in Nairobi. There she was fed and clothed and had a roof over her head, but the uncle's promise to provide her an education seemed to have been forgotten. She had become an unpaid domestic servant, but at least no one was beating her anymore. Over time she became an unpaid nanny to that uncle's grandchildren. After a year or more of that, the children's parents asked Shiyayo what she most wanted from them as a thank-you. Shiyayo asked her cousin to help send her to high school.

Shiyayo was then seventeen and had been out of the school system for five years. She was sent to St. Anne's, a Catholic boarding school situated not far from her hometown. She loved it there and grabbed the opportunity to learn with both hands, so grateful was she to be given the chance to get an education. During holiday times she went to stay with her cousin to help look after the kids, but that was a small price to pay for the gift of learning. One year's fees at St. Anne's was twenty-five thousand shillings—less than five hundred dollars—but it was still a large amount of money for most Kenyans.

In her final exams she scored a C class, which was a fine result. She was more than happy. "They'd sponsored me all the way, for four years," Shiyayo told me. "It was a lot of money, even for them. I'll never forget them for helping me like that."

When she graduated from high school, Shiyayo was twenty-one— the same age as I had been when I was locked up in a Nairobi jail. She thought she might try for a nursing career, but it cost around five hundred dollars a year for three years' training. She had no way to pay the fees. Instead, she spent a year looking after her cousin's kids, to repay their generosity in putting her through high school.

But then the husband lost his job, and the family couldn't afford to feed everyone. Desperate for somewhere to live, Shiyayo went to visit her kindly uncle living in Huruma. By now he'd divorced his violent wife and he welcomed Shiyayo in. He lived with his three kids in a one-room shack with a tin roof and bare brick walls. It was already crowded, but he welcomed Shiyayo in, as she had nowhere else to go.

Her uncle slept on his bed, which was curtained off from the rest of the room, while Shiyayo took one sofa and the eldest cousin another, with the two young boys on a mattress on the floor. Anyone who needed to use the loo in the night would have to step over sleeping forms and out into the yard. And in the daytime they'd cook on a charcoal stove, eat, chat, and watch TV all in that one room.

"My uncle was generous to have invited me in," Shiyayo told me. "He explained that my mother had been kind to him when he was little. Over time, he became something of a father to me, and everyone started to call him my dad. If he hadn't taken me in, I don't know what would have happened. Maybe I'd have ended up on the streets.

"When I see street kids now, I can understand how they got there," Shiyayo continued. "It's only ever a small step away. And for those who commit crime—stealing bags, snatching wallets, pickpocketing—I can understand how they end up doing that. If

I'd ended up on the streets, I'd have tried to look for work, because I'd have tried to resist falling down that slippery slope. But there's never any guarantee."

I thought of Scram, Cheesy, and Jeff, and how Shiyayo might have fared living life on the edge. It was rare to find a girl on the streets, and only the truly desperate ended up there. Shiyayo was right: her uncle had been truly generous to invite her into Huruma and to give her a home. But I knew of families in similarly cramped conditions who'd taken in orphaned kids who were no relation to them at all. To see that orphaned child wandering lost was a wound to the whole community.

With no funds to study nursing, Shiyayo had to find a job and start earning money. She got work in a beauty salon, doing pedicures and manicures. She'd work six days a week and spend Sunday morning at a Catholic church that served Huruma. In the afternoon she did chores around the home, and then Monday was the salon again. But the salon work was commission-only. Some weeks she earned nothing at all, and she'd have to ask her uncle to loan her a little money to pay for the *matatu* journey to work.

Even in a good week she might earn only a thousand shillings, less than twenty dollars. The bus journey alone would cost twenty-five shillings a day, and double that if it was raining, when the demand for seats was far higher. Some days she couldn't afford to eat. Some days the girls in the salon would boil water, add tea and sugar, buy a loaf of bread, and that would be their lunch. And on a day when she was feeling really wealthy, she'd treat herself to a plate of rice and beans.

Her uncle scratched out a precarious living by selling secondhand clothes in and around Huruma, yet still he found the time and the space to coach ghetto kids at football. His example had inspired Shiyayo to try to give something back and propelled her to join the One Love Youth Group and the garbage cleanups in Huruma.

"Once I got used to living here, I kind of liked it," she told me. "I felt safe and at home, and I got used to the security of having people around me the whole time. I'd spent so much of my life alone and insecure, and I love the community and sense of unity here. People are truly united. They're for each other. Does that make sense to you?"

I told Shiyayo that it did. I knew exactly where she was coming from.

"There's a magic in the ghetto," I told her, "a togetherness, 'cause we're all in this together. In the ghetto we share the same wall, the same door, the same air, the same food, so you have to know your neighbor and to get on with him. No one is ever alone. That's one of the upsides: you'll never be alone in the ghetto. That's guaranteed."

"Never be alone." Shiyayo smiled. "That's good. But you know, there's a lot of downsides. How many times have I come back from the salon, gotten off the *matatu*, and heard gunshots? Not knowing what to do—do you go into the ghetto, or back onto the bus? You don't know where the gunshots are coming from or who is shooting. Is it safe to sneak through the darkened alleyways, or will you run into a gunfight on the way?"

Two years ago it would have been me doing the shooting, as Shiyayo well knew. She'd heard about the darkest parts of my past, and we'd been neighbors for long enough for her to have seen me at my worst. Hearing the story from the other side made me realize just how messed up those years had been, for when I was playing at being the badass gangster, others—innocents like Shiyayo—had been in mortal fear for their lives.

"And then there is the *community*," Shiyayo continued. "You can't just come here from somewhere outside; you have to have a way in. People defend each other and look after their own. We know all our neighbors. We talk to them and greet them, and borrow stuff from each other. Those are qualities that aren't found anywhere else in Nairobi."

I told Shiyayo that she was right, that there was a singularity about this place. We were a tribe—the ghetto tribe. We were united and unbreakable in our spirit.

"My uncle has spent his whole life living here," Shiyayo concluded. "And you know what? *He's happy.* He wouldn't live anywhere else. He wouldn't want to. And I don't know if I'd want to either."

In a way I was the same. For better or worse, Huruma had become my community and my home.

As time went by, Shiyayo and I grew closer still, but she was more like a sister to me than a lover, and I'd given up hope of our ever becoming an item. In a way I was fine with that. There was a sense that we both were orphans—I with my father literally and my mother geographically—and we needed each other more as family than we ever did as lovers.

Shiyayo was still trying to stay positive, still searching for a source of funds for nursing school. Her uncle was doing his best to help her find someone to sponsor her. But for Shiyayo, like most ghetto dwellers, the next shot of pain was always just a step away. No matter how hard you tried to clean up the ghetto, some horrors always seemed to be with us.

One evening we heard a shot ring out. It sounded close by. A crowd peered out from behind windows and corners. Shiyayo was there with her young cousin, and we watched, aghast, as a policeman opened fire on a figure lying on the ground. We recognized the victim. He was a young slum dweller who had tried petty crime but couldn't hack it. He was too soft to mug anyone or to make a career out of crime. He was a layabout, but no villain.

The gun-wielding policeman was notorious. We knew him by his nickname—"Killer"—and he was infamous for gunning people down. The young man on the ground had been shot in the leg and was pleading for his life. The crowd was growing in size, but everyone was afraid of Killer and his gun. Killer yelled at the wounded man to walk, and we watched as the terrified young guy stumbled to his feet and tried to drag his wounded leg after him, his face a rictus of agony and fear.

Killer goaded him up the hill that led toward the police station. The crowd followed, restive and angry. Killer could sense our anger and our threat. Yelling at the wounded man to go faster, all of a sudden he just lost it. He shot the man in the other leg, and he collapsed onto the ground. Some of the crowd rushed forward, but Killer brandished his pistol at them.

The wounded man had fallen beneath a tree that had a makeshift streetlight attached to it. The next stage of the horror played out under its glare. The young man was lying on the ground with both hands up, begging for his life. We could hear his cries of agony and his pitiful pleas for mercy. But Killer was lost in a crazed bloodlust.

He shot the wounded man in the body, putting bullets all over his torso. Then he bent forward and placed the muzzle of his pistol against the young man's head. For an instant the ghetto seemed to hold its breath, and then Killer pulled the trigger, the shot ringing out through the muffled darkness and echoing around the crowded alleyways. That bullet blew the guy's head apart in a shower of blood and brains.

Killer had executed him—that innocent, layabout youth—at point-blank range. As we surged forward howling with rage, Killer raised his pistol and began firing over us, driving people back. At the same time he pulled out his radio and started yelling for backup. Killer retreated up the hill and was soon lost in the shadows. We searched the blood-soaked body, just to make sure that the dead ghetto youth didn't have a weapon on him. There was nothing. No gun. No knife. Nothing.

Before we could move the corpse, Killer was back with reinforcements. We retreated to a safe distance and watched as the police taped off the "crime scene." Then they pulled out an old jacket and placed it over the body. And in the inside pocket of that jacket they placed a pistol. They didn't try to hide what they were doing. They planted that weapon on the body of the dead man in full view of us all. They wanted us to see how powerless we were in the face of their death squads. This way, the next time they did a roundup in the slums, they knew we wouldn't dare to stand against them. They did those roundups on a regular basis, forcing all those arrested to pay a bribe. If you didn't pay, they'd haul you down to the station, and the least you could expect was a good beating. The amounts paid were tiny by Western standards—the equivalent of just a few dollars—but they were crippling to the victims.

In the cold-blooded murder of that innocent youth, the police sent out an unmistakable message: *We can do anything*. The killing was reported as a case of "an armed criminal resisting arrest." Not for the first time, Killer went unpunished. He'd killed before, and on some days he'd carried out multiple executions in and around the slums. He clearly got a kick out of killing and getting away with it.

In the ghetto, we were deprived even of the right to life. The injustice left me burning with rage. If I had gotten my hands on Killer, I know for sure that the Mamba would have resurfaced, and that I would have ripped his head off. Sensing the rage and resentment burning in the ghetto, the police transferred Killer to another area. If they hadn't, there would have been war.

In the face of such horror and injustice, it was hard to remain positive. But in the ghetto something always happened that would lift you up again.

CHAPTER 21

The Brotherhood

I WAS TALKING to Shiyayo and some of the other veterans of the Pendo Moja Youth Group. We'd reached a stage where we felt the group was too large and unwieldy; we'd outgrown it. We wanted to do things that pushed the envelope, that were truly innovative, and we couldn't do them at One Love. So we decided to set up our own community organization. The name we chose for it was the Huruma Centre Youth Group.

We called it "Huruma Centre" because we wanted it to be the heartbeat of the ghetto. Shiyayo was proposed as the group's treasurer, because she was the only girl among us and we felt we could trust her to handle the funds. But as things turned out, her work in the salon was taking up too much time, and she was forever missing meetings, so Lawrence took her place. He was a part-time *matatu* tout, so he had more time to dedicate to the role. John, a young and ambitious guy born and brought up in Huruma, was made the chairman, and I took the role of coordinator.

This was a job I felt particularly suited to. My responsibilities were to organize functions and events and programs and to raise money for some of the more unusual things we were planning. For example, one of the movers and shakers in the group, a guy called Clyde Kagondu, was a member of the Kenyan Air Force tae kwan do team. He was a part-time tae kwan do instructor, so our idea was to find a place where we could enroll the ghetto kids in tae kwan do classes. It was my job to find such a venue and raise the money to fund the training sessions.

We formed an arts and culture section, which was about teaching the ghetto youth the traditional dancing and music of their tribes. I wasn't so closely involved in that, for I was a useless dancer, but I did manage to find a venue. There was a hall in central Huruma that belonged to another community organization, and they agreed to allow us to use it for our cultural activities. I also had my eye on that hall for the tae kwan do classes.

Rajab was an informal adviser to our group—an older pair of hands to help steer us. He suggested we start a handicrafts section, so the ghetto kids could make curios to sell to tourists in and around Nairobi. The kids could keep the wire and tin they scavenged from the garbage heaps and use it to fashion toy cars, animals, and Maasai figures.

One member, John Ukiru, could make stunning bangles, necklaces, and earrings out of copper and twisted wire. He wanted to teach the ghetto kids his skills, but you needed money for the raw materials, so once again, it was all down to raising cash.

John's life was a lesson in how the untold suffering of the ghetto dwellers pulled people together and inspired them to help others. John hailed from the same tribe as Shiyayo, the Luhya. Soft-spoken and gentle, he had been born and bred in Huruma. He was a fifth child, but by the time he came into the world, his parents had divorced. John never knew his father—he died not long after the divorce—and the most he ever saw of him was a photo his mother kept.

It was up to the mother alone to raise the five—subsequently seven—kids in the family. Their house was a one-room shack with a tin roof, from which his mother brewed and sold *changa'a*. She'd sell her brew at fifty shillings for a liter, or by the tot, to drinkers visiting her home. At the end of her day, she would prepare a meal for the family on a charcoal stove in one corner of their home.

Every day they ate *ugali* with greens, and often they survived on just the one meal. Come evening, John's mother and the kids would clear away the cooking things and place a single mattress on the floor, next to their mother's bed. Five, six, and then seven kids would sleep crosswise on that one mattress, with a cloth on the floor to rest their legs where they hung over the edge.

When John started to go to the nearby Kariobangi North Primary School, his mother had to pay school fees for five children, and all from the money she made from selling *changa'a*. The family was desperately in need of a bigger house, but she couldn't afford to rent one and pay the school fees. She chose to give them all an education, and so they were forced to remain in that horribly claustrophobic home.

John's first school uniform was a hand-me-down from his older brother, Timothy, and it was worn thin, with patches over patches. The wealthier kids used to laugh at him in his scruffy clothes. Having a pair of school shoes was another impossible dream, so John went to school barefoot, which led to more teasing. John tried to turn the other cheek: as far as he was concerned, it was a luxury just to be getting a little learning.

John's was a relatively happy childhood, for he hadn't known anything else in his life. He loved school and was a gifted pupil, his favorite subjects being English, Swahili, and history. Once or twice a month the mother might buy the family a treat—a hunk of goat or cow meat, which she would boil into a thick stew. John and his siblings would each get two lumps of meat on their plate, swimming in juices. On Christmas day the big treat would be a plate of spicy chicken with chapati, and a soda to share.

John's mother was a Christian, and every Sunday she'd troop the kids to the local Huruma church. John would pray quietly that when he grew up he'd be rich and successful, so he could help his mum. He'd rent her a bigger house, but still in Huruma so she could be with her family and friends, and she'd be able to stop selling *changa'a*. John prayed that he would become a doctor or a pilot, so he could ease his mother's later years.

But it was not to be. At age fourteen John graduated from primary school, but there was no money to pay the thirty thousand Kenyan shilling ($500) secondary school fees. His older sisters had gone to high school, but neither finished before the money ran dry. John and his elder brother, Timothy, started selling peanuts that their mother roasted at home. They'd wander around Huruma with a tin tray piled high, each rattling a handful of coins to attract customers.

John's friends laughed at him now that he had become a street hawker. He felt shamed by what he was doing, but he knew his mother needed the money. He did this work for two long years, and then his elder sister's husband made John his informal apprentice in his jewelry business. John quickly realized he had found his calling, for he was crafting more unusual and beautiful jewelry than the man he was working for.

The tools of the trade were a vise to hold the wire, and pliers of various shapes and sizes to bend, weave, cut, and twist. You also needed dextrous hands to thread beads and fashion clasps, and John had a gift for such work. But what he didn't have was the money to buy the tools. He continued working for his brother-in-law, who sold the jewelry in the Nairobi tourist markets, paying John a hundred shillings a day for his labor.

Meanwhile, John's older brother was learning to drive, his mother paying the fees in installments whenever she could afford to. Once Timothy passed his test, he got a job as a *matatu* driver and started to earn some real money, around a thousand shillings a day. That enabled Timothy to help his mother and to pay the youngest siblings' school fees, and life became easier for the family. But after a year driving the *matatu*, Timothy had a quarrel with his boss and was sacked. He got a new job driving a pickup truck.

One evening some guys in Huruma asked Timothy if he would collect some cargo for them. Timothy drove to the spot and waited in his pickup as the goods were loaded aboard. Suddenly there was a commotion outside, and the truck was surrounded by an angry mob. It turned out the goods were stolen, and the guys who had hired Timothy had fled.

The crowd dragged Timothy out of his cab. He feared the mob would beat him to death. The police arrived and beat the hell out of Timothy anyway, refusing to believe a word of his story. They caught the gang of thieves, and all of them, including John's brother, were thrown into the cells. They were charged with robbery-with-violence and spent two years on remand in the same prison where I had languished. One of the gang died, and during his monthly visits John saw Timothy losing hope and wasting away.

John and his mother attended the trial, but the family couldn't afford to hire a lawyer for Timothy. When the inevitable guilty verdict was given, John's mother fainted, and her health never recovered. John's brother was sent to the Kamiti Maximum Security Prison for fifteen years. The prison conditions were inhuman; he was starving to death before John's eyes. John tried to smuggle in a little money, but he had to bribe the guards to get just a few shillings to his brother.

Deprived of Timothy's earnings, the family fell on hard times. Two years after Timothy was jailed, John's sister Violet died from tuberculosis. There was no money to pay hospital fees. John's mother passed away in 2005 from a suspected heart attack. John was devastated, and when he told Timothy the news, his big brother tried to hang himself.

John and his remaining siblings were now orphans. As the new head of the family, John had to provide for his younger sisters, and all from the 150 shillings a day he was earning from the jewelry trade. John joined the Pendo Moja—One Love—Youth Group about the same time I did. He'd gotten into the garbage patrols as a way to earn a little extra money on weekends.

But more tragedy befell John's family. His youngest brother, Patrick, was twenty-one years old and a giant of a man. He refused to listen when John tried to steer him away from a life of crime. Patrick was sucked into a group of ghetto gangsters of the kind that I had been when I was the Mamba. One day John heard that his brother had been shot. He went to the city morgue along with his surviving sisters, and there they found Patrick's body.

The others in Patrick's gang hid for many days, and it was only when they returned to Huruma that John learned how his brother had been killed. Several gang members had been arrested by the police during a robbery. The police had driven them to an isolated patch of bush, where Patrick was the first one ordered out of the vehicle. He was marched into the woods and forced to lie facedown. The other gang members heard gunshots, and at that moment they managed to break free and flee.

John went to the police to try to find out the truth about who had killed his younger brother and how. But the police told him to go and investigate it himself, and if he secured any evidence of police wrong-doing, then they might open an investigation. John had no money to pay for private investigators or lawyers, so there was little more he could do.

Yet still he didn't lose hope. John became a founding member of the Huruma Centre Youth Group, and in his jewelry-making skills he saw a way to give kids in the ghetto a trade—something to stop young boys and men from ending up in the kind of trouble that had befallen his brothers. He planned to form a cooperative with those he taught, to sell their necklaces and bangles and earrings in the Nairobi markets. All he needed was a small amount of capital to buy the tools.

We drew up a budget of 17,500 shillings—some $250—and I managed to find a Western sponsor to put up the funds to start the handicraft workshop. John proved to be a fine teacher—patient and gentle and calm. Fifteen kids from the youth group enrolled in the handicrafts program. With the workshop up and running, John had achieved his dream.

Shiyayo contributed a much-needed feminine slant to the youth group's plans and aspirations. She proposed a beauty contest for the ghetto girls, and a modeling competition. She joked that she couldn't take part, for she was too short and too shy, but that those with the beauty and the courage to show it off should be given the chance. We'd call in the Nairobi press to report the event, and that might open a route into a golden future, for modeling was a dream career for the ghetto-dwelling girls.

The youngest kids in the youth group were in their teens, but my real desire was to expand our scope and draw in the street kids, for my experiences from my earlier life had opened my eyes to their plight. I felt as if I owed them.

We had many dreams and aspirations, but to make them a reality we needed money. I hoped I had the education and the erudition, plus the charm, to talk people into providing resources to support our work, because a lot of hopes rested upon my ability to raise some cash. In the face of such daunting challenges, my life took an unexpected turn that opened up a new promise of opportunity.

Two years or so after my stint in prison, I was at home in Huruma, watching the news on CNN. We had a tiny TV in our cramped living room, with a sofa and comfy chair squeezed before it so we could gather as a family to watch. On the wall facing the TV were some calendars, plus a few family photos—formal, black-and-white shots taken in a Nairobi studio.

There was one of Auntie Sarah dressed in a frilly white blouse and looking deep into the camera with her unyielding eyes; one of Rajab, complete with mortarboard and gown, at his university graduation ceremony; and one of my father in heavy, dark-rimmed spectacles, hands clasped in studious and pensive contemplation. That picture epitomized the spirit that Auntie Sarah had so often evoked during my lost years—the spirit of my father's serious professional, academic, and personal endeavors.

I was hoping to catch some sports news on CNN, for like many young men in Kenya I was an avid follower of world soccer, and especially the English Premier League. I'd been a fan of the top British club Chelsea FC for a decade or so, and I rarely missed a match on TV. But mostly the channel was showing international news. I must have drifted off, for I awoke to Auntie Sarah jabbing me in the ribs.

"You should be watching this," she hissed, pointing at the screen. "Your big brother in America . . ."

I rubbed the sleep from my eyes and stared at the screen. The news report was about a promising young black lawyer and politician getting elected to the United States Senate. That man was Barack Obama, the former head of the *Harvard Law Review*, and my brother. As I watched the story unfold, I felt a thrill of excitement. I hardly knew my American brother and had heard little of him since the first time we had met, eighteen years before. Even so, I hadn't forgotten he existed, and in large part that was because others in the family used to talk about his ongoing success in the USA.

But this topped it all. Having an American senator for a brother—that was really something.

"So, what d'you think of that?" Auntie Sarah asked, once the report was done. "An Obama makes a senator in the USA!"

"That's pretty damn cool," I replied, smiling.

She glanced at the photos on the wall behind us. "Your father would have been truly proud of his American son, you know that?"

"Sure. He's an inspiration, achieving all that he has."

"I knew that he was going places," Auntie Sarah continued. "He came over to visit us once, you know, here in Huruma, and I recognized the spirit that he had within him. He was always going to be a big man. Like you are—he's your father's son. He's your father's son. He's got that same sharp mind, and ambition." She rolled her eyes at me. "Only difference is he didn't fritter away his youth and his education misbehaving."

"He's still an inspiration to me," I told her. "If *he* can make it like that, well, you never know. He's an inspiration to push ahead with my studies. Like Rajab says, it's never too late."

Auntie Sarah gave me one of her looks. "You're right, Hussein, and it's good to hear you talking like that. It's a good way to look at things." A smile lit up her normally stern features. "And you know something, Hussein? You really have changed. I'm proud of you, you know that?"

Barack Obama *was* an inspiration to me, but at the same time I recognized the gulf between us. I was the ghetto-dwelling rebel who'd blown my education, he the American law school whiz who was making a name for himself in politics. I was his youngest half brother, but the only time we'd ever met was during that brief encounter at my primary school. For a moment I wondered what it would be like if we were to see each other now. What, if anything, did we have in common? Sure, we were brothers, but our lives were worlds apart.

It was hard to know what we would talk about, for what were the ties that bound us, apart from a father whom neither of us had ever really known?

CHAPTER 22

Barack, My Brother

MY LIFE WAS far more settled than it had been during my teenage years. I was doing my thing with the Huruma Centre Youth Group, driving the *matatu* to earn a little cash, and pressing ahead with my studies.

Then, in the spring of 2006, I got my second chance to meet my American brother. This time he was coming to Kenya with his family, and he was doing so partly in his role as a U.S. Senator. A part of me hoped that by meeting him, an American politician and a man of real stature and substance, I might boost my ability to secure funds for what we wanted to achieve in Huruma. I might even talk him into providing some assistance.

Uncle Ezra, one of my late father's cousins, drove me up to the Obama clan's homeland in Kogelo, a small village in rural western Kenya. It was my first visit to Grandma Sarah's place—the grandma that I shared with my American brother. Their compound reminded me of Grandma Dorcas's, where I had fished and laughed and swum and fought with my cousin Omondi, for it was typical of a rural Luo homestead.

I was nervous during the drive to Kogelo. We would be staying for the one night only, so if I was to make an impression on Barack, this was my chance. I wondered what my American brother might make of me. I was the kid from the slum, the Obama son who had been a gangster and served time. He was a U.S. Senator and Harvard graduate. If there was a leading light in the Obama clan, then he was it; and if there was a shadowed place that no one liked to talk about, then I guess that was me.

I tried not to let it bother me. I didn't know him, but he was still my brother. And I was proud of his achievements, just as all in the Obama clan were.

We arrived in time for the welcome feast that had been prepared by Mama Sarah, as everyone called our Obama grandma. The compound was crammed full of people. Barack and his family were there, together with the U.S. ambassador and other dignitaries, plus dozens of Obama relatives.

My American brother was unmistakable—a tall, lean, bronze-skinned guy with close-cropped hair. Even at a distance he projected an air of supreme confidence, as if around him everything might be possible. Yet there was still something familiar about him from when we'd first met, something that tugged at painful memories of a different time, when I was a young boy and everything had been possible in my life.

I reckoned that I wasn't going to get much of a chance to talk among the crush, and I didn't feel confident enough to thrust myself forward. After all, who was I to interject myself into such a crowd? So I ate and drank the good food on offer, by which time much of the evening was done.

It was then that my cousin Pascal, one of Auntie Zeituni's sons, seized the moment and led me by the elbow to where the senator— my brother—was standing. Pascal and I knew each other passably well, and he said that it was silly for two long-lost brothers to be in the same room and not to have the chance to talk.

"Senator, this is your other brother," Pascal announced. "He's come all the way to Kogelo to greet you."

Barack thrust out a hand, a smile of welcome crinkling the corners of his eyes.

"George, isn't it?" he remarked. "It's good to see you again. It's been too long."

"Yeah, I'm George." I smiled, taking his hand in mine. "It's good to see you too . . . brother."

There was a ripple of gentle laughter around the room, before he introduced me to some of the others who were standing nearby, including his wife and children.

"So, how've you been over, how long is it, twenty years?" he asked.

"Something like that, yeah," I replied. "I've been good, and I've never forgotten you."

He laughed, half turning to face the others. "Gee, it's good to see the little brother of the clan."

There followed a series of comments from the onlookers as to how we looked so alike, but to me the remarks felt somewhat hollow. Barack was smart and fresh and groomed, whereas I was pretty much direct from the dust and dirt of the ghetto. I felt as if I were meeting a superstar, but a superstar who was still my long-lost brother.

Barack Obama had last seen me when I was five. Yet something in his manner told me that he was curious—curious about what I had lived through and seen and survived, and about what I had learned from it all. And I was curious about him and the life that he led. He moved in a different universe, one of high power, populated by high achievers. That world was one that I could barely conceive of. It was so alien, yet still it fascinated me.

I wondered if it was simply an accident of our births that had bequeathed this gulf between us. I wanted to ask him what he thought and explore this idea, but there was little private space in which to do so. He seemed to want to hear about how I was managing in life and how I was surviving, and I got the strong impression that he cared. As we talked, we tried to hold this special moment between us.

"So, how are you keeping, George?" he asked, half turning me away from the crowd so we could share a few, quiet words. "I hear it's been tough. But you're doing good now?"

"Yeah, I'm trying to study, to catch up on some of what I've lost," I told him. "I saw the reports on CNN of your election to the Senate. You know, you're a big inspiration to me. You've kind of helped me turn my life around."

"Thanks, George, that's good to hear." He paused for a second, as if lost in thought. "And you know something, I never forgot you either. That little kid I ran into at his primary school, all dusty from playing a wild game of football."

We both laughed. "You remember that?" I asked him.

"Sure I do. I wrote about it in my book."

"I know. I've read it. *Dreams from My Father.*"

"You did? What d'you think of it?"

"Well, truthfully, I read it a couple years back to find out some more about my father. Our father. It was kind of great for me on that level."

"So did you learn much about him?"

"Enough to know that I'd have liked him to be alive when I was growing up." I smiled. "Enough to know that I'd like to have known him."

The more we talked, the more I felt as if I'd like to get to know my brother better, but the one thing that we didn't have that evening was time. I got the sense that he wanted to achieve greater things in his life, and perhaps even try for the U.S. presidency. I was in awe of such ambition, and almost embarrassed to raise the issue of Africa's dispossessed and the slums. If I could just get him alone and have a few private minutes, then I felt certain that I could reach him, even if the world of the ghetto was so far removed from my American brother's reality.

But most of all I'd have liked to have asked him more about his memories and impressions of our father. They shared the same name—Barack Hussein Obama—and that had to signify some kind of unique bond. Were our father alive today, what would he have thought of Barack, I wondered, and what would he have thought of me?

I was left with the indelible impression that Barack was the kind of guy who would accept me for who I was regardless of the past. I departed Kogelo the following morning with a strange mixture of emotions. On the one hand I was glad that we had met. I felt just a little bit closer to this brother whom the clan so admired. But I had also failed to talk to him about the issues in the ghetto that Shiyayo, Clyde, John, and I were trying so hard to address.

Back in Nairobi I received a message that he wanted to meet again. I left Huruma and caught a *matatu* into central Nairobi. Barack and his family were staying in the Serena Hotel, an island of manicured serenity between Nairobi's Central and Uhuru Park, with views over the lush expanse of green toward the city's high-rise skyline. It is perhaps the best hotel in the entire city, and it is popular with aid workers, UN officials, diplomats, and businessmen.

The Serena isn't exactly a hangout for those from the Nairobi ghetto. On my reaching the hotel entrance, there was a moment when the uniformed hotel guards looked as if they were going to refuse me entry, but when they learned whom I was meeting, I was whisked inside. I ran into my big brother in the lobby. He was surrounded by his security detail and looked as if he was just leaving.

"George," he smiled, thrusting out a hand. "It's good to see you again. But listen, I got to rush to a meeting. I've got two days in Nairobi, and I'll call you. We'll arrange a time so we can meet and have a proper talk, okay?"

"Okay," I confirmed. "I'd like that."

I returned to Huruma and waited for that call. It didn't come, and it was some days before I learned what had happened. My American brother had wanted to spend some time alone, so he could have that one-on-one with me. Unfortunately, his plans had been frustrated. Word was that one of the Obama clan was supposed to have come and fetched me, but at the last minute they'd managed to "forget" to do so. I got a strong sense that the failure to fetch me was less by forgetfulness and more by design.

I was raised by my mother and her side of the family, and to some in the Kenyan Obama clan I was an unwelcome impostor. Moreover, in their eyes I was the "black sheep" of the family. I'd broken the law and served the best part of a year in jail. Worse still, I chose to live in the ghetto. One or two of my relatives thought that Barack Obama raised the family up, while my presence dragged it down, and that I was not the sort of person suited to meeting an American senator.

No one in Huruma viewed it that way, of course. To Rajab and Auntie Sarah I was family, and I was pretty much family to Shiyayo, Clyde, and my fellows in the youth group. I'm certain that my American brother hadn't seen things that way either. From reading his book, *Dreams from My Father*, I was aware of the tough streets that he had walked, especially when he worked with the poor communities in Chicago. No, I felt certain he wouldn't resent my fall from grace or my time spent in the ghetto.

Along with Shiyayo, Clyde, John, and the others, I tried to bring in whatever money we could to fund the work of our youth group. We started a trash collection service, just as we had with Pendo Moja, to help raise funds. Within six months we'd transformed the area where we operated. Considering what a mess and a health hazard it had been, it was a miraculous result. Shiyayo and I really got a kick out of the work, so once again, we spearheaded the cleanups.

Once we'd had piles of rotting rubbish all around our area, and it was like a symbol of the community's lack of self-respect that we could dump our refuse right in the midst of where we lived. But now all that was gone. It was a powerful testament to what we could achieve on a tiny budget.

In the months following Barack Obama's visit, Auntie Sarah faded fast. Day by day Rajab and I witnessed her life ebbing away. During the years after prison she had become like a second mother to me, giving me a home in my darkest days and trying to guide me through my hardest hours. I was devastated when she died. Losing her was a bitter blow, and I felt as if my struggle to find a family—to not be an orphan—was never-ending.

Muslims must be buried before sundown on the day of their death, and so the funeral was a hurried affair. Most of the clan were unable to make it in time for the lowering of her body into the Nairobi dust. A period of forty days' mourning followed, during which the compound filled with friends and family, who came to share their memories of Auntie Sarah's life.

This collective mourning proved a real palliative, and by the time it was over I felt ready to face the world again. Rajab was now the head of the household, and he, my niece Mwanaisha, and I made up our Huruma family. Mwanaisha had a three-year-old boy, called David, and I had become like a father to him. After Auntie Sarah's death, walking little David to nursery school each morning proved to be a simple joy that lifted my spirits.

It was a five-minute stroll through the narrow alleys of the ghetto to his school. I taught him to make the return journey completely on his own. I knew that it was safe and I wanted him to learn to find his own way. If he strayed, all he would need to do was announce that he was Hussein Obama's "son," and he'd be brought home, for everyone in the ghetto knew me as his father.

I'd taken it upon myself to furnish David with his gray shorts, smart white shirt, and blue satchel with "Back to School" written on it. I'd taken him to the tailors myself, and had felt a warm glow as he'd stood there proudly in his first school uniform. Each afternoon he'd come home from school with pictures he'd drawn of cars or bananas or carts and donkeys—the things he saw in his daily life. And I tried to find the time to help him with the letters of the alphabet or the numbers that he was learning.

When I was a young child I'd learned to embrace difference—the difference of having a white man as a father. As time went on I craved notoriety, which in turn led me into a life of crime and rebellion. After the prison year I'd found a new path, that of the close embrace and the easy anonymity of the ghetto. But I was about to be thrust into the light as never before, and it was the difference between my American brother and me that would force me into the world's spotlight.

Most restaurants and bars around Nairobi have a TV set, and many show international news channels like CNN. Via the TV news the Kenyan people followed the unfolding battle in America for the Democratic nomination for president. Kenya celebrated the rise of

Barack Obama, its "lost" African son and the possibility that the first Luo president was going to be elected—in America! The reggae hit "Barack Obama" by Cocoa Tea boomed out from *matatus;* bars set up wide-screen TVs so customers could watch Barack Obama in action. Like everyone else, I found myself gripped by the powerful rhetoric of this man.

> *And because of what you said, because you decided that change must come to Washington, because you believed that this year must be different than all the rest, because you chose to listen not to your doubts or your fears but to your greatest hopes and highest aspirations, tonight we mark the end of one historic journey with the beginning of another—a journey that will bring a new and better day to America.*
>
> *Because of you, tonight I can stand here and say that I will be the Democratic nominee for the President of the United States of America.*

As my American brother went from underdog to odds-on favorite, the interest in his Kenyan roots and African heritage mushroomed. His face peered out of every Kenyan newspaper and magazine: T-shirts sported his most popular slogans, like Change You Can Believe In. He seemed to be everywhere, and I suppose it was hardly surprising when the world's press came looking for me.

Apart from a few close family and friends, I hadn't told anyone that I was the U.S. presidential nominee's youngest brother. Obama isn't such an unusual surname in Kenya, and there are many Obamas who are only distant relations of ours. A couple of months after Barack won the nomination, I was contacted by a European journalist. She explained that she wanted to do an interview with me as a profile piece on the U.S. candidate's brother. I talked it through with Rajab, and he suggested that it might be a good thing: I could use it to raise the profile of our work and goals in the slums.

I did the interview, and because I'm not ashamed of where I live,

I showed the journalist around the Huruma compound. And I let them take my photograph in the gate leading into my late Auntie Sarah's home. Unfortunately, the article that appeared didn't cover any of the things that I had wanted it to. Instead, it headlined the news that the U.S. presidential candidate's brother had been tracked down to a "ramshackle shantytown," where he survived on less than "one dollar a month." No one could live on a dollar a day, let alone on three and a half cents a day, not even a Nairobi ghetto dweller like me.

One aims for the White House, the other lives in an African slum— that was the tone of the headline. It was true to say that I lived in a poor African slum, while my brother was running for the White House. But it wasn't true to say that I resented that fact or felt that my brother should have done something about my situation. That wasn't true. No way.

The article would have been laughable if the impact of its publication hadn't been so detrimental to all that we were trying to achieve. It was syndicated all over the world, and in an instant a pack of journalists came into the ghetto to track down the presidential candidate's ghetto-dwelling brother who lived on a dollar a month. I felt both hunted and betrayed.

I'd brought that first journalist into Huruma and into my community to shine some light into the ghetto, but she'd made it sound as if I were ashamed to live there and resentful of my American brother's success. I'd told the journalist the opposite. I'd said that I was happy living in Huruma and proud of my brother's achievements and his dreams. I'd even let them take a photograph of me standing beside my father's photo, and one alongside the newspaper report of Barack Obama's success that I had pinned on the wall.

That one piece of skewed reporting destroyed my faith in the media, but at the same time it raised my profile so high that the world's press came clamoring. Most reporters were pursuing the same angle—to discredit my American brother by comparing the difference between our two lives. I refused to speak to them.

Eventually Rajab persuaded me to do something to counter the damage caused by that first rash of articles. I was offered an interview on CNN, and Rajab argued that because it went out live, I could say what I wanted without having things twisted. I could counter the lies of the original stories.

I did the interview with CNN's David McKenzie, on location in Huruma.

"The magazines distorted everything," I told him. "I was brought up well; I live well even now. I kind of like it here. I'm Kenyan, so I definitely love to live in Kenya."

I told him that I knew Barack Obama was going to be the president of America.

"It's because he wants to be," I said. "I think in life, what you want is what you are supposed to get."

The CNN interview went well, and I concluded that Rajab was right—I could use the media to get out a message that I wanted to communicate. I did some further interviews, including one with the *London Times* published under the headline "Life Is Good in My Nairobi Slum, Says Barack Obama's Youngest Brother." "Life in Huruma is good," I was quoted as saying. "In other places you must lock yourself in to keep yourself safe. Here I am surrounded by friends and family and I feel safe and secure."

Rajab told me to be myself and to do the things that I wanted with this. It was both an opportunity and a challenge, and I should use it to take me wherever I wanted to go.

CHAPTER 23

Slaying the Shame

THE U.S. ELECTION was an extraordinary event in Kenya, and most of all for the extended Obama clan. We gathered in the family's rural homeland and celebrated for days. None of us had had any doubt that our brother/cousin/nephew/grandson was going to win. I was convinced of it. Yet the relief and joy of seeing him win the presidency was overwhelming.

I sent him a message of congratulations: To my brother, soon to be the new man in the White House.

We gathered as a clan to watch his victory speech, and I was caught up in the driving power of his rhetoric and his inspirational message, expressed with such eloquence and heartfelt conviction.

> *If there is anyone out there who still doubts that America is a place where all things are possible; who still wonders if the dream of our founders is alive in our time; who still questions the power of our democracy, tonight is your answer. . . .*
>
> *It's the answer spoken by young and old, rich and*

poor, Democrat and Republican, black, white, Latino, Asian, Native American, gay, straight, disabled and not disabled—Americans who sent a message to the world that we have never been a collection of Red States and Blue States: we are, and always will be, the United States of America.

Having my brother elected to the White House did open up some new and unusual avenues of support for our work in Huruma. Recently we had set up a Huruma Centre Youth Group football team. I was the coach, and the team had become my driving passion. I wanted them to compete in the forthcoming Nairobi-wide tournament, but they didn't possess a single football uniform between them. There were few if any football boots to go around, but what we did have in bucketloads was a hunger to win. A prime example of that was our star midfielder, Jonathan Mbeu Mweu.

Jonathan was from the Kamba tribe, and he'd taken his Kamba name, Mbeu, from his grandfather. As with me, he was supposed to be the double of his grandpa. Grandpa Mbeu must have been a fine football player, for Jonathan was a prodigy. By the time he turned fifteen, he was the head boy of the local Huruma School and the captain of their football team.

Jonathan's sports teacher, Mr. Mwangi, used to watch him juggle the ball on feet and head and marvel at his skill. He'd tell Jonathan that with proper training he could make it on the world stage. But Jonathan's parents worked as casual laborers in the ghetto and had barely enough money to put food on the table, let alone to pay for training for their son, the budding football star. Jonathan's father had been a fine football player in his day, but Jonathan was in a different class. He could shine just about anywhere on the field, and few players could match his foot-dancing talent.

Jonathan had left school at sixteen, when the money for school fees ran dry. He was the eldest of three kids and his parents needed him to help bring in money. Jonathan found an ingenious way to combine work with his love of football. In Huruma there was a very basic football ground, complete with a khaki green tin hut that acted as the community sports office. Around the back was an outside tap, and Jonathan started offering a carpet-cleaning service. For a full set of automobile carpets he'd charge 50–100 shillings, and for a household carpet 150, tops.

Word soon got around, and Jonathan built up a base of customers. On a very good day he might earn five hundred Kenyan shillings, about seven dollars. He still lived at home, and he gave the money to his mother to buy food and clothes and to help pay his two sisters' school fees. Working out of the football ground meant that he could join in the training sessions whenever he didn't have any customers. He earned himself a place on the Huruma Youth Football Club team for the under-eighteen players.

Jonathan nurtured the dream that one day his talent would get noticed and that he'd make it onto the international soccer circuit. But the only income coming into HYFC was the ten-cents entrance fee that fans paid to watch matches. Money for travel to away matches, for team uniforms, and for football boots was always lacking. Sometimes, the team would travel to a match, play the game of their lives, and have to trudge home on foot. But at least Jonathan was playing, and in spite of the far better-resourced clubs that they were up against, his youth team ranked at the top of their league.

Just as soon as Jonathan turned eighteen, he was snapped up by the senior team—my team—the Huruma Centre Football Club (HCFC). Via the Obama connection and the profile it had earned me, I'd managed to pull in a little sponsorship, and just about every player had his own set of boots by now, even if they were battered and broken, with worn or missing studs.

It costs less than a thousand shillings—under fifteen dollars—to buy each player a uniform. We wanted green and yellow colors, with each of the player's number on the back of his shirt. I got a journalist to pay for the entire team's uniforms, in exchange for doing an interview with me. It wasn't quite what I'd imagined when I'd envisaged how the Obama connection might help, but as Rajab had said, I should make it work for me in whatever way I could.

It was just days before the tournament when I presented the players with their kits. All I did was announce that they had a friend in the UK who'd decided to sponsor the team, and then I revealed the box of pristine new uniforms. It came as a complete surprise and the team went wild, the players cheering and mobbing me.

"But guys, now you have your strip, you have to win!" I cried out, over the noise of their cheering. "No excuses anymore. You've got to go out there and knock them dead."

Our team was playing against a dozen others in the Extreme Tournament, and if we won that, we'd be promoted to the Super League—a short step before hitting the big time, the Kenyan Premier League. Like Jonathan, every player in the team shared the dream to make it big on the world soccer stage. And I reckoned at least three—Jonathan included—had the potential to do so. I was determined to build the team into a top Kenyan club, and to give the players the chance in life that they had never had.

By now our Huruma fans knew the club affectionately as "Obama's team." I guess some of my "celebrity status" as the U.S. president's youngest brother was rubbing off on the players. Jonathan told me that having me as coach had lifted him up and made the entire team feel special. And perhaps fittingly, our club nickname had become "the Mambas." I'd reclaimed my badass gangster identity and transformed it into a beacon of hope for my ghetto football team.

With our newfound confidence and our kit, sure enough, we won the Extreme Tournament. The sense of achievement was unbeatable. The sense of being on a mission, and of achieving something the guys had thought was beyond them, was both thrilling and deeply gratifying. Jonathan was pushing twenty by now, and he and I had become close. Along with Tony Odiyo, my deputy coach, we were the driving force behind the Mambas.

"You know, I feel like that dream to be a pro, it's getting closer and closer every day," Jonathan told me. We'd gone to our favorite Huruma bar to celebrate our success. "You've lifted us up, Hussein, you know that? It's you who's taken us where we are today."

"To the Mambas!" I grinned, raising my bottle of Pilsner lager.

"The Mambas," Jonathan and Tony echoed.

"To Obama's team," Jonathan added. Then, at me, "And to Huruma's very own president!"

The football team had become the most important thing at the Huruma Centre Youth Group, for it offered young men a real and tangible alternative to getting into trouble. None of my players were doing drugs or crime or gangster stuff anymore. Playing football, and the self-respect and hope it inculcated, was keeping them away from the dark side.

The most high-profile football project in the Nairobi slums is called MYSA, the Mathare Youth Sports Association. MYSA has been running slum-based football clubs and tournaments for years, and they've taken players from the ghetto to compete in soccer tournaments all over the world. The players have been recruited onto the international football circuit, a dream for any young ghetto kid who could kick a ball around.

With my team I hoped to achieve something similar. And even those who couldn't make it internationally could still compete locally. The captain of our team was called Mathenge. He was a ghetto youth in his early twenties and he had no job, but he was a good captain and a great leader. Soccer was his life, and his work with our youth group was the biggest break that he'd ever had.

As a result of my media profile, a Western philanthropist contacted me. He put up several hundred dollars of his own money to fund our work. We aimed to use the funds to build the team's prowess and to finance a couple of Shiyayo's modeling competitions as well.

I started working with the Mwelu Foundation, a slum-based charity that uses photo and video images to document life in the slums. Like me, Julius Mwelu, the organization's young founder, is an ex-gangster from the ghetto. I was fascinated by his life, and our shared stories drew us together.

When Julius was eight years old, his father had died. His mother was left alone to fend for seven children in a tiny one-room shack in the Mathare slum. In an effort to earn some money, one of Julius's older brothers became a child soldier in Uganda, fighting the Lord's

Resistance Army. Another became a slum gangster, breaking the law to help provide for his family. Julius decided to join that brother's gang, rather than to go and fight with his other brother in a foreign war.

By the age of nine Julius had learned to pickpocket and mug. A year later he was using guns. By the age of twelve he'd been shot twice and survived, and shot people in return. It was then that Lana Wong, a Chinese American photographer living in Kenya, recruited Julius into her charitable project, called Shootback, which gave disposable cameras to slum children to photograph their own lives. Julius and the program were made the subject of a Dutch documentary and he and his photography won international attention and acclaim. Overnight almost, Julius's life had turned around.

At age fourteen Julius traveled to Holland to exhibit his work and talk to the European press. His career as a young photojournalist took off. Ten years later he had won several international press and journalism awards for his groundbreaking photographic work, and had traveled to Belgium, Spain, France, Holland, and South Africa. He'd won particular praise for his photographs of the terrible violence that had engulfed Kenya following the disputed 2007 elections.

Like me, Julius had decided to give something back to the ghetto, to recognize the special chance that he had been given. Using his prize money, he established the Mwelu Foundation, to provide slum children with the chance to pursue photography and filmmaking about day-to-day life in the slums. After just a few years, Julius was achieving amazing things with the young Mwelu students.

"I want them to show the world how they see life, from the eye level of the slum," he told me. "We have forty-five children documenting our lives as we live them, with cameras. That's like a dream come true for me. I'm hopeful about the future, for their work proves that they have enormous talent—if only the world will give them a chance, a chance for their talents to shine, a chance to do more than simply survive here."

"I like the fact that it gives the kids such a break," I told him. "It's a chance to document their own lives for themselves, from their own perspective. No one's ever given them that, or even suggested that it might be valid."

"I tell you, just give the kids here one chance—*just one chance*—and you'd be amazed what they can achieve," Julius enthused. "They have such potential here, such talent, such a hunger to learn and to better themselves. And imagine the frustration when such talent is blocked at every turn. All we need is the resources, and look what we can achieve."

Julius urged me to use my position as the youngest brother of the American president to further the Mwelu Foundation's aims, to help publicize their work and raise money. I was keen to get involved and became an honorary ambassador for Mwelu's work. Working with Julius, I started taking my own photos in Mathare, the ghettoland that I had once been afraid to set foot in.

Most celebrities—Kenyan and foreign alike—never set foot in the slums. If they came from the slums originally, once they'd achieved their celebrity status they'd leave and never return. The fact that Julius returned to the ghetto was unusual, and it struck a real chord with me.

Julius had a great way of putting it: "I love living in the slum, and I tell you something, if there's a slum in heaven, that's where I want to end up. At least I'd know that all my friends and my community would be there too."

People kept asking me the same thing: why was I still living in the ghetto when I'd become something of a celebrity? I told them that while I may have earned some renown, I was still the same guy underneath, with the same life story. Julius didn't try to hide where he'd come from or what he'd done in the past. It was the same with me.

The idea of documenting life in the slums was vital. Generally, the ghetto dwellers don't talk about what they've been through or how they ended up where they are today, because to do so is upsetting. Most are ashamed of their lives. And so a program that puts pride back into people's lives, that slays the shame, has to have priority. Photography, football, handicrafts, even modeling—these programs give people pride in who they are.

To help strengthen people's self-respect, we set up a Children's

Parliament, one populated by kids from the ghetto. It was the Mwelu kids' own idea, and the aim was to raise an alternative voice to that offered by our political leaders—those who continue to ignore the calls for justice and development from the slums. As with any normal parliament, we elected "ministers," and Julius or I would introduce a resolution, dealing perhaps with corruption, the lack of infrastructure, or the needs of the community. We'd send the "ministers" away to research the problem and to develop a policy to address it.

We tabled a resolution for the anticorruption minister to come up with ways to combat bribes being demanded by the police; for the minister of health to look at ways to combat the pollution of drinking water; for the minister of sanitation to look at ways to combat the so-called flying toilets, where a slum dweller defecates into a plastic bag and flings it onto a neighbor's roof.

The kinds of answers that the kid ministers came back with helped them learn about the problems in the ghetto and how we might address them. The parliament was like a ghetto think tank. In Kenya there is a formal Children's Parliament, but all the ministers hail from the educated elite. They have zero sense of the problems and challenges the ghetto kids face on a daily basis.

I loved working with those kids. I'd use humor to encourage their hopes and their dreams. Treating them like small adults, you could really start to turn their lives around.

One thing especially struck me about those Mwelu kids: a lot of them were orphans, which meant in a way that they were just like me. By making a future for them, I was making a family for myself. For as I'd said to Shiyayo, in the ghetto you're never alone.

On a baking hot September day in Nairobi, a crowd gathered at the Huruma football ground, seeking the shade cast by the twelve-foot concrete walls that surround the stadium. Men, women, young girls, and boys crouched in the shadows, waiting. The easy laughter and chat went rippling back and forth, as they speculated on the forthcoming match. A group of toddlers kicked a battered, semi-inflated football back and forth in the blinding light, their shouts and tumbling enthusiasm testament to a new generation of players to come.

A buzz of excitement swept the crowd as the first figures in shimmering sky blue and sunflower yellow uniforms jogged out onto the sunbaked dirt of the pitch.

"Hussein's champions!" the crowd started yelling. "Obama's champs! Obama's champs!"

As I watched my guys doubling back and forth across the field, their boots kicking up a thick cloud of dust, I felt an odd mixture of embarrassment and pride. The fact that everyone saw this as my team now was great for team morale, but it did make me feel a little awkward. My thirst for difference was far behind me. I hungered for other satisfactions now, like winning this particular match.

It was crunch time for the team. We had three matches to go in the Super League, and we were top of the league table. If we won this match, we would be pretty much unbeatable and heading for the National League. A year back such achievements were only vaguely dreamed of, yet here we were with everything to play for. And to add a touch of nervous excitement to the game—not that it was needed— a sponsor had offered to buy the entire team brand-new football boots if they won. None of the players had ever owned a new pair of football boots. They'd buy the cast-offs and hand-me-downs from more affluent Nairobi families.

It was approaching four o'clock in the hot and airless stadium. Kickoff had been scheduled for three, but this was Kenya and everyone was running on "African time"—the referee, the linesmen, and the fans included. No one seemed overly bothered that the crucial match of the day—Huruma Centre Football Club (HCFC) versus Sports Connect—was three-quarters of an hour overdue. But the longer the match took to start, the cooler the temperature would be, which would be a huge relief to players and spectators alike.

I gazed out over the stadium. On each of the four walls a group of kids had found themselves a good vantage point. It was an unspoken understanding that those kids would call out for the ball to be returned if it sailed over the wall after an extra-powerful kick and landed among the tin-roof shacks and alleyways that clustered against the stadium's walls.

For this match, a fellow player had loaned my star midfielder, Jonathan Mweu, a pair of bright red boots. Jonathan still hadn't managed to buy a pair of his own, so the promise from the sponsor was like manna from heaven. He'd been dreaming of a snow-white pair of Nikes for years. With white boots, he promised me, he would play even better than ever.

During the warm-up kick-around, a cry went up from the fans. "Obama's enemies! Obama's enemies! Obama's enemies!" I turned to see our opponents, Sports Connect, jogging onto the field in their bright white uniforms. On average they looked bigger than my guys, which was hardly surprising. Brought up on a diet of *ugali* and greens—and often not enough even of that to fill their bellies—my boys were typically small in stature. But what they lacked in size they more than made up for with their toughness and speed, plus their burning desire to win.

I felt the stab of nerves gripping my stomach as the teams lined up for kickoff. The referee's whistle blew, and a roar went up from our supporters. In a swirl of sunlit dust, battle had been joined. But within the first five minutes Sports Connect got a lucky break and kicked the ball into the back of our net. For a moment their goal was met with a shocked silence from our fans, and our lads hung their heads in dejection.

But then a bellow of support went up from Lelo, a giant of a man with a booming voice and our single greatest fan. *"Go Obama's Mambas! Go! Go! Go! Obama's Mambas! Go get 'em!"*

We had a rule that no match could start without Lelo, for he'd become our team cheerleader. I took up his call and the crowd did likewise. The players took the ball from kickoff, and Jonathan Mweu danced and weaved and flew past half a dozen Sports Connect lads, passing the ball to Frank Zola, our ace striker. Seconds later Frank had slammed it past the opposing goalie, and the crowd went wild.

Goal!

We were tied 1–1, and it was time to turn the game our way. By halftime the score was 5–2 to us, and I reckoned we had it in the bag. Jonathan had scored the third goal from a free kick, curling it over the opposing team's wall and into the top corner of the net. It was the best goal of the match so far. At halftime the team threw their heads under the water tap to cool themselves down—the same tap that Jonathan used to clean his carpets.

A few minutes into the second half Sports Connect got another lucky break and scored their third. Once more I felt the cramp of nerves, for we hadn't won yet. But I needn't have worried. As a goat herder drove a long line of goats through the stadium, our players danced and twirled and weaved in the fine evening light. Jonathan Mweu, Frank Zola, Frank Kamawe, and Patrick Njgona slammed the ball forward toward the Sports Connect net. By the time of the final whistle, we were ahead 7–3.

Lelo had roared out a continuous stream of support for the team and abuse against bad refereeing decisions, and I have to confess that I joined him. And he chased the crowd of ghetto kids back from the touchline whenever they pressed forward to see the best of the action.

The meaning of our victory didn't escape any of the players. I could see it written on their sweat- and dust-streaked faces as they came striding off the field. Each was a picture of happiness. We'd beaten Sports Connect, which would keep us at the top of the league, with forty-seven points. The nearest team to us, Guerrillas FC, had forty-five. Barring a complete disaster, we were going to win the Super League, which would place my guys one step nearer to achieving their dream. And perhaps just as importantly, our sponsor would have to buy the entire team the new boots that he'd promised them.

If we did win the Super League, we'd then move on to competing nationally. I knew that would present its own set of challenges for the team, and most of all for me. We'd have to raise funds to take the team all across Kenya. They'd need meals and overnight accommodation, and the team would be relying on me—and the Obama connection—to make the money materialize.

In fact the entire Huruma Centre Youth Group was relying on

me to raise the money for the drama workshops, the handicrafts, the tae kwan do classes, and beauty contests. Even with the Obama factor, it hadn't gotten any easier to raise funds inside Kenya. Affluent Kenyans still seemed unwilling or unable to embrace change and promise from the ghetto. The drip-drip of support that we had attracted came from Europe and the United States.

In Kenya, the people of the ghetto still have no voice. And in the wider world people largely do not see the ghetto dwellers or want to hear them. Kenya is about safari animals, sun-kissed beaches, and exotic tribes like the Maasai, not the slum tribe. I want to change all that. I want people to see. There is much human misery in the slums, but much human courage and potential as well. The ghetto dwellers need to be given one chance, just a glimmer of hope. The extraordinary success of our football team, the Mambas, is only one example of what we can achieve with just a little help.

I'd started my life as a dreamer, on Grandma Dorcas's knee. And I finish the story of my life so far with a dream. My American brother has risen to be the leader of the most powerful country in the world. Here in Kenya, my aim is to be a leader among the poorest, most powerless people on earth—the people of the ghetto.

My dream is to shine a light into the ghetto, to bring a ray of hope, and to lift up my slum homeland.

EPILOGUE

I'VE NEVER FORGOTTEN the street kids with whom I once made my home. Their tragedy is the tragedy of the slums, because their potential, their hunger for a future worth living, is so universally quashed. Those like me who have an escape route out of the ghetto or the streets are few and far between. For the millions of others, a life of shattered dreams appears to be preordained. Today, one sixth of the world's population live in slums. *One sixth of the world's population.* Or one billion people. So this isn't a problem that is simply going to fade away.

The street kids that I have spoken to have incredibly moving life stories, and I hope to start a program to document them. The majority have never talked to anyone about what their lives have been like. Mostly they try to avoid speaking about the struggle embodied in their young lives, for to do so is too upsetting. But in the controlled and sheltered environment of a community program, it can be cathartic and healing.

Along with documenting their stories, we'd like to get them off the streets and into educational or vocational programs so they can learn life skills. We'd like to do so within an environment like the Huruma ghetto, somewhere where those street kids won't feel so out of place or looked down on. Our intention is to motivate those kids so that their voices can be heard, and so that they will have a better alternative for the future. We also want to prove that not all street kids have to be criminals, and that there is a rich vein of talent there to tap, if only the outside world will give them a chance.

My onetime sweetheart and fellow community worker, Shiyayo, has found a sponsor for her ongoing studies, which came about via the Obama connection. Suffice it to say that the sponsor is living in the affluent West and met her after hearing my life story. Shiyayo and I remain best friends, and she has been one of my greatest supporters in writing this book. She flew to the Tanzanian island of Zanzibar with me—the first time she had ever been on an airplane—so I could work on the writing in peace. We stayed at the wonderful Pongwe Beach Hotel. It was the first time that Shiyayo had ever seen the sea.

Sadly, Grandma Dorcas—who taught me so much about Luo and rural life—passed away during my lost years. As a result I never got to attend her funeral or pay her my last respects. I regret that deeply. I have fine memories of my times spent with her, and I hope that I've started a strong relationship with Grandma Sarah, the grandmother I share with my American brother, Barack Obama.

One day soon I'd like to travel to the United States to be reunited with my mother, and to meet my little sister, who's turning eight this year, and to get reacquainted with Marvin. I speak with them regularly on the phone, but it's not the same. My mother has not been back to Kenya since the day she left, so seeing her again is long overdue. And when I get to the United States, I'd like to meet my American brother, the president. I'd like to have the chance to chat about life, about our father, and about my work in the Nairobi ghetto and with the street children.

Before the news broke about my story, very few in Kenya knew that I was the brother of a U.S. presidential hopeful. After those articles were published, everyone knew. This has proven to be both a blessing and a curse. On the one hand it has given me a platform upon which to say some of the things that I want to say. On the other, it's tough, because everyone now expects the world from me. In a sense, my life is exactly as it was before; but people presume I have a direct line to the White House, which I do not, and so that has placed a lot of weight on my shoulders.

I honestly believe that without having experienced the dark side of Kenya, the dark heart of Africa, I would be a very different person. I wouldn't feel the pulse of the ghetto in my blood; I wouldn't bleed for its suffering; I wouldn't thrill for its people, for its youth and their promise. If I hadn't sunk so low in life, I wouldn't *be one of them*, while at the same time having access to a very different world via the Obama connection—that of the affluent, urbane, global citizens of this earth.

It is because of who and what I was—the lost years—that I can do the type of work that I do in the ghetto, especially with the youth. Julius Mwelu and I share the same dubious pedigree—we both walked on the dark side—and that means that we can relate and empathize, and that we do not judge. I believe I wouldn't be able to do this were it not for my past, and so in that sense I wouldn't change a day of it. I wouldn't have my life any other way.

When I was first approached to write my life story, I discussed it with Rajab, my best friend and sometime father figure. Rajab backed the idea, for he felt that my story could be the story of Huruma, and the wider Kenyan slums. If I could use my story to raise the issues that the ghetto dwellers face, and in particular the need for hope to shine a light into the slums, then it would be a fine thing. I hope that I've achieved that, and that some who read this book will help us shine that light. It's long overdue, and just a little illumination will go a long, long way.

Recently, I was invited to Turkey at the behest of a Turkish company. On the flight I watched an in-flight movie, *Slumdog Millionaire*. For me it captured much of the essence of the ghetto—the hopes and the fears, the love and the brutality that coexist there. In many ways, the movie's protagonist is a typical slum kid: one with huge potential, but whose life would never have gone anywhere without the lucky break he's given. Few slum kids get the chance to appear on *Who Wants to Be a Millionaire,* but there's many practical ways to help them to achieve their dreams.

They're hungry for it. It's time the world listened.